Dangerous Women

LARRY A. MORRIS

Dangerous Women

WHY
MOTHERS,
DAUGHTERS, AND
SISTERS BECOME
STALKERS,
MOLESTERS, AND
MURDERERS

 Prometheus Books

59 John Glenn Drive
Amherst, New York 14228–2119

Published 2008 by Prometheus Books

Inquiries should be addressed to
Prometheus Books
59 John Glenn Drive
Amherst, New York 14228–2119
VOICE: 716–691–0133, ext. 210
FAX: 716–691–0137
WWW.PROMETHEUSBOOKS.COM

12 11 10 09 08   5 4 3 2 1

Library of Congress Cataloging-in-Publication Data

Morris, Larry A., 1936–
Dangerous women : why mothers, daughters, and sisters become stalkers, molesters, and murderers / by Larry A. Morris.
     p. cm.
ISBN 978-1-59102-633-4 (hardcover)
1. Female offenders—Psychology. 2. Violence in women. 3. Women—Psychology. I. Title.

HV6046.M365 2008
364.3'74—dc22

2008026156

Printed in the United States of America on acid-free paper

For Duane Ragan

His legacy lives on

CONTENTS

FRA

PATANIA,
KENEDI F
Sun May 12, 2019

(Estimated hold expiration date)

Transit Date: Fri May 03 2019 12:

Dangerous women : why mothers,

33029059990960

Hold note:

*
*
*
*
*
*
*

FRA

PATANIA,
KENEDI F
Sun May 12, 2019

(Estimated hold expiration date)

FOREWORD

Robin Sax Katzenstein

E very day as a deputy district attorney, I witness the reper-
cussions of bad behavior. I see people whose actions and
behavior have led them to poor choices that go beyond unwise—
these choices are criminal in nature. They can cost a lot of money,
break up families, and land people in jail. I see the worst acts, conducted in horrific circumstances, leaving lasting marks on individuals, families, and our world as a whole. Some of these crimes you
may hear about, but most you will not.

The crimes people do hear about are those that interest the
media, such as celebrities misbehaving (Lindsay Lohan and Paris
Hilton earned themselves jail time despite their exalted status as
actresses). Other high-profile individuals may find themselves
facing criminal charges when their passions overrule their
common sense, as in the case of astronaut Lisa Nowak, whose
cross-country drive to confront her lover's new girlfriend nearly
resulted in a crime of passion.

But what about the 95 percent of cases and crimes involving
"ordinary people" whose lives slip into violence? How much do
we really know about them?

Like Larry Morris, I, too, handle a variety of cases, from high to low profile, from newsworthy to news blackout, from dramatic court confrontations to settlements outside of court.

Each and every day, our court system is faced with the challenge of understanding some of the most despicable acts that one person can perpetrate upon another. As a prosecutor, I am constantly trying to understand why and how a crime happened. Larry Morris, from a much broader perspective, also seeks to understand what makes people — specifically women, in this fascinating compilation — become dangerous to themselves and others.

Very few people can provide answers to my questions and those of jurors hearing these cases. My job, as a prosecutor, is to convince twelve people in the community that a defendant committed a particular crime beyond a reasonable doubt. While there is no requirement for me to prove why someone committed a crime or acted (or didn't act) in a particular way, today's jurors want to know why. They want to understand *what's behind the crime*. Therefore, the more light I can shed on the inner world of a particular perpetrator, the greater my odds of ensuring that the perpetrator will no longer threaten others.

As a prosecutor, I have another responsibility besides helping jurors understand why people do the things they do. I also play an integral role in assisting the court as to deciding appropriate punishment or consequence for the bad conduct in question. In order to decide whether someone is suitable for rehabilitation or simply deserves to be punished, I (and the court) need to understand who we are dealing with, the chances of recidivism (or criminal relapse), and how likely the person is to offend again. For example, is the teacher who molested her thirteen-year-old student likely to molest again, or was this an isolated case?

When it's time for me to decide which penalty or consequence is appropriate, I rely on the opinion of a forensic psychologist. It is the forensic psychologist who puts a crime into context and can educate the court, the jurors, and the lawyers about the dynamics of the crime, the criminal, and the victim.

A forensic psychologist is more than a shrink, more than a doctor, more than an expert witness. A good forensic psychologist is worth his weight in gold if he or she can answer the court's burning questions with insight, expertise, and knowledge. Even more important is the ability to answer technical questions clearly and simply to ensure that everyone (regardless of educational background) can understand.

Larry Morris is just such an expert. He is the person who brings criminal behavior into perspective. He is the person who understands how people think and why they do what they do. He understands crimes, evaluates cases, and draws conclusions. But what makes Dr. Morris different from many other forensic psychologists is that he answers questions with objectivity, insight, and integrity.

Those who know him say that Larry Morris puts 110 percent into every case he handles. He doesn't just provide cursory conclusions—he analyzes facts, case histories, and the individuals who are under the microscope, assessing their unique qualities and characteristics. He then takes what he has learned during his countless hours of examination and reconciles the new information with what he has gleaned from over thirty years of professional experience.

Perhaps no area of courtroom practice is more complicated and subject to greater controversy than the opinions of a mental health expert. While much has been written about mental health, little has been written about how this aspect pertains to actual court cases.

Even less discussed is the answer to the question that has been gaining momentum in court these days, and it is this question that Dr. Morris analyzes in *Dangerous Women*: "Why are more females committing violent crimes?" It's a question that I, as well as judges, jurors, and society, ask with increasing concern. Why are we seeing an increasing number of women in court, and why are their crimes becoming increasingly dangerous?

Dr. Morris shows us that it's not only shortsighted but dangerous for us to ignore the phenomenon of "dangerous women." He recognizes that understanding female perpetrators is critical to understanding current trends in crime. His theory is not lodged simply in statistics, which are telling, but also in the denial that our society perpetuates when dealing with the reality of women in crime.

In truth, the statistics only show one part of the picture:

- Nearly one in three (30 percent) juvenile offenders entering the system is female
- Women account for 14–20 percent of all violent crime (mostly assault)
- Approximately 1 million women, or 1 in every 109 adult American females, is in the criminal justice system (prison, jail, probation, parole)
- Women under supervision are the mothers of an estimated 1.5 million minor US children

Dr. Morris provides a framework to understand these women and helps us understand what to do with them. Throughout this book, he offers a wide variety of examples of the woman as perpetrator, one who is a danger to herself and to society as a whole.

The media loves to focus on crime but offers only a superficial look at criminals who happen to be women on such shows as those hosted by Nancy Grace and Greta Van Susteren. For more depth to these stories, we turn to *Dangerous Women*, where Morris offers answers to the questions we all ask: How can a woman murder her own child? Why is a female teacher who has sex with her thirteen-year-old student simply the butt of jokes? How could a woman drown not just one but all five of her children?

What if we could understand behavior *before* a crime has occurred? What if we could find warning signs and use them to deter potential criminals? What if we could understand the women who might commit a dangerous act, or have already done so?

One of Dr. Morris's objectives in writing this book is to help readers do exactly that—prevent a crime from occurring that might even include a reader's family member or loved one. He offers tips on potentially dangerous or antisocial behaviors that we might not ordinarily notice, such as depressions or irrational behavior, which can presage acts of greater seriousness.

While Dr. Morris takes us through several fascinating examples of dangerous women, he concludes with a path to prevention. Not only does he examine *why* girls may become dangerous, but he also brings forward suggestions as to what we can do to prevent "bad behavior" from becoming criminal behavior.

And as a prosecutor, I couldn't be more grateful for a book that concludes on a hopeful note. Perhaps, after all, some women might be spared from becoming the next dangerous women.

INTRODUCTION

THE MAKING OF
AN ORDINARY
FORENSIC PSYCHOLOGIST

When I was twenty-one years old, I received an official-looking document from the government. It was my draft notice. I didn't care. After all, I'd spent four years out of high school trying to find my place in the world, and didn't. Maybe the military would show me the way.

I wasn't sure how much danger I'd be in because the conflict in Korea was supposed to be behind us, but we still maintained a strong military presence there, just in case. Vietnam was starting to get a lot of attention and seemed next in line. But none of that mattered to me, as most of the men in my family had fought in one war or another, including the Civil War. I would be just another body in a long list of young Morris warriors sent into harm's way.

But I was one of the lucky ones. Korea stayed calm and I finished my tour of duty before all hell broke loose in Nam. I thought about reenlisting to preserve the unbroken string of brave Morris men marching off to war, but during my stint in the army, I realized I'd changed.

Actually, my army buddies at Fort Lee, Virginia, had changed me—they'd turned me into a college student. College graduates all, my army buddies schooled me in the fine art of educational enlightenment. They told me on numerous occasions that I was college material, and when I seriously considered the army's offer to enter Officer's Candidate School, my buddies told me to consider college instead. They challenged me to pursue my secret passion for learning everything I could about why people acted the way they did by enrolling in at least one college course offered by the University of Virginia at the fort.

I resisted at first, fearful of a disastrous outcome because I *knew* I was not college material, in spite of my buddies' firm reassurances. But eventually I accepted their challenge. I found that I reveled in the learning experience and, much to my amazement, I earned a top grade in the course.

The professor also joined ranks with my buddies and encouraged me to enroll in another course. I did — with the same positive results. Inspired, I then marched off to Indiana University, instead of off to war.

As an undergraduate I put my passion to work. I declared a major in psychology right away. In addition to the required core of psychology and science subjects, I also studied sociology, religion, and criminology. My goal as an undergrad was to learn all I could about human behavior, then keep the passion alive by pursuing graduate studies. Not only did I have a burning need to understand how and why we human beings work, but I was intensely interested in learning how and why we *don't* work, and how to fix those problems. A doctorate in clinical psychology was, I decided, just what I needed.

I was drawn to the University of Arizona for my graduate studies because the clinical psychology program offered unusual opportunities to get involved in research and therapy projects focused on child development, juvenile delinquency, psychiatric disorders, and adult criminal behavior. My clinical supervisor was Ted Rosenthal, one of the best and brightest who had studied under the esteemed social psychologist Albert Bandura. Rosenthal also had studied at the famed Maudsley and Middlesex Hospital in England, where the staff developed and applied state-of-the-art behavior modification techniques for all sorts of sordid behavioral problems. My passion for studying aberrant behavior rose sharply when I was assigned a child sexual abuse case as a second-year graduate student.

I was asked to develop and implement a behavioral program to eliminate a father's voyeuristic behavior with his eight-year-old daughter and replace it with appropriate responses—no small task for a second-year clinical psychology student. I was excited by the challenge, and even more so about what I could learn from this assignment.

Before I could even consider a therapeutic procedure I had to research the case. The case records revealed that one evening the previous spring, Joyce Barnes* sent her eight-year-old daughter, Mitzi, to take a bath while Joyce read to her other daughter, six-year-old Mindy, in the family room. When Mitzi didn't return after a reasonable time, Joyce went to check on her. She knew her daughter tended to dawdle in the bathroom, but the problem seemed to be getting worse.

Now, Joyce went over to the bathroom door and opened it. To her surprise, she found Mitzi standing naked. She was facing an outside window, opened just a crack for ventilation, that was covered with a curtain. Joyce thought she saw her husband, Paul, standing at the crack, then he disappeared.

Disturbed, Joyce quietly put the girls to bed then asked Paul about seeing him outside the girls' bathroom window. He said he was just passing by the window on his way to a storage shed next to the house. But Joyce didn't buy his story, and the next day, Joyce held Mitzi close and asked why she was always taking so long in the bathroom.

At first Mitzi giggled, "I don't know." Joyce repeated the ques-

---

*An asterisk denotes the use of a pseudonym or pseudonyms to protect the identity of those involved.

tion, and Mitzi squirmed in her mother's lap, then admitted, "Because Daddy wants me to."

When confronted by a Child Protective Services investigator, the father confessed to telling Mitzi to spend a lot of time in the bathroom while he watched her take off her clothes and bathe. Paul told his daughter that it was a secret game, and she wasn't to tell anyone about it. He told the investigator he had begun peeking through the bathroom window at Mitzi around the time he and his wife decided Mitzi was old enough to bathe herself safely.

The court ordered the father out of the home, placed him on probation, and required him to participate in individual and family counseling. At first the therapy plan seemed to work, and Paul was gradually reunited with his wife and two girls. But soon his sexual interest in his daughter not only resumed — it escalated.

During an individual therapy session, Paul revealed that he told Mitzi to go in the bathroom and touch her private area while he peeked through a keyhole. He also admitted that he was now becoming aroused by his younger daughter, Mindy. Child Protective Services decided that a new therapeutic approach was needed and referred the Barnes case to the University of Arizona's Department of Psychology.

When I interviewed Paul, he reported that, as a teenager, he often watched a preteen girl next door undress. He lived in a neighborhood with houses built close together, and his bedroom window was opposite his neighbor's bathroom. Carelessly, the girl often left her curtains open.

At first, Paul was curious, but his curiosity grew into sexual excitement and one night he masturbated for the first time while watching the girl dry herself with a towel after taking a bath. After that, watching and masturbating became routine.

He remembered being disappointed when the girl's family moved but denied having any other peeping experiences. He also reported being surprised when he first became sexually aroused by seeing his little daughter, Mitzi, nude in the bathroom.

Armed with this information, I was not surprised that traditional individual and family counseling had achieved only a temporary success. Research shows that traditional insight-oriented therapies alone seldom reduce conditioned sexual attraction to children.

Therefore, I proposed a comprehensive behavior modification program to tackle the conditioned responses. The program would include a controversial component—electric shock—to eliminate Paul's inappropriate sexual responses to his daughters. At the same time, it would be used in a way to reinforce appropriate non-sexual responses.

Paul agreed to try this approach, and over the months that followed, he struggled with the electric shock component. However, he responded well, and when he and his family reported that his inappropriate sexual responses to his daughters had ceased, I shifted the case to follow-up mode.

The next year, Paul had no relapses. Nor did he transfer his inappropriate sexual behavior to other children. I was both pleased and relieved over the successful outcome of this difficult first case. A failure would have left two young children at risk and a family destroyed.

In order to develop my therapeutic plan for this family, I first had to find answers to several questions: Why would a father become sexually aroused by a very young daughter? Why did he get aroused when he saw his daughter in the bathroom? What were the risk factors associated with acting out outside of the home? What therapeutic techniques should we use to change the behavior? What will happen if we fail?

Answers to these and many other related questions were vital to the success of my chosen approach. They were also important to resolving the case in court. This was my first experience with a clinical case in the criminal justice system, and it sparked my desire to learn more about the application of psychology to the law. But exploring that link would have to wait, as I now had to successfully complete the requirements of a stringent clinical psychology program.

After I received my doctorate in clinical psychology in 1970, I embarked on an exciting journey with several highly skilled psychologists to probe the depths of human behavior. Among us were research, developmental, educational, and clinical psychologists, and as a member of the group, known as Behavior Associates, I found myself specializing in research, evaluation, and training related to parenting, child development, child abuse, and juvenile delinquency. While these activities increased my understanding of both normal and aberrant human behavior, it was my work with perpetrators and victims of antisocial behavior that brought me back to the courtroom.

I was often asked to testify in court about my patients, especially the perpetrators. This is called being a "fact witness." It's pretty easy because a fact witness testifies only to the facts, but does not render an opinion. For example, I would testify that I was indeed seeing a patient, using certain treatment techniques, and report whether or not the patient was making progress. Although many attorneys would try to trick me into giving an opinion, especially about my patient's risk of recidivism, or relapse into criminal behavior, I knew enough about forensic psychology and the law to realize that rendering opinions was the purview of an expert, not a fact witness. Only qualified experts are allowed to render opinions in court because they are considered expert in the issues before the court. Fact witnesses may know a lot about a patient but may not be expert in the issues.

However, I found that my growing reputation as an expert in child abuse cases and other forms of interpersonal violence was spurring a stream of referrals for psychological evaluations and expert testimony. I declined at first, unsure that I wanted to spend that much time being hammered in court by attorneys. However, I eventually succumbed to the excitement of a new learning challenge, accepted my first nonclinical referral, and launched an exciting career in both clinical and forensic psychology.

Most people know about physical forensic science due to the popular *CSI* series on TV, but what is forensic psychology?

Is it *CSI* with a Freudian slip? Not quite.

Is it performing psychological autopsies? We're not there yet.

Is it criminal profiling? No, it's much, much more.

While definitions of forensic psychology are still a bit murky, purists view it as a two-part discipline. The first part is science, which involves researching aspects of human behavior that are directly related to legal proceedings. These include criminal behavior, psychiatric disorders, risk factors, jury selection, and eyewitness memory. The second part is applying one's psychological knowledge to the court systems. Psychologists who become forensic experts must be trained in both the law and psychology.

Forensic psychologists work in civil courts, family law courts, and the criminal justice system. Some forensic psychologists also assist law enforcement agencies by performing fitness-for-duty evaluations, pre-employment psychological evaluations, and evaluations to determine if an officer is psychologically fit to work in special units, such as a SWAT team.

In civil court, a forensic psychologist might evaluate someone to see if they suffer mental health problems because of another person's noncriminal negligence. In family court, issues of child custody dominate. As a forensic psychologist and child development expert, I would be asked to evaluate everyone in the family, including the child, then offer my opinion about what would be in the child's best interest.

Most forensic psychologists tend to work on criminal cases, which require unwavering objectivity, a wide range of expertise, and skin as thick as a rhinoceros. Not only are forensic psychologists exposed to a steady diet of the worst acts of interpersonal violence human beings can devise, but also the criminal court itself operates under an adversarial process not for the faint of heart.

Most people think a forensic psychologist just shows up in court and looks impressive. But I've put in hundreds of hours preparing for appearances in court. I rereview every piece of information I used in formulating my opinion. I check testing results for errors in scoring or interpretation. And I do a last-minute search for the latest relevant research. In short, I do my homework, hone all my skills, and gird myself for battle.

But all of my expertise and efforts are for naught if an attorney is not prepared to ask a proper line of questions or offer objections to improper questions on cross-examination. For example, while under cross-examination in a murder trial, I noticed that the prosecutor had begun asking me questions about the defendant's response to one item out of hundreds on a personality inventory I used in the evaluation. I explained that the test was not designed to draw inferences from one individual response, and I proceeded to explain to him and the jury the proper scoring and interpretation protocol.

The attorney listened then asked the same questions about another individual item. My response was the same. When the prosecutor repeated his questions about a third individual response, I knew he was going to ask about each of the hundreds of items, one at a time. He was trying to discredit the test by showing the jury how silly some of the items seemed when taken out of context.

I waited for the defense attorney to object, but he said nothing, even though I had prepared him for this strategy, which was often used by this prosecutor. Undaunted, the prosecutor continued his questions.

Finally, I turned to the judge and told her my answer would remain the same for each of the items. When the judge called the defense attorney's name, he finally woke up and produced an objection. Most experienced trial attorneys are more alert than this, and they spend considerable time preparing for court with their experts and remain diligent while the expert is testifying.

For an expert witness, a "typical" criminal case, if there is such a thing, ordinarily has eight components:

1. *The Referral Question.* A forensic case usually begins with an attorney asking a question, such as: "Would you evaluate my client to see if he is a raging pedophile, or if he molested this girl for other reasons?" Or, for instance, a prosecutor might say: "We are convinced this woman is a sociopath who should be put away forever. Would you evaluate her and testify in court?" And the court routinely has questions about how competent a defendant might be to stand trial.

2. *Review of Collateral Documents.* Before I move forward with any case, I learn as much about it as possible. I review all documents pertaining to the case including police reports, previous forensic evaluations, and any other investigative reports. Medical, psychiatric, school, job, and military records can be essential to the evaluation. By the time I receive a criminal case, considerable information will have been generated. Sometimes I'll even ask the referral source how many new filing cabinets I should buy to store the expected documents!

3. *The Evaluation.* While the procedures may vary from case to case, I usually conduct a lengthy clinical diagnostic interview, making sure I cover the defendant's social and psychiatric history, as well as corroborating all the information I learned from the supporting data. If I believe psychological tests will help answer the referral questions, I select and administer the most appropriate ones. If necessary, I also interview family members or others who may have relevant information about the defendant and the case.

4. *The Consultation.* Once I complete my evaluation and can respond to the referral question with an opinion, I contact the referral source. I usually start my consultation with a statement like this: "If you ask me to testify in court, my testimony will be . . ." Then I give my opinion.

   For example, I might say, "If you ask me to testify in court, I will say that in my opinion, your defendant is a pedophile with a documented history of molesting children to satisfy his own sexual needs. He does not consider the damage to his victims."

If my opinion does not support the attorney's theory of the case, my involvement usually comes to an abrupt end. If my opinion is supportive, my involvement may continue.

5. *The Written Report*. In my experience, most attorneys request a written report if my opinion helps their case. Court-referred cases, such as competency cases, nearly always require a written report. My written reports always summarize my work on the case, and I document everything I did to reach my opinion. Then I present and discuss the results of my evaluation as they relate to the current criminal proceedings, ending with my opinion.

6. *Disclosure and Depositions*. If referral sources decide to use expert witnesses in a criminal case, they must disclose their intentions and the names of the experts to the other side, who has the right to depose those experts before they testify. In my experience, depositions can be informal, such as submitting my work results and being interviewed by one of the opposing attorneys.

Other times, depositions are formal affairs featuring court reporters and teams of attorneys. The attorneys can ask you almost anything about your credentials as an expert and your involvement in the case. Your previous testimony in court, as well as anything you ever published, is also fair game. I have had attorneys ask questions about a sentence or two from one of my books or other publications.

Essentially, the opposing side is looking for chinks in your professional armor and faults in your proposed testimony so they can develop strategies to destroy you and your opinion in court. And thus, the battle begins.

7. *Preparation for Court*. I believe in thorough preparation, being somewhat of a perfectionist. I recall on one occasion I

told a new public defender that I wanted to meet with him to discuss my report and review my proposed testimony a week before his client's trial for murder. Surprised, he replied, "Why? You're a recognized expert with tons of court experience. I have your report. I'll just ask you questions from it." He paused, then added, "Hey, are you trying to run up the bill?"

I ignored the insult and tried to tutor the fledgling attorney in the proper care and feeding of expert witnesses. I explained that no matter how much professional experience an expert witness has had, a well-prepared attorney can always mount a powerful challenge to poorly prepared testimony on cross-examination. Without strong preparation, an attorney and his expert can suffer real damage.

8. *Testifying in Court.* The battle is joined.

While I may think I'm an expert, I am not an expert in a court of law until the judge rules I am. This involves the jury-numbing process of having to present all my training and relevant experiences that have brought me to the level of "expert."

Sometimes the process of qualifying as an expert is abbreviated or waived just to expedite the trial. Once the judge declares me an expert about the issues before the court, direct questioning begins. Usually the attorney asks questions, and I'll turn to the jury or judge and give an answer the attorney already knows I am going to give.

After direct questioning comes cross-examination, which allows the other side a chance to discredit me and my testimony. If the jury or judge finds the defendant guilty, I may be asked to testify again in the sentencing phase.

Now that your tutorial in forensic psychologist-as-expert is completed, I'd like to share why I've decided to write this book.

Over the past three decades, I have studied, evaluated, and

treated hundreds of perpetrators and victims of all kinds of inter-personal violence. Much of that time was spent in the criminal justice system as a clinical and forensic psychologist, evaluating and treating female perpetrators and victims of crime.

To my growing alarm, I've become aware of a steady rise in violent crimes by females of all ages. For example, a decade or so ago most researchers still thought sexual abuse of children by females was extremely rare. However, the number of females arrested for sex crimes rose for five out of six years since 2000. An alarming 20 percent of students in a 2004 US Department of Education survey reported sexual misconduct by a female teacher or aide. Some researchers are now estimating that nearly four million children have been sexually abused by females.[1]

The purpose of this book is to help answer questions about why girls and women commit violent crimes, including sexual crimes. The information in the book comes from four major sources:

1. My clinical and forensic experience involving girls and women perpetrators and victims of interpersonal violence.
2. The professional literature relevant to the female perpetration of murder, sexual abuse, and other forms of interpersonal violence.
3. The public record of highly publicized cases of criminal misconduct by girls and women.
4. Media coverage of female celebrities behaving badly.

Because this book contains actual cases from my practice over the past thirty years, I have taken steps to mask the identity of the people involved, consistent with ethical procedures and standards. Even though many of their names and crimes are public record and have previously been revealed by the media, each girl or woman and their family members were given a fictitious name. Many demographic characteristics such as age, education, and occupation, as well as location and dates were altered. To illustrate a point, as well as to protect identities, I exchanged some information among some cases according to the accepted process of hybridizing.[2] And as an extra precaution, professionals involved in the case, including attorneys and judges, were also given fictitious names. The procedures just described were used for my forensic and clinical cases only. Information from other cases, especially highly publicized cases, are reviewed and presented as documented in the public record. Because many of the persons from the public domain were never my patients, I offer my views not as a treating psychologist but as an educator in psychology. My theoretical interpretations should be taken in this context.

I've chosen a few fascinating cases to help reveal answers to such questions as:

- Why does a young mother drown all her children?
- Why does a woman put a bullet in the back of her partner's head?
- Why do women murder strangers?
- Why do girls and women sexually abuse children?
- Why does an attractive female teacher molest a student?
- Why do nuns molest children and each other?

While I have had some difficult times personally dealing with a steady diet of murder, mayhem, and child abuse, I remain as compelled by my current work as I was with my first case in graduate school. I believe that the more we know about people who become dangerous, the better prepared we are to prevent interpersonal violence. The personal histories within this book offer signals and clues about the motivations behind such criminal acts. It is my hope that by recognizing these signals, you will be able to avoid, prevent, or minimize similar acts from affecting you and your loved ones.

NOTES

1. For a review see Robert J. Shoop, *Sexual Exploitation in Schools: How to Spot It and Stop It* (Thousand Oaks, CA: Corwin Press, 2003).

2. K. Heilbrun, G. Marczyk, and D. DeMatteo, *Forensic Mental Health Assessment: A Casebook* (New York: Oxford University Press, 2002).

1
GROWING UP DANGEROUS
The Warning Signs

A scantly clad young girl flaunted her nubile body as she sang and danced across a stage cluttered with equally nubile bodies. After prancing and getting the most of her jiggles, she paused with legs spread wide. The camera zoomed in, providing an eager audience with a great crotch shot, then she bent low to reveal a titillating view of teenage tits. The beginning of a pornographic movie? No. It was the first TV commercial aired at half time of a college football game between opponents I no longer remember. The product? Viagra.

The camera shifts from crotch and tits to a smirking Senator Bob Dole sitting in his living room. Dole turns to his golden retriever who is moaning with excitement and says, "Easy boy." Dole then admits to having ED (erectile dysfunction) and urges men to talk to their doctors about their erection problems and the wonders of Viagra, as though any man would need Viagra after watching the former Mouseketeer Britney Spears display her newly grown goods.

Senator Dole and his golden retriever are not the only ones who have been watching with wonder and appreciating Britney's talents. Millions of adoring fans flock to her concerts, buy her albums, dress like her, and want to be like Britney. So who is this teenage phenom and why is she dangerous?

BRITNEY SPEARS

Britney Jean Spears was born December 2, 1981. She grew up in the small town of Kentwood, Louisiana, upstream from New Orleans toward the Mississippi state line. She was one of two daughters and one son born to her parents, James Spears, a building contractor, and Lynne Bridges, a grade school teacher.

As a young girl Britney performed locally as a singer and dancer, then wowed a national television audience on *Star Search*. At age eight she auditioned for the *New Mickey Mouse Club* and was turned down, not because she didn't have talent, but because she was too young. However, Britney's audition led her to a New York agent, the Professional Performing Arts School, television commercials, and off-Broadway plays. By age eleven, Britney was ready for another shot at Mickey Mouse, and Mickey was ready for her. For two seasons, Britney wore her ears proudly alongside other notable Mouseketeers such as Justin Timberlake, J. C. Chase, Christina Aguilera, and Keri Russell. Then the show was cancelled, tossing an early teenage Britney out of a job. But not for long.

At age fifteen, she headed back to New York, where she eventually worked out a deal with Jive Records, again joining good company with pop stars like Whitney Houston, Backstreet Boys, and *NSYNC. At barely seventeen years old, her debut single, "Baby One More Time," shot to the top of the charts. Fans, including millions of young girls, couldn't get enough of her. Never mind that Britney and a troupe of dancers pranced around in Catholic schoolgirl uniforms titillating any male within eyeshot. About a year later her first album with the same title started at the top of the charts and stayed there seemingly forever while spinning off single hits like a musical centrifuge.

Britney was too young to vote, drink, or have legal sex in most states, but she was a superstar, a teen queen. And the media was all over her, knowing that anything they published about Britney would be bought by millions of fans, including those same young girls dreaming of stardom. Be like Britney.

In 2000 Britney's follow-up album, *Ooops! I Did It Again*, hit the top of the charts upon release and set a record for single-week sales by a female artist. In 2001 Britney was no longer a teenager and her next album, *Britney*, tried to reflect a coming-of-age quality she and many of her fans were experiencing. Although *Britney* debuted at number one, the spin-off singles didn't fare as well and never reached the Top Ten. Like a lot of musical superstars, Britney looked to the movies for more star power. After her feature-film debut in *Crossroads* pretty much fizzled as a commercial success, Britney made a cameo appearance in *Austin Powers: Goldmember*, singing a remix of her hit "Boys."

In her early twenties, Britney's reign as a teen queen slipped. Sales stalled. Could she be all washed up at the age when most people are just getting started? She took a break from all performances to work on a new album. When her new album *In the Zone* was released in 2003, Britney again hit the mother lode. The album shot to number one on the Billboard 200 and spun off several megahit singles, including "Toxic," which won a Grammy for Best Dance Recording. It appeared Britney was back. But all was not well.

Soon the tabloids would be reporting about Britney's wild times at clubs and parties, wardrobe malfunctions including panty-less nights on the town, rumors of drug abuse, career-risking bad behavior on photo shoots and during interviews, serious family squabbles, and other self-destructive behaviors. It seemed to start when Britney ran off and married a childhood friend, Jason Alexander. The marriage lasted two days. When Britney's financially successful but highly sexualized Onyx Hotel tour was canceled, fans were told she had injured a knee. Britney watchers worried that she was cracking, heading for another meltdown. Brit on the brink.

Bizarre behavior by superstars always drives the media into a feeding frenzy, especially the paparazzi, who picked up the scent of wounded prey. When the rumors that Britney was having a relationship with bad boy Kevin Federline were confirmed and the couple planned to wed, the media moved in for the kill. Photos and stories of Britney's personal life appeared everywhere for months. The couple even participated in the carnage by showing awful home movies on a television reality show, *Chaotic*, a harbinger of things to come for Britney.

In the midst of her new life as a wife, this time longer than two days, Britney released her album *Greatest Hits: My Prerogative* and made an announcement. The highly sexualized former teen queen was with child.

Sean Preston Federline was born on September 14, 2005. His birth was marked by a fierce bidding war for the first baby photos. A celebrity at birth. What else do you need as a baby? A celebrity mother? How about a celebrity mother with two babies? About twelve months after Sean was born, biology spoke again: Britney gave birth to her second child, Jayden James.

Biology dictated that Britney was indeed a mother. But could she be a parent? How about a single parent? Britney and Kevin separated and set about to divide their fortunes and children. Their divorce was final in July 2007. But which one would step forward as the parent with the best interest of the children?

Hints at Britney's questionable parenting skills came from the tabloid photos of her driving around with Sean sitting on her lap, not strapped into a car seat. She blew off the criticism and pointed to her upbringing in rural Louisiana where, according to Britney, most parents just toss their kids in the car and go. Visions of another pop star gone bad—Michael Jackson, dangling his baby out of a second-story window so the media could get good shots—flashed in my mind. I also wondered what else in Britney's upbringing would dictate how she would raise her babies.

Another hint came when twenty-five-year-old Britney and her

mother, Lynne, locked horns in a battle about Lynne's role as mother, grandmother, and as a member of Britney's management team. Showing tough love, Lynne insisted Britney enter rehab and she drove Britney to the front door. Tabloids reported that Britney was furious and that she told her mother she would never speak to her again. After rehab, which Britney insisted she did not need, Britney's feelings about her mother soared to the top of the anger charts. According to Britney, her mother was plotting with her ex-husband Kevin to take her children. Britney wanted to file a restraining order against her mother, but her legal eagles advised her against it.

In the end, Britney fired Lynne as mother, grandmother, and from her management team. Her mother fired back allegations that Britney was not a good mother and the children may be in physical danger. This from a mother who raised her own baby daughter to become the tween queen of sleaze.

Surely Britney's mother, like most mothers, began to teach her daughter values before she allowed choreographers to teach her to twist and grind. Surely she was a good role model for morals and values. And surely she was a great role model for how to parent and protect children. But what if she wasn't? Where in Britney's young life would she have learned these important skills, if not from her mother? Perhaps from her idol, Madonna? And if she didn't have these skills, how was she going to be a good role model to her own children? Did Lynne or anybody really expect Britney would grow up, ditch all the sleaze-tease, and become mother of the year? Or did anyone care?

Britney's estranged relationship with her mother shocked most Britney watchers. Before the falling-out Lynne and Britney seemed to be very close. In *Heart to Heart*, a book they published together in 2000, Britney claimed that her mother was her best friend and the strongest, bravest, and most generous person she had ever known.[1] So what happened?

Britney does what Britney was packaged to do. Her childhood

life was all smoke and mirrors. Some make-believe is healthy for children, but a steady diet is toxic. And as children move from childhood into the demands of adult reality, new skills are necessary for survival. Someone steeped in a steady diet of make-believe will be tested and sorely ill-equipped to negotiate this developmental task.

Once Britney left her teens, she seemed to fall apart. For the next five or six years she went on a rampage of dysfunctional behavior including impulsive sexual exploits, two ill-fated marriages, suspected substance abuse, severe body image changes, a sudden estranged relationship with her mother, and a careless disregard for her children.

On September 17, 2007, I watched Matt Lauer of the *Today* show ask the self-proclaimed first supermodel, Janice Dickinson, "Is thirteen too young to be on the runway?" She responded without hesitation. Dickinson warned that parents abandon their children to a dangerous adult world when they allow young children to be exposed to such a provocative profession as modeling. She then took a swipe at Britney's mother as an example. "Look at Britney's mother, she's bad. She's a stage mom. Now Britney can't keep her clothes on."

So why did I include Britney Spears in a book about dangerous women, women who commit crimes much more heinous than taking clothes off? Isn't she just a simple country girl looking for love in all the wrong places? According to most Britney fans her only "crime" was to almost single-handedly resurrect teen pop when most had declared it dead. But along with the music she gave preteens and teenagers a message. Sex sells. Sure, her videos and commercials were highly sexualized, but she openly sang a different tune in her private life: abstinence until marriage. So what's the danger? So what's the harm in tweens strutting around showing cleavage they don't have and belly buttons they do? Why is Britney dangerous?

Because she has two children who need good parenting and will probably not find it. She has millions of adoring fans who still want to be like her and do not have parents capable of guiding them away. But Britney is not the only dangerous celebrity out there.

LINDSAY LOHAN

In the early morning hours of July 24, 2007, a Los Angeles 911 operator received an emergency call from a frantic woman pleading for help because she was being followed by another car. When the police arrived they found Lindsay Lohan, who was barely twenty-one, and Michelle Peck, the mother of Lindsay's personal assistant who had just resigned a few hours earlier, standing nose to nose outside of Peck's SUV engaged in a heated argument.

When approached by the officers, a disheveled and belligerent Lindsay stepped aside sporting a clunky alcohol-monitoring bracelet wrapped cozy around her dainty ankle. She screamed that she was not the driver and pointed to one of two young men who had been in her SUV. She was the driver, though. Both young men, obviously shaken by the experience, told police they were just along for the ride and had been fearful for their lives. They also said they pleaded with Lindsay to stop the SUV and let them out, but she refused.

After Lindsay refused to take a breathalyzer test and failed her field sobriety tests, she was carted off to a police station. Her blood tested above the California legal limit. Officers also found cocaine in Lindsay's pocket. NBC News reported that somewhere along the way she shouted something like "I'm a celebrity and I can do whatever the f— I want." Maybe so, but she was charged with DUI, driving with a suspended license, and felony charges for possession of cocaine and transportation of a narcotic. Who is this belligerent celebrity and why does she think she's above the law and can do anything she wants?

Lindsay Dee Lohan was born in the Bronx on July 2, 1986, to

troubled but financially secure parents. Her father, Michael Lohan, was a one-time actor who came into money when he inherited and sold his family's pasta business. He used the money to trade in futures and became the president of New York Futures Traders for a brief period. Then he was convicted of securities fraud and spent most of Lindsay's preteen years in prison. In 2005 her father was sentenced to a maximum of four years for DUI and assaulting his brother-in-law. He served two years.

Lindsay's mother, Donata "Dina" Sullivan, claims she had been one of the famed Rockettes at Radio City Music Hall, but no credible records have surfaced to support her claim. There is no dispute, however, that she worked on Wall Street as an analyst until she became Lindsay's manager.

Lindsay has three younger siblings, two brothers and one sister, each an aspiring model or actor. Early in Lindsay's childhood, the Lohan family moved from the Bronx to more upscale neighborhoods on Long Island.

At the age of three, Lindsay began her career with Ford Models in New York. She wasn't an instant success but eventually found steady work as a child fashion model for magazine advertisements and television commercials, including spots with Bill Cosby. When Lindsay was ten years old her young career got a tremendous boost. She landed the role as Alexandra "Alli" Fowler on the popular television soap *Another World*. Next in line was the critically acclaimed dual roles as estranged twin sisters in the Disney movie *The Parent Trap*. At a mere eleven years old Lindsay was declared a major talent.

Over the next few years Lindsay landed major roles in television movies (*Life-Size*, 2000; *Get a Clue*, 2002), a series (*Bette*, 2000), three movies (*Freaky Friday*, 2003; *Confessions of a Teenage Drama Queen*, 2004; *Mean Girls*, 2004), and she turned down a role in *Inspector Gadget*. Ironically, Lindsay also turned down the lead role in *Mean Girls* played by Rachel McAdams because she worried the character was too mean and her young fan base wasn't ready for her to be that mean. How old would her fan base need to be to accept Lindsay's heightened meanness on or reportedly off the screen?

Most Lindsay watchers claim that Lindsay started to melt down shortly after she turned sixteen, the age most adolescent girls are looking forward to friends, parties, and proms. She sort of got stuck on the party part, along with her mother, who often partied hearty with her daughter. Lindsay also had a long string of celebrity "boyfriends," and a longer list of well-publicized feuds with other teenage female celebrities.

At work she gained a reputation for being exhausted and difficult. Even so, Lindsay continued to land major roles in movies (*Herbie: Fully Loaded*, 2005; *Bobbie*, 2005; *Just My Luck*, 2006; *Prairie Home Companion*, 2006; *Georgia Rule*, 2007; *Chapter 27*, 2007) and garner votes as one of the top one hundred sexiest women. But by the time the teen movie queen turned twenty, her personal and professional problems were coming to a head. The entertainment media was full of Lindsay's heavy partying and bad behavior, and her young fans couldn't get enough. Party on dude!

In February 2007 Lindsay decided she needed help and admitted herself into an upscale drug and alcohol rehabilitation facility. According to scattered interviews with the media, Lindsay expressed doubts about rehab and being addicted to drugs or alcohol. In May 2007 Lindsay was arrested for DUI after she lost control of her Mercedes-Benz convertible and struck a curb. Police also found a small amount of cocaine in her car.

Two days later Lindsay checked into another upscale rehabilitation clinic. Even after a second try at rehab and another arrest, Lindsay's attitude did not change much. According to some reports, Lindsay didn't take the treatment seriously and preferred to text-message rather than follow the treatment regimen. She broke the rules by coming and going whenever she wanted. Staff also offered complaints about her hygiene and the condition of her room. With that kind of attitude, few were surprised when Lindsay left rehab after forty-five days and went right back to her wild child ways. And she kept the party going in her new film, *I Know Who Killed Me,* as a red-hot pole dancer.

Those familiar with the stresses of stardom point to her troubled background for answers to her dysfunctional behavior. Actress Christine Lakin told *Us* magazine, "It's difficult growing up in this business. Hopefully she can get her life back on track." Jane Fonda added, "We can't know what it's like to grow up famous starting at age twelve with such family problems."[2]

Yet some girls from lofty backgrounds also become wild childs.

PARIS HILTON

Paris Whitney Hilton, born on February 17, 1981, is the oldest of four children of Richard and Kathy Hilton. A child of plenty, Paris had the advantage of living in several exclusive homes and swank hotel suites in New York and California. Paris also attended high school in California and New York but dropped out after her junior year. She subsequently earned a GED.

Paris was a heiress to the vast Hilton Hotel fortune until her grandfather, Barron Hilton, became disgusted with her bad behavior and stripped her of her inheritance. She is still in the good graces of her father and may share in her father's real estate fortune, but she may not need it. Paris has become a valuable piece of property herself.

Paris pursued a modeling career as a child. Her first appearances were at charity events, then in a number of major advertisement campaigns. At nineteen Paris cavorted as a New York socialite. In 2003 she landed a costarring role with Nicole Richie in the reality television series *The Simple Life.*

Then Paris became a sensation and media favorite when a three-year-old homemade sex video with her then-boyfriend was leaked one week prior to the premier of *The Simple Life.* Although Paris told the press that she was humiliated by the sex tape, it was subsequently produced and released on DVD as *1 Night in Paris*, with Paris listed as the director.

Perhaps boosted by Paris's greatly heightened celebrity status as a porn star, *The Simple Life* was a commercial success and ran for three seasons before Paris and Nicole had a major dispute and Fox cancelled it. E!, the Entertainment Channel, picked up the show for two additional seasons. Paris has also appeared in other television shows as a guest star and in music videos. Her movie credits include mostly cameo appearances and minor roles. She founded Heiress Records in 2004 and released her own music productions to modest success.

Even though her movie credits are mostly forgettable and her musical talent questionable, Paris had a vast fan base. They hungered for information about her personal life and the paparazzi worked hard to feed them. Paris was featured everywhere doing just about anything from the mundane to the sensational. Encouraged by the vast amount of media coverage of her every movement, Paris decided the world wanted more of her, so she released *Confessions of an Heiress: A Tongue-in-Chic Peek behind the Pose*, an autobiographical book cowritten by Merle Ginsberg.[3] In the book, Paris presents a long list of advice for aspiring young celebrities such as never have only one cell phone, never wear the same clothes twice, and, of course, act ditzy. Critics panned the book, but Paris's tip on acting ditzy was good advice for success. The book became a *New York Times* best seller. She and Ginsberg followed up with *Your Heiress Diary: Confess It All to Me*, a designer diary. More success came with the creation of a perfume line.

During the year the homemade sex video was released, Paris earned $2 million according to *Forbes*. The following two years after the release, her income more than tripled to $6.5 million in 2004–2005 and $7 million in 2005–2006. Apparently sex and notoriety pay well. Young girls, are you taking notes?

Notoriety may also give license to behave badly and to drive drunk. In 2006 Paris was arrested in California and charged with

DUI. Her license was suspended. In January 2007 Paris pled no contest to a reckless driving charge related to alcohol. Paris was fined and sentenced to thirty-six months on probation with stipulations that she attend an alcohol education program. But in January and again in February 2007, Paris was caught driving with a suspended license. The February episode also included speeding and driving without headlights on after dark. Paris had also failed to enroll in the court-mandated alcohol education program. Unlike Paris's adoring fans, the Los Angeles City district attorney was not amused and charged her with violating the conditions of her probation.

When a judge sentenced Paris to forty-five days in jail, he set off a firestorm of protests and counterprotests. While Paris and her attorneys prepared an appeal, one of her most strident fans organized an online petition asking Governor Schwarzenegger to pardon Paris. Of course Paris strongly supported the petition, as did thousands of fans. Opponents to the pardon started their own petition in support of the sentence. After the controversy settled, Paris dropped her plans to appeal. But another firestorm was brewing.

Two days after Paris attended the 2007 MTV Movie Awards, she checked herself into the Century Regional Detention Facility, an all-female jail with a special section for high-profile inmates, located in a Los Angeles suburb. Four days later, Los Angeles County Sheriff Lee Baca reassigned Paris from jail to home confinement with an electronic monitoring device, contrary to the court order that Paris would serve all her time in jail. The judge was not impressed by Baca's actions and ordered Paris into court the next morning. He voided the sheriff's order and sent Paris back to jail. The twenty-six-year-old protested loudly and cried for her mother before officers escorted her out of the courtroom.

Paris got one concession, however. Since the sheriff's order of reassignment was based upon an unspecified medical condition, Paris was transferred to the medical wing of the Twin Towers Correctional Facility in Los Angeles. After about three days of jail medical treatment, Paris showed improvement and was moved back to the Century all-female facility to complete her sentence. Her medical condition? She said she suffered from claustrophobia.

With time off for good behavior, Paris served twenty-two days of her forty-five-day sentence. On June 28, 2007, two days after being released from jail, Paris appeared on *Larry King Live*. She told King that the time in jail gave her an opportunity to reflect and she now planned to start a new life. Paris repeatedly denied she had used drugs. She also talked about being inspired by prison minister Marty Angelo, who previously petitioned the court to serve Paris's jail sentence for her if Paris was placed in an alternative treatment program. Paris went on to say that she read the Bible a lot while in jail. When pressed by King, Paris seemed uncomfortable and was unable to quote any particularly inspiring scriptures. In the end, she promised to use her celebrity status to help others.

The next day most media journalists who watched the King interview reported that Paris was not believable. Her friends reported that Paris was hurt by the criticism but grateful that her loyal fan base continued to support her.

In July 2007 Paris announced that she was getting serious about her music career. She was taking singing lessons and learning how to play the guitar in preparation for a new album and a concert tour. Just how this helps other people is unclear.

When I mentioned to a colleague that I planned to begin the first chapter of this book with Britney Spears, Lindsay Lohan, and Paris Hilton, she said, "Good, I think they are horrible role models for our kids." After a pause and a mischievous grin she continued, "I think you should call them the Triple Xs of Evil." I got the pun and agreed that each was a dangerous role model and collectively they certainly deserved an XXX rating. But I wasn't quite ready to declare them evil. Even so, I was encouraged that others confirmed that the trio was, indeed, dangerous. But who else cares, other than a few obscure colleagues trying to mend fractured families and myself? Maybe a few parents.

A recent *Newsweek* poll found that 77 percent of Americans believe that Britney, Lindsay, and Paris have too much influence on young girls, 84 percent of adults said sex plays a bigger role in popular culture than it did twenty or thirty years ago, and 70 percent said that sex playing a bigger role in our culture was a bad influence on young people. Columnist and editor Kathleen Deveny writes, "Like never before, our kids are being bombarded by images of oversexed, underdressed celebrities who can't seem to step out of a car without displaying their well-waxed private parts to photographers."[4]

But the truth is the increase in narcissistic, oversexualized tweens is only one part of an even uglier trend facing young girls today.

MEAN GIRLS

No one is sure when girls started to get meaner, but warning signs were posted a number of times by educators and mental health professionals since the mid-1980s. At first it was just educators talking with colleagues about how surprised they were that girls were getting so difficult to discipline in class and how aggressive they were with peers. Then teachers were concerned that they had to break up more physical fights between girls on high school campuses. One reported that two boys were fighting and a girl, who was smaller than both the boys, jumped in and started wailing away on one of them. It took two male teachers and a female hall monitor to drag the girl off. All of this talk was considered just a spurt in aggression, often seen with adolescents, mostly boys. The episodes of girl aggression were still pretty rare.

Then official reports from national law enforcement agencies about criminal violence by adolescents during the 1990s provided a wake-up call. While the rate of aggravated assault among boys under eighteen years of age decreased by about 5 percent, the rate increased for girls by about 57 percent. In addition, girls were arming themselves. Weapons violence for girls rose about 44 percent, while for boys it decreased by about 7 percent. And just plain criminal offenses against people by girls rose a staggering 157 percent, while the rate increased for boys by less than half that amount (71 percent).[5] What would the twenty-first century bring? It didn't take long to find out.

My wife is an educator. We have many friends and colleagues who are educators. I have also consulted school staffs about disciplinary problems with students. Over the past two decades or so, my contact with educators revealed that the age of girls behaving badly was getting younger and younger each year. At one time the behavior was mostly in high schools, but now it was trickling down farther into the lower grades with each succeeding school year. While assaults by girls in high school were becoming way too common, I was startled recently when a kindergarten teacher told me she had been attacked by a five-year-old girl brandishing a screwdriver. When the teacher tried to disarm the little girl, the girl bit the teacher with such force that the teacher was taken to the emergency room for treatment. A human bite is a serious medical matter, even if it is from a "sweet" little girl.

At first I thought this was simply an isolated episode of a troubled young girl until other teachers in all grades reported a scary increase in seriously aggressive behavior by girls in their classes. One teacher summarized many other teachers' concerns when she said, "Girls are a lot more disobedient, use foul language, dress like whores, even the little ones, and are mouthy, mouthy, mouthy." Another said, "I didn't think I would ever say this but I am very careful when I approach a girl who is being disruptive in class. I don't know what she might do. In the past, I used to handle the problem myself, now I just call for the disciplinarian. I love my job, but it's not worth getting killed for."

While the number of girls who kill is still small, the teacher's concerns were justified. Some girls do not stop at being mouthy and hitting; they kill. The rate of murders by girls in the United

States is higher than that of boys in some other industrialized countries. Overall, juveniles commit about two thousand murders per year (12 percent of the total murders in the United States), and girls commit about 10 percent of all juvenile murders.[6]

Researchers are quick to point to media images of aggressive females as an important link in the growing problem of mean girls. A favorite target for researchers is MTV, which is watched by 78 percent of girls and 73 percent of boys between the ages of twelve and nineteen. One study found that females were 22 percent of the aggressors in violent interactions and almost half of the victims. Another study found a positive correlation between the amount of MTV watching and physical fights among third through fifth grade children. In addition, frequent MTV watchers were reported by peers as more verbally, relationally, and physically aggressive than other children. Teachers rated them as more relationally aggressive, more physically aggressive, and less helpful.[7]

But you don't have to be a sophisticated researcher to see the messages depicted by music videos on MTV and shown in other forms of media. Watch most television programs and the chances are good that violence is a major theme and much, if not all, of the violence is justified in some way and embraced as socially acceptable. It offers a simple way to solve conflicts — smack somebody in the mouth, run over him with a car, or just shoot him. Don't worry about pursuing a peaceful solution or considering possible consequences associated with the violent act, such as the pain and suffering of the victim or other empathic feelings that might dissuade most compassionate people from violence. Just do it!

The portrayal of "justified" violence with no consequences is even more prominent in children's programming. If children could distinguish real violence from fantasy violence with certainty and regularity, the problem would be less severe. But most children cannot. And the more a child accepts the violence as real, the more likely he or she will act out aggressively, especially if the aggressive character is the same sex as the child. And guess what? Over the past couple of decades, more female violent characters have shown up in television and movies.

Initial long-term studies begun in the 1960s of the effects of television violence on children's aggression showed convincingly that the more boys watched television, the more physically aggressive they became. The impact for girls was not so pronounced. But a big shift was found in similar studies of children raised in the 1970s and 1980s. The impact of television violence on girls caught up with the boys. Why this shift? What happened? By far, most of the aggressive characters depicted on television in the 1950s and 1960s were male. But, starting in the 1970s and up to today, girls have been exposed to a rising number of increasingly violent female characters.[8] Girls are kicking ass!

With all the warning signs about the negative impact of violence on television for boys and, now, girls too, why don't parents simply pull the plug? One answer is that many of today's parents were also children who sat in front of the television. Many of these parents are so desensitized to violence that they accept it as part of everyday life. They have come to believe that aggression is the major problem solver with few, if any, negative consequences.

Remember the little girl who attacked the teacher with a screwdriver? When the little girl's mother, a child of the 1980s and 1990s, was called in for a teacher-parent conference, the mother showed up wearing a T-shirt with the words "Fuck You!" on the front and "Warning, Bitch on Board" on the back. The mother quickly preempted the conference by confronting the teacher and the principal with angry accusations that the teacher must have done something to provoke her little girl. The little girl defended herself just as her mother taught her to do. The mother said, in part, "I don't take no shit from nobody and I teach my kids to take no shit from nobody." How about the pain and suffering of the teacher who had to undergo several painful medical procedures to ensure the bite did not become infected? The mother's attitude was clear: Too bad for her. She had it coming.

It would be unfair to blame the mother's attitude on her child-hood experiences with television. Many other factors are usually present in severe cases such as this, but the mother did report a personal history of watching a lot of television and the use of tele-vision as a babysitter for her daughter. *Sesame Street* was not one of their favorites.

Still not seeing the warning signs? In 2001 the American Psy-chological Association issued a report based upon an analysis of the most recent and reliable research on the impact of television violence on boys and girls. The inescapable conclusion was that 10 to 15 percent of the changes in children's aggressive behavior was related directly to television violence.[9]

Recent research on criminal violence by juveniles also shows the gap between boys' violence and girls' violence is narrowing. One girl for every ten boys was involved in some form of criminal violence in the early 1980s, but now one girl for every four boys is charged for a violent act, and 7 percent of female students have been involved in a physical fight on school property compared to 18 percent of male students.[10]

For example, one of the leading authorities on juvenile vio-lence, James Garbarino, warned in his 2006 book, *See Jane Hit*, "For the first two decades of television viewing in America, girls were mostly immune to its toxic effect with respect to aggression, but in the last two decades that immunity has ended."[11]

An increase in aggression toward others is troubling enough, but young girls are also turning the violence on themselves at an alarming rate. In 2007 the Centers for Disease Control and Preven-tion reported a disturbing reversal of recent trends in the suicide rate of girls. For the general population between ages ten and twenty-four, the suicide rate rose 8 percent from 2003 to 2004, the largest single-year increase in fifteen years. As troubling a figure as that is, the suicide rate for girls increased by a staggering 74 percent.

At the time of writing this book, no one has been able to iden-tify the reasons for the changes in young girls' suicide rates. Some mental health experts speculate that recent stern warnings about prescribing antidepressants for children have scared away parents with girls who may need the medications. Others believe that young girls are becoming more depressed and anxious overall.

Now that we have seen the warning signs, let's look at what some girls and women have been doing to live up to a dangerous reputation.

NOTES

1. Britney Spears and Lynne Spears, *Heart to Heart* (New York: Three Rivers Press, 2000).

2. "Lindsay Lohan's Cocaine Scandal," *Us*, May 21, 2007, pp. 48–49.

3. Paris Hilton and Merle Ginsberg, *Confessions of an Heiress: A Tongue-in-Chic Peek behind the Pose* (New York: Paris Hilton Entertainment, 2004).

4. Kathleen Deveny with Raina Kelley, "Girls Gone Bad?" *Newsweek*, February 12, 2007, pp. 40–47.

5. For a review of research showing mean girls are getting meaner, see James Garbarino, *See Jane Hit: Why Girls Are Growing More Violent and What We Can Do about It* (New York: Penguin, 2006).

6. Ibid., pp. 174–93.

7. Ibid., pp. 90–113

8. Ibid.

9. C. Anderson et al., "Influences of Media Violence on Youth," American Psychological Association report, 2001.

10. Garbarino, *See Jane Hit*, pp. 3–21.

11. Ibid., p. 92.

2

FEMALE PREDATORS

WOMEN WHO KILL OUTSIDE THE FAMILY

W hen most people think of those who kill outside of their family or partner relationships, they think of serial killers like Jeffrey Dahmer, Ted Bundy, the Green River or BTK killer, and Dennis Rader—all male. And when people think of women who kill outside of their family, they usually focus on Aileen Wuornos, who created quite a stir when the media erroneously reported that Aileen was the first female serial killer in the United States. While more males kill outside of the family, females are no strangers to predatory killing. Criminal psychologist Eric Hickey reported that of the four hundred serial killers officially identified from 1800 to 1995, about 16 percent were female.[1] According to Hickey's math, one in about every six serial killers is a woman.

Investigative journalist Peter Vronsky lists about 125 female serial killers who had at least three confirmed victims each.[2] The first one was not Aileen, although her case may have been the most sensational due to the media coverage at the time and the public's lingering fascination with her. Yet, more than five years after her execution in 2002, Aileen remains the queen of female serial killers. Why? Let's take a look.

AILEEN WUORNOS[3]

As I look at photographs of Aileen taken in the 1960s, I see a lovely young girl with sparkling eyes and an engaging smile. It's hard for me to imagine such a beautiful freckle-faced child would grow up to leave a legacy of dead bodies strewn up and down the country's highways. But the smiling face in the photographs belied the trouble in her young life.

A lot of kids were born and raised in the factory-feeder suburbs that sprung up around Detroit during and shortly after World War II. Aileen was one of them, born in Troy in 1956, a dingy mix of mostly low-income housing and run-down strip malls, a few miles north of Detroit. A look at Troy left no illusions that it would ever live up to its namesake.

Aileen's mother, Diane, a battered spouse who at sixteen years already had one child, Keith, separated from Aileen's father, nineteen-year-old Leo Pittman, when she was pregnant with Aileen. In addition to physically and emotionally abusing Aileen's mother, Leo had a penchant for young girls. When Aileen was an infant her father was arrested and convicted of kidnapping and raping a seven-year-old girl. Leo was sent to prison for life, which he shortened by committing suicide. Aileen never met her father.

As a teenage single mother with no marketable skills and two young children, Aileen's mother was ill-equipped to raise Aileen and Keith. She often neglected the children when she was around and frequently left Aileen and Keith alone or in the care of a roommate or babysitter. When Aileen was about six years old, her mother told the kids that she was going out to dinner. She never returned. After about a week Diane's roommate called Aileen's maternal grandparents, Lauri and Britta Wuornos. Aileen's life was about to change dramatically, and it wasn't going to be all for the better.

Aileen went into the home where her mother was raised. Lauri and Britta had three older children of their own including Aileen's mother. Even though two of the children, Barry and Lori, lived at home, Aileen's grandparents took Aileen and Keith into their home as their own and eventually adopted them. Aileen was raised believing that her grandparents were her parents and her aunt and uncle were her sister and brother, a strange situation for most, but not unusual for children who have been abandoned by their parents then raised by grandparents or other family members.

I couldn't help but wonder how healthy the Wuornos household was for Aileen. One only has to review the emotional problems Diane displayed to fear that the parental practices in the Wuornos household may have been suspect. At first Aileen seemed to thrive, but by age eight she was showing signs of a desperate need for affection and a deep-seated anger barely under control.

Children with this very bad mix of twisted emotions often demand attention in inappropriate ways and when they don't get the love they need they fly into angry tirades. They are deficient in the skills that most children learn naturally and use to handle complex social interactions with other children and adults. They don't know how to play well. Aileen's "stepsister," Lori, remembers trying many times to include Aileen in her playgroup. Although Aileen would try to play nice, she seemed to always spoil the fun, mostly with lots of whining and outbursts of anger. At one point Lori's playmates refused to include Aileen in any of their activities. They had become afraid.

Although Aileen earned high marks in school for the first two years, her behavioral problems at eight years old erased whatever potential she had for succeeding at school. Teachers were concerned and recommended evaluations of Aileen's vision, hearing, and intelligence. Aileen's IQ testing showed the classic marginal level of verbal abilities and the high level of nonverbal abilities often found in children with learning disabilities. Many children with learning disabilities are often deficient in social skills and exhibit behavioral problems.

According to some reports Britta refused to have Aileen tested for vision and hearing problems and resisted remedial counseling and treatment for her learning problems. But for whatever reason, Aileen did not receive the treatment she desperately needed at a point where it might have made a significant difference in her young life. Prisons are full of adults who were never adequately treated for learning disabilities and behavioral problems.

At her trial, Aileen testified that she received harsher discipline than her "brother" and "sister" by both Britta and Lauri. She described episodes of beatings with a leather belt on her naked buttocks and legs by Lauri and particularly cruel acts of discipline that the other children did not suffer. As examples, Aileen said that Lauri withheld Christmas presents, made her eat food out of the garbage, and drowned a kitten she was not supposed to have. To drive home the point, Lauri forced Aileen to watch the drowning. She also described frequent episodes of Lauri and Britta abusing alcohol. Aileen's "stepsiblings" later disputed Aileen's account of alcoholism and abuse in the family.

Somewhere between the age of eight and eleven years, Aileen discovered sex, lots of sex. As a tween, she traded sex with most of the boys in her neighborhood and school for money and cigarettes, sometimes participating in gang bangs with groups of boys. If Aileen was using sex to find love and acceptance, she didn't find it in the arms of neighborhood boys willing to pay her in order to pass from boy to man but nothing more. I was not surprised that Aileen gained the reputation of the neighborhood whore girl. And nearly every neighborhood with a whore girl has a nickname for her. Aileen was called "Cigarette Pig." Aileen also had sex with her brother, Keith.

Aileen's inappropriate sexual behavior as a young girl strongly suggested to me the possibility of sexual abuse. Even her mother's emotional problems and behavior suggested that Diane may have been a victim of sexual abuse. I wondered if Aileen's predicament was an incestuous family. Some evidence of this possibility is found in a report where Diane had described tension between she and her mother, Britta, because Lauri seemed interested in his daughter sexually. Diane never accused Lauri of sexual abuse but her description of his inappropriate touching and kissing raised a lot of concern for me, and especially for a vulnerable granddaughter like Aileen. The incest perpetrator often goes from child to child. Diane was out of the house, but Aileen was now in; and, like her mother before her, Aileen never accused Lauri of sexual abuse. However, Aileen described at least one attempt by Lauri to French kiss her.

I had a lot of questions. Why would a father/grandfather, who should be interested only in the well-being of his children, try to French kiss his daughter and, later, his granddaughter? When lots of alternative forms of effective discipline are available, why would a grandfather expose his granddaughter's genitals and beat her on the butt with a belt? A family like this often has secrets, deep secrets. Aileen took whatever secrets she had to the grave.

By the time Aileen was a teenager she had failed at nearly everything. Her mother abandoned her, she was rejected and denigrated by her peers, she had conflicts with teachers, and she had alienated her adoptive family. Aileen followed the path many troubled children follow and found some comfort in the world of drugs and alcohol. After experimenting with marijuana and LSD, Aileen found the cocktail that worked best for her, alcohol and tranquilizers. The dangerous combination eased her pain and calmed her, but only temporarily. More trouble was on the way.

Like a lot of troubled kids on drugs, Aileen began shoplifting. Few actually target stores where family members are employed, unless a family member is complicit. Aileen tried to shoplift at the retail store where Bitta worked and managed to get caught. I wondered about the message Aileen was trying to give. If Aileen was trying to punish her adopted mother, it worked. Britta was so humiliated she quit.

Following in her mother's footsteps, Aileen, at fourteen,

became a pregnant teenager. Her various stories about the pregnancy, including a kidnapping and rape by an Elvis impersonator, showed how disconnected she was with her sexual behavior. When Lauri found out he was outraged and took control. He took Aileen to a home for unwed mothers in Detroit and left her there with specific instructions that the baby be given up for adoption and Aileen be forbidden from seeing her child. Lauri also told the family that they were to have no contact with Aileen while she was in the home. Britta secretly disobeyed Lauri and wrote several letters to Aileen. But when Aileen gave birth to a baby boy, whom she called Keith, Lauri's instructions about adoption and the prohibition on seeing the baby were followed completely.

Aileen returned home devastated that she had not been permitted to see and hold her baby before he was taken away. But she tried to put her life on a corrected course by going back to school and reentering family life. It didn't work. Conflicts at home and school soon resurfaced. She ran away from home several times and had a few minor brushes with the police. Lauri told her that she was no longer welcome at home. At fourteen, Aileen was on the street, alone.

It didn't take much time before Aileen became street-wise. She learned early on that lots of men stopped for pretty, blond-haired teenage hitchhikers and the men were always good for some money or a place to sleep for the night. And cigarettes. But times were still tough and Aileen lived a vagrant's life, begging or stealing food and sleeping in abandoned cars.

When Aileen was fifteen, her stepsister, Lori, found her in an abandoned car just outside of Troy. She had bad news. Britta, the only mother Aileen had known, died of cirrhosis of the liver. Grieving comes in different forms. Aileen's was incomprehensible to most. She showed up at the funeral home in jeans and proceeded to act out in most inappropriate ways. When Aileen approached Britta in her coffin she bent over as if to kiss her goodbye, but instead she took a long drag off her cigarette and blew smoke in Britta's face. The family threw Aileen out of the funeral home. I wondered what had transpired between grandmother and granddaughter to fuel such anger and contempt. I remembered the shoplifting episode and wondered if both were expressions of pent-up anger Aileen had no idea how to express appropriately. But Britta's death brought an unexpected visitor from Texas.

Shortly after Britta was laid to rest, her estranged daughter and Aileen's natural mother, Diane, showed up in Troy. She hadn't changed much. Diane had produced two more children as a single mother and was living on welfare. But she seemed genuinely concerned for Aileen and Keith, the children she had abandoned about a decade before and, according to some reports, she offered to take the children back to Texas with her. It didn't happen. Diane said later that her plans were thwarted by social welfare authorities in Texas who had concerns about Diane's ability to care for two let alone four children. By the age of fifteen, Aileen had lost her natural father, been abandoned by her natural mother twice, and lost her adoptive mother. But there is more.

After Aileen's brother, Keith, managed to overcome serious substance abuse problems and join the army, he died of cancer. And Aileen's reviled stepfather/grandfather committed suicide.

Aileen put her pretty young face and body on the road. She hitchhiked across the Midwest then into the Deep South, getting by on the road by selling herself and stealing from clients or people kind enough to help her out. Then in Florida she hit what she thought was the mother lode. Lewis Fell, a sixty-nine-year-old retiree from a wealthy and respected family in Philadelphia, stopped to pick her up. Fell, like a lot of older men, was drawn to beautiful young women, often known as "trophy women" because they become a symbol of an older man's ability to still attract sexually desirable women. Never mind that Aileen was a vagrant prostitute. He could clean her up and parade her around.

And Aileen didn't mind being paraded around. She, like a lot of other emotionally disturbed and socially deficient women, hoped someday to find a "trophy husband" like Fell who looked reasonably good, had money, and would overlook past transgressions. With Fell on her arm, maybe she would now get the attention and respect she so desperately needed. In short fashion, Fell and Aileen got engaged and married. As I looked at the wedding photo published in the social section of the Daytona newspaper, I knew that the smiling face of Aileen the married woman was the same as the smiling face of Aileen the eight-year-old I saw in her childhood photo. Nothing in either revealed the trouble to come.

Aileen quickly returned to Troy to show off her "trophy husband." She flaunted her diamond ring to anyone who would look. But Aileen didn't know how to make an intimate relationship work, any more than she knew how to make relationships work as a child. Within days she was doing what she knew how to do best. She was getting drunk, hanging out with lowlifes, and raging. Reports surfaced that Aileen had actually beaten Fell with his walking cane because he was stingy with his money. Her trophy husband had seen enough. He went back to Florida without her, filed a restraining order, and got a divorce. Within one month Aileen had reached the highest point in her young life only to lose everything again.

Aileen went back on the road again. Maybe she could never be a trophy wife, but she knew how to negotiate the mean streets. Always on the move, Aileen's deficits in developing long-term intimate relationships didn't matter. She could hook, steal, rage, change her name, then move on. Over a ten-year period Aileen was arrested for a number of criminal offenses not uncommon for a vagrant lifestyle and alcohol abuse, such as DUI, theft, and drunk and disorderly. But Aileen's rage was taking a new turn; she got a gun.

At age twenty-five, Aileen tried another intimate relationship with an older man. She moved in with fifty-two-year-old Jay Watts. Watts was not a wealthy socialite like her first husband but an autoworker like her deceased grandfather, Lauri. Watts was good to her, and Aileen managed to be a good companion and to keep her rage in check for about two months. Then one night the couple argued. Watts and Aileen have given conflicting accounts of the argument but the outcome is not disputed. Aileen got up the next morning, armed herself with a six-pack of beer, and drove to the beach in a car restored and given to her by Watts. After polishing off the six-pack she bought more beer, then a .22 caliber handgun at a pawnshop, ammunition at a K-Mart, and whiskey at a liquor store. To this already lethal mix she added Librium, a powerful tranquilizer.

Aileen later reported she was convinced her relationship with Watts was over and she was going to commit suicide. Instead, a drunk, tranquilized, bikini-clad Aileen staggered into a convenience store, waved her .22 around, and demanded money. When the police caught up with her a few miles away, she offered no resistance. Aileen later explained that she staged the holdup as a test of Watts's love for her. In Aileen's mind, if Watts really loved her he would bail her out of jail, forgive her, and take her back home. Convoluted? Yes, but remember, Aileen had been caught stealing from the store where her adopted mother worked. Although Watts didn't rescue Aileen the way she had hoped, he did find her an attorney. Later, after Aileen was sentenced to three years in prison, Watts visited her and they corresponded for about a year.

While in prison, Aileen tried a new tact to find someone to love her: She placed an ad in the personal section of a biker magazine. Not surprising, she was flooded with suitors. Aileen corresponded with a few men until she was released from prison in 1983.

Back on the road again, Aileen hitchhiked to Washington, DC, the home of one of her paper suitors, Ed, a forty-seven-year-old engineer. Not only was Ed surprised to see Aileen, but he was also in for a bigger surprise: Aileen told Ed she was gay. Even so, Aileen moved in. And she wasn't finished with Jay Watts just yet.

During the three months she lived with Ed, Aileen made several trips to Florida to stay with Watts then returned. Ed reported that Aileen was drinking constantly and raging with little or no provocation. Both men reported Aileen was seemingly consumed with violent fantasies, including stomping bikers and living a Bonnie and Clyde existence.

One day Aileen surprised Ed with an offer of sex. She denounced her claim of being gay and took Ed into the bedroom to prove it. After a few minutes of afterglow, Aileen got up. She went to the kitchen, got a knife, went back to the bedroom, and threatened to kill her surprised lover. Ed became a good crisis negotiator very quickly and with a lot of patience and effort got Aileen settled down. Ed knew right then that he had to get Aileen out of his apartment and out of his life as soon as possible. But he had to be careful. Aileen was a dangerous woman and getting more dangerous.

On another night Aileen really got on a drinking binge. She drank so much she collapsed. Ed seized the opportunity and took Aileen to a hospital and left her, much like the way Lauri took her when she was fourteen to a home for unwed mothers and left her.

For the next few months after Aileen was discharged from the hospital she went back on the road. She hooked and stole from clients and innocent people who offered her a ride, like she had done since she was fourteen. Then her criminal activities began to escalate. Using a number of aliases, Aileen added stealing cars and handguns, forging bad checks, and fleeing to avoid arrest, prosecution, and sentencing to her criminal repertoire.

In June 1986 a thirty-one-year-old Aileen walked into a gay bar in Daytona where she met who she thought must be the love of her life. She had been wrong before, but this was not an older man who would try to control her or a friend who would abandon her. This was Tyria "Ty" Moore, a woman six years younger than Aileen. Ty was quite taken by Aileen's energy and fun-loving ways. Aileen was quite taken by Ty's looks and laid-back approach to life. They seemed to fit each other's needs. They became a couple.

Together, Aileen and Ty joined the ranks of the downtrodden

who eke out an existence in the dingy motels and backwater apartments of Florida seldom touched by well-heeled tourists on their way to sun, sand, and fun. They lived mostly on Ty's meager wages as a housekeeper at low-end motels. While Ty worked, Aileen stayed home getting drunk, until money got tight, then Aileen would get on the road again and hook.

Like a lot of intimate relationships, the couple had differences. Aileen dominated Ty and showed hot flashes of jealously. At times Ty would bring friends home from work. Aileen appeared sociable on the surface but her anger seethed just below the façade. I was reminded of the playmates Aileen's stepsister, Lori, would bring around whom Aileen would find some way to run off. She still did not know how to play well. She still needed to be the focus of attention. She was still scary.

When money got tight Aileen would try to pull herself together and turn tricks on the highways. But no longer was Aileen peddling exciting sex as a forbidden teenager or a sexy twenty-something. After nearly two decades of drug, alcohol, and cigarette abuse, Aileen's thirty-something wares were roughshod, flabby, and shabby. Most of the easy money and sugar daddies waved and whizzed on by, and the men who did stop could be as scary as Aileen. The mean streets were about to get meaner, at least in Aileen's mind.

On November 30, 1989, Aileen threw on a pair of cutoff jean shorts and a sleeveless T-shirt, then headed for the highway. She and Ty had been looking at a new apartment but they needed more money before they could move in. Maybe she would have a good night.

Aileen thought she got lucky when a Cadillac slowed then pulled over to pick her up. The man behind the wheel looked to be in his fifties and was well dressed. Maybe he would be good for some extra money. Certainly good for some alcohol and cigarettes.

The next morning, Aileen came home with the Cadillac and by her own account, lots of money. She told Ty the car was borrowed and she had to return it, but in the meantime they could use it and the money to move into an apartment they both wanted right away instead of waiting. After moving their belongings and some items unfamiliar to Ty from the car into the new apartment, Aileen said she needed to return the car to its owner. Aileen tossed a bicycle into the trunk and drove off.

When Aileen returned that evening, she and Ty celebrated their new home with beer and television, then Aileen suddenly announced that she had killed somebody. Ty sat motionless and silent, watching television while Aileen described shooting the owner of the Cadillac and hiding his body in the woods. When Aileen tried to show Ty a photograph of the man as though she were a proud mother showing pictures of her kids, Ty kept her eyes glued on the television.

A few days later, police on a routine patrol discovered the Cadillac parked off the side of a rural road. The car was empty of personal belongings and wiped clean of fingerprints, but somebody failed to wipe the blood from the backrest in the driver's seat. Officers called in the VIN number and the number on the plates. Partially hidden nearby, the police found a couple of plastic tumblers and a half-empty bottle of vodka. The police also found a wallet with business cards and some expired credit cards. When the call came back identifying the owner, the name on the business and credit cards matched. The owner was fifty-one-year-old Richard Mallory, owner of an appliance repair shop who had a reputation for soliciting prostitutes.

On December 13, 1989, several men were scavenging a wildcat garbage dump about five miles from where police found the abandoned Cadillac. When the men pulled a large piece of discarded carpeting aside, they didn't find valuable recyclables, they found Mallory. He stared up at them with four bullets in his chest. He was fully clothed with nothing amiss except for pockets turned inside out.

Forensics determined that at least one bullet hit him while he was seated in the Cadillac. Ballistics identified the bullets as .22

caliber copper-coated hollow-points, small but very effective in ripping the inside of a body to shreds with tiny shrapnel. Toxicology tests showed Mallory was a little drunk when he was killed. One last drink, but not the last victim.

On Saturday morning, May 19, 1990, forty-year-old David Spears crawled into his pickup and headed toward Orlando for a routine weekend stay with his ex-wife and their three children. But this weekend was more than routine; one of his daughters was graduating from college and celebrating her twenty-third birthday. Dave had a nice cash graduation/birthday surprise for his daughter. If the traffic was not too bad he would arrive at his usual time, about two in the afternoon. By everybody's account David was a hardworking, soft-spoken nice guy who was predictable, reliable, and honest. He also always showed up on time or called to let you know he was running late. On this very special day, he did neither.

Several days later, Spears's pickup truck was found looted and abandoned on a remote roadside. When police examined the truck they found blood on the inside running board on the driver's side and a condom package. It was empty.

On June 1, Spears's badly decomposing body was found about eighty miles beyond his wife's house. He was naked. The autopsy and ballistics showed that Spears had been shot at least nine times with a .22 caliber. He had been shot at least once but more likely twice in the back.

When asked later about her second murder, Aileen told investigators she was hitchhiking near the I-4 and US 27 intersection when Spears stopped to pick her up. She said Spears drove to a deserted area near Homosassa, arriving at about one or two in the morning. They drank beer, got naked, and started to fool around. When they crawled into the bed of his truck to have sex, Spears started to rough her up.

According to Aileen she got really scared when she saw he had a lead pipe. She jumped out of the bed and ran to the passenger side to get her handbag. Hidden in the handbag was Aileen's tidy little .22. Aileen told police she shot Spears once while he stood at the back of the truck, once when he tried to get into the truck to get away, then another time, which knocked Spears to the ground. How about the rest of the bullet holes?

Aileen thought about it but said she couldn't recall shooting Spears more than three times. She admitted, however, that she was angry and shouting at Spears that she was going to kill him because he tried to get violent with her. It was the second chorus of her theme song: He was going to rape me.

Aileen left Spears to the cruel critters of the Chassahowitzka marshes and headed home with his truck and a graduation present meant for somebody special. When she got home she took anything she could sell from the truck then abandoned it along one of Florida's many remote roads that lead to nowhere. Ty remembered Aileen bringing another vehicle to the house, a pickup she thought, and Aileen again saying that she borrowed it.

There seems to be no doubt that Aileen killed Spears, but her story about how and why it happened has always been suspect. Even a quick look at a Florida map shows that Spears was only about thirty to forty-five minutes from his destination if he encountered Aileen at the location she told police. Most of Spears's family and friends are certain he would not have forgone a joyous celebration for his daughter and driven another eighty miles beyond his destination for sex with a highway tramp. At the very least he would have called to say he would be late. And why did it take nearly twelve hours to get from the purported hitchhiking spot to the killing zone, a route a little over one hundred miles. Most people can drive from one end of Florida to the other in that length of time.

What we know for sure is that Spears and Aileen ended up together in his pickup, and at some point his body was found riddled with bullets in a remote area off US 19 near Chassahowitzka. It would be consistent with what we know about Aileen's anger and violent fantasies that something transpired between Aileen and Spears other than her account of the events that triggered her rage response. We also know Aileen shot Spears many more times than she recalled or was willing to admit. Some have speculated that Aileen's method of getting money had changed with Mallory. Aileen wasn't turning cheap tricks on the highways anymore, she was robbing and killing. Like Bonnie and Clyde. But Aileen never wavered from her story and she took the truth about her second murder with her into the execution chamber.

About two weeks after Spears was killed, Charles Carskaddon was driving his Cadillac near Tampa on his way to pick up his fiancée. They had plans to move to Missouri, where he had found a steady job as a punch press operator. Somewhere along the way his path crossed with Aileen Wuornos. When he didn't show up as expected, Carskaddon's fiancée alerted law enforcement.

At her trial, Aileen calmly described how she shot Carskaddon when he got into the backseat of his Cadillac, then rummaged through his car for valuables. When she found a .45 automatic pistol in the glove compartment, Aileen went ballistic. Somehow she felt betrayed and was certain Carskaddon had planned to kill her. She reloaded her trusty .22 and pumped Carskaddon full of lead, even though he was already dead. This episode is telling. Aileen's theme that everybody was out to get her played out even after she had removed the threat. Her rage was always fueled and ready to go.

Aileen was not only robbing and killing; she was also taking the bounty home to her lover, Ty, who seemed to pretend that nothing untoward was happening. They even drove Carskaddon's Cadillac out to a remote area and used his .45 for target practice. They hung onto the Cadillac for a couple of days before dumping it.

A few days later, Aileen was on the prowl again. Her unwitting prey this time was Peter Siems, a sixty-year-old preacher who was taking a break from interstate driving in a coffee shop near Bunnell. He was on his way to meet a Christ Is the Answer Crusade caravan. At some point he and Aileen got into his Sunbird full of Bibles.

According to Aileen she shot the preacher after they both got naked because she thought he was going to rape her. Like she did with the other highway murders, Aileen discarded the body then drove home to Ty with the car and the loot. But this time Aileen deviated from her usual game plan. She kept the vehicle instead of disposing of it right away, a mistake that would soon put the police hot on her trail.

About a month later, Aileen and Ty decided to celebrate the Fourth of July by getting drunk and taking the Sunbird out for a spin and more beer. When Aileen became too drunk to drive she turned the wheel over to an equally drunk Ty, who promptly crashed the Sunbird into a ditch. As Aileen and Ty scrambled out of the car, some people from nearby houses came out to help. In spite of being so drunk they could hardly walk, Aileen and Ty managed to run away, but not before the would-be rescuers got a good look at them and called the police.

When the police discovered that the wrecked Sunbird belonged to the still-missing Siems, the forensics team examined it carefully. They found Aileen's handprint. Peter Siems, Aileen's fourth victim, has never been found.

Only a few weeks after the close call with the Sunbird, fifty-year-old Eugene "Troy" Burress and the company truck he used to deliver sausages went missing. Burress was married with children and grandchildren. He had no history of unreliable or inappropriate behavior on the job or at home. A check of his route the next day led police to his truck, abandoned on the side of the road. A few days later, Burress's body with two bullet wounds was found lying facedown off a dirt road. Aileen had struck again.

When Aileen confessed to the Burress murder, she said that Burress picked her up in his sausage truck and they agreed to have sex. But Burress turned mean, threw some money at her, and said he was going to rape her. She pulled out her gun and shot him once in the chest. When Burress fell face-first on the ground, Aileen shot him again in the back.

On September 11, 1990, Dick Humphreys, a child abuse investigator and former Alabama police officer and chief, did not come home as expected. Humphreys was happily married and had no history of staying out late or not coming home. The next day some children riding their bicycles near a housing development found Humphreys' body. He was fully clothed but his pockets were turned inside out. He was also still wearing his wedding ring and watch. He had been shot seven times, and, for the first time, Aileen shot one of her victims in the back of the head, execution style. But he wouldn't be the last.

On November 17, 1990, sixty-year-old Walter Jeno Antonio picked up Aileen Wuornos while she was hitchhiking. Antonio was engaged, a trucker, a security guard, and a member of the reserve police. According to Aileen, Antonio agreed to give her money to have sex in the backseat of his car. But, when she undressed, he flashed a badge and threatened to turn her over to police if she didn't have sex with him for free. They got out of the car and argued. When Antonio headed toward the passenger side of the car, Aileen pulled her gun. Antonio tried to disarm Aileen but failed. When Antonio tried to flee, Aileen shot him in the back, then two more times to make sure. Then Aileen walked up to her victim and shot him once in the back of the head, execution style, to make absolutely sure he was dead.

As Aileen Wuornos finished off her seventh victim, the police were already closing in on her and Ty. As careful as she had been she still left a thumbprint when she pawned Mallory's booty at a pawnshop and a palm print on the Sunbird. Police now knew Aileen had used an alias and they were watching her very carefully. Witnesses to the Sunbird incident also helped prepare an artist's sketch of Aileen and Ty, which had been shown on television and published in the newspapers. When Ty realized that police were connecting her to the murders, she left Aileen in Florida and headed north.

Alone again, Aileen crashed a party at a biker bar in Daytona and got completely drunk. When she passed out on a car seat in a corner, the police dragged her out and took her to jail. Her seventh victim would be her last.

Law enforcement was also hot on Ty's trail, catching up with her in Scranton, Pennsylvania, where she was hiding out with some relatives. Ty quickly made a deal to save herself. In the end, the only person with whom Aileen Wuornos managed to maintain a long-term relationship betrayed her. Her lover finally did her in with a series of police-guided, secretly recorded phone conversations; Aileen exonerated Ty and essentially confessed to the murders.

About a week later, Aileen gave a lengthy confession during which she started to assert her self-defense defense. According to Aileen each one of her seven victims had turned violent and tried to rape her. She shot each of them in self-defense. Later some of her stories changed, becoming more fantastic in their violent content. Aileen's revised story about Mallory included bondage, anal sex, and torture, none of which was mentioned to Ty when Aileen showed up at home, without a scratch on her, in Mallory's Cadillac. I was reminded of Aileen's previous violent fantasies about stomping bikers and how her later story about Mallory sounded like a fantasy. We will never know for sure why Aileen killed seven men in about a one-year period. But it is curious that her murders all happened while she was living with Ty.

Aileen's trial garnered lots of attention from the media, people sympathetic to her plight, and others driven to save her. One of these, Arlene Pralle, a born-again Christian, became one of Aileen's spokespersons with the media, testified at Aileen's trial, and legally adopted Aileen. Another, Phyllis Chesler, an author and professor at City University of New York, Staten Island, voluntarily jumped in as an "expert" on battered women who kill their abusers. She took a strong stand in the media that Aileen was a perfect example of the victimization of women by a phallocentric, heteropatriarchal society. At times her outrage seemed to equal Aileen's raging responses.

When Chesler offered her services to Aileen's attorneys they refused, but Chesler managed to meet with Aileen anyway and she supported Aileen's story of self-defense against rape. After Aileen was convicted of murdering Mallory, Chesler hired an investigator to look into Mallory's past for purposes of an appeal. The information the investigator found was equivocal. According to Chesler's investigator, Mallory at age nineteen broke into a home and made sexual advances toward the woman who lived there. When she resisted he ran off. For this offense (housebreaking for the intent to commit rape), Mallory spent four years in a Maryland prison and received psychiatric treatment for "irresistible urges to make sexual advances to women." For ten years after his release from prison, Mallory was registered as a "defective delinquent." The investigator found that, for at least twenty years before he was murdered, Mallory frequented strippers and prostitutes, none of whom reported any abusive behavior. One reported that Mallory drank too much at times and would have mood swings. While Mallory had business problems, the investigator found no records that Mallory was ever arrested for another criminal offense. When this information was presented to the appeals judge, it was refused on the grounds that it was not admissible because Mallory's arrest was too remote in time and the information would not have added to Aileen's self-defense claim of a brutal rape by Mallory.

During her first ten years on death row, Aileen remained firm in her claim of rape by Mallory and her other victims. She lashed out at the victims' family members and anyone else who disputed her claim. Then, with the help of Arlene Pralle, she found Jesus. She dropped all of her appeals and told the media that she killed the seven men because "I wanted to." She also revealed that Mallory did not rape her but she "snapped" when he told her that he had been in prison for rape.

Aileen was not the first female serial killer, but she generated more public interest and a larger media cottage industry than that of any other female killer. In addition to the widespread media coverage, including the Court TV coverage of her trial, Aileen's case has inspired a TV movie, a TV documentary, a comic book, a *True Crime* trading card, an opera, and an Academy Award–winning movie.

Aileen was a throwaway child, a child who probably should never have been conceived because no one wanted to be her parent. It wasn't her fault that no one wanted to hold her, love her, teach her, and share in the joy of her upbringing. What Aileen did as a throwaway child was learn survival skills. These survival skills got her to adulthood but did not foster the skills necessary to find the love and affection any human needs.

On October 9, 2002, at the age of forty-six, Aileen Wuornos became the tenth woman in the United States to be executed since the death penalty was reintroduced in 1976.

Unlike Aileen, most female serial killers target family members or acquaintances rather than strangers. But one does not have to be a serial killer like Aileen to pose a danger to strangers. Women kill strangers or people they know for a variety of reasons.

THE BADDEST BITCH

Shauntay Henderson's mother died when she was young, and it wasn't long before her father abandoned her. Her childhood was spent trying to grow up in a tough housing project in Kansas City, Missouri, a breeding ground for wannabe and real "gangstas." Like a lot of disenfranchised children trying to survive the mean streets, Shauntay turned to the protection and excitement of a violent street gang. She found a home. Shauntay also found a vicious mentor with a penchant for high-powered weapons and settling disputes ruthlessly. She liked what she saw and soon earned the reputation of the "Baddest Bitch" on the street.[4]

After she shot a rival gang member while he sat in his car with his girlfriend, Shauntay went underground. But not for long.

Authorities say Shauntay was at least partially responsible for a series of about fifty shootings, about five or six murders, and a surge of gangstas killing gangstas or anybody else their bullets would hit. The Baddest Bitch was back—with a vengeance.

For her efforts, Shauntay became the eighth woman to make the FBI Ten Most Wanted list. The girl from the projects loved the limelight. She proclaimed her glory on her MySpace Web page and rapped about the virtues of the gangsta life until police caught up with her in an alleged drug dealer's apartment. At age twenty-four, if convicted of her alleged crimes, the Baddest Bitch on the street may soon become the Baddest Bitch in prison.

THE BARBIE DOLL

Pretty and popular Karla Homolka dreamed the dream of most teenagers—find the perfect husband. When she met handsome Paul Bernardo she thought she had found her dream mate. She did. They were perfect together, like Ken and Barbie. But unlike the Barbie dolls, Karla and Paul had a dark side. Very dark. By the time they married in 1991, they had raped and murdered at least two teenage girls. One of the victims was Karla's fifteen-year-old sister.

The couple enjoyed the attacks so much they captured their fun on videotape. Karla first gave her sister to Paul as a Christmas gift, then gave the videotape of the rape to him as a wedding gift. During the first year of their marriage, the couple kidnapped another teenage girl, whom they raped, brutalized, and murdered. They added another videotape to their growing collection of self-produced horror films.

When apprehended, Karla claimed that her perfect husband, Paul, beat her into participation. She said she was a battered wife. The videotapes were discovered after she struck a deal with the prosecution, and they showed something quite different. As the videos played, no sign of coercion or battering was revealed. Karla was a sometimes active, sometimes indifferent, but always a more-than-willing participant in the vicious attacks.

Paul was sentenced to life in prison. In 2005, after serving twelve years in prison, Karla was released to search for another perfect husband.

THE BABY SNATCHER

On September 15, 2006, twenty-year-old Tiffany Hall summoned police to a local park in East Saint Louis, Illinois. She told the dispatcher that she was going into labor. When first responders arrived they found Tiffany holding the body of a dead baby. Tiffany and the baby were taken to a hospital where Tiffany refused to be examined. According to police, Tiffany gave conflicting reasons why she went into labor, including rape and consensual sex. An autopsy of the baby showed no signs of trauma and examiners were unable to determine the cause of death.

Tiffany made arrangements for a nice funeral service and burial. While a couple of relatives waited for Tiffany to arrive and for the funeral service to begin, Tiffany called the funeral director to reschedule the services for another day. She said she wanted more time so more relatives could attend. The funeral director was unable to grant her request and Tiffany arrived about two hours later, accompanied by her boyfriend. At the funeral, Tiffany told her boyfriend a fantastic story: The baby was not hers. She had killed a friend, Jimella Tunstall, and had stolen her baby. The boyfriend called the police and Tiffany was arrested.

When the police arrived at Tunstall's apartment they found a gruesome scene. Tunstall was lying in a pool of blood, her womb ripped open and empty. A pair of scissors lay nearby. Tunstall's three children, ages seven, two, and one, were found stuffed in a washing machine and dryer in the basement of the apartment complex.

Tiffany has been charged with four counts of first-degree murder and one count of intentional homicide of an unborn child for these alleged crimes. The prosecutor says he will seek the death penalty. I await news of the defense strategy.

NOTES

1. Eric W. Hickey, *Serial Murderers and Their Victims* (Belmont, CA: Wadsworth/Thomson Learning, 2002), pp. 213–15.

2. Peter Vronsky, *Female Serial Killers: How and Why Women Become Monsters* (New York: Berkley Publishing Group, 2007), pp. 435–43.

3. Ibid.

4. Catharine Skipp and Arian Campo-Flores, "One of America's 'Baddest,'" *Newsweek*, April 16, 2007, p. 42.

3

UNTIL DEATH
DO US PART

WOMEN WHO KILL THEIR PARTNERS

P sychologist Donald Dutton, a preeminent expert in interpersonal violence, points out that until the middle 1970s, research on intimate partner violence was overshadowed by studies on aggression toward strangers and was virtually absent from scientific literature. Today, we know that violence between intimate partners is common and as many as one out of two women have experienced some form of physical, sexual, or psychological abuse. We also know that approximately one-fourth of the nation's homicide victims are related to their assailants, and of the homicides occurring within the family, about half involve a spouse killing a spouse, with wives being the majority of victims.[1]

While the results of recent studies question the widely held belief that only males perpetrate intimate partner violence, women don't usually kill other people; they perpetrate less than 15 percent of the homicides in the United States. When women kill, they do so more often in self-defense when compared to men. Women charged in the death of a mate typically have much less of a criminal history than female offenders do, but they face harsher penalties than men who kill their mates and are sentenced to longer prison terms than men.[2]

I am reminded of an infamous 1970s case in my home state of Indiana where a man brutally beat his wife then raped her as she lay bloodied and dying. In spite of a credible eyewitness account, the prosecutor refused to charge the man with murder, filing a manslaughter charge instead. The prosecutor explained, "He didn't mean to kill her. He just meant to give her a good thumping."[3]

Sometimes wives thump back.

LORETTA FONTAINE[*]

A little before noon Randy Longacre heard popping sounds followed by what he thought were moans coming from a next-door apartment occupied by seventy-five-year-old Phillip Fontaine. Without hesitation Longacre rushed to his neighbor's front door. He feared Fontaine, who lived alone, had suffered a heart attack. When Longacre shouted and banged on Phillip's front door, the latch clicked and the door opened slowly. Inside Longacre faced Phillip's estranged wife, seventy-year-old Loretta. A nickel plated Smith & Wesson .357 Magnum was tucked into a thin belt cinched tightly around her tiny waist. "I just shot my husband," Loretta said, "Please call the police." As Longacre ran back to his apartment, he heard another shot.

When sheriff's deputies arrived, they found Phillip slumped in a chair, his head and chest covered with fresh blood. An overturned coffee table and a broken lamp lay at his feet. Loretta sat quietly at the dining room table.

Paramedics examined Phillip but could do nothing for him. He had taken four shots to the head and one to the chest. Any one of the wounds could have killed him; taken together, death was certain. When Loretta confessed to investigators at the scene that she had shot her husband, they toted her off to jail. She was charged with first-degree murder and first-degree burglary.

At her arraignment the next day, Loretta's public defense

attorney, Sean Stoneback, entered a plea of not guilty. In a statement to the press, Stoneback didn't deny that his client killed her husband. "She certainly shot him," he said, "but it was self-defense and we plan to prove that to a jury." Stoneback planned to use a history of domestic abuse spanning over nearly two decades of marital disharmony as a basis for Loretta's lethal act against her husband. This defense is derisively called the "abuse excuse" by most prosecutors. But to mount this type of defense, Stoneback needed a mental health professional expert in the impact spouses suffer as a result of years of domestic abuse.

When Stoneback called me, I recommended clinical and forensic psychologist Dr. Lenore Walker from Denver. Walker was considered the leading researcher on the effects of partner abuse on women and had recently published two books detailing her findings: *The Battered Woman* and *The Battered Woman Syndrome*. She also developed a theory of "learned helplessness" that helps explain why many abused women fail to effect significant change in their lives.

Stoneback said he preferred to work with me because we had worked on similar cases before and he felt confident that my knowledge base and experience in this type of case would provide the forensic information he needed. I asked him to send me a complete file and set a tentative appointment for Loretta, who was out of jail after posting a hefty bail.

When Loretta entered my office she seemed frail but confident. She was very well groomed and wore a stylish dress and pumps, attire uncommon to the overly casual look popular with desert dwellers in and about Tucson. I thought she would make a good candidate for the cover of a senior citizen version of *Cosmopolitan*.

Loretta sat composed in her chair while she told me she was born and raised in New York City. She was the oldest of three children. Her father earned a good living as an electrical engineer and her mother was a traditional housewife and mother. She admitted that she was favored by her parents but denied parental favoritism created any undue stress in the family.

Although Loretta told me about childhood experiences that seemed fairly typical for children raised in middle-class families, she also admitted that all was not well in her household. She said, "My father had a drinking problem and my parents had a lot of verbal fights about his drinking." As a child, the parental fights made her sad and frightened her. Loretta hoped her father would stop drinking. He didn't. Her parents separated shortly after Loretta graduated high school then divorced a couple of years later.

Loretta said she was always motivated to get a higher education and enrolled in New York University, but she quit school after about two years. She had decided to pursue a career in retail management instead of college and was employed by an upscale New York department store.

Loretta's eyes grew bright and the lines in her face fell soft as she talked about her first husband, Gary. She said she fell in love with and married a dashing young real estate broker from a wealthy New York family. For two years they lived a near honeymoon existence with love, companionship, and numerous social and entertainment events. Then Gary got the bad news—he was drafted.

Loretta worried and waited for three years while Gary served his tour of duty. When he returned home safely, Gary's employer transferred him to an office in New Jersey. While Loretta was overjoyed to have Gary home safe and sound, she was not happy about the move to New Jersey. She said, "I was forced to give up my job to which I was devoted. I had worked there for over ten years."

Once settled in their new home in New Jersey, Loretta and Gary decided to have a baby. Their only child, a son, was born. The couple decided that Loretta would be a stay-at-home mom until their son was in the first grade. Loretta loved parenting her son and both parents were active in their son's school, scouting, and other family activities. Once her son was in school Loretta decided to return to the work force. She secured employment at a public relations firm.

Loretta smiled and became animated as she continued to tell me about her first marriage, then her face turned sad. She hesitated for a moment then said, "We got a divorce after twenty-seven years because I had to." She went on to explain, "Gary got mixed up with the Mafia and couldn't get out of it. He didn't lie to me about it. He told me he had made a mistake and fronted for the Mafia on a project building a state highway. Now he was stuck with them unless he wanted to go to jail or worse." Loretta reported being frightened and felt she couldn't tolerate Gary's involvement in criminal activities. "I didn't want to get a divorce but I felt I had to," she said. "I was very sad."

Shortly after her divorce, Loretta began dating Phillip Fontaine. She said, "I met Phillip several years ago through bridge lessons. He and his wife had a son, too, and we all became friends over the years." Phillip's wife died at about the same time as Loretta's divorce, so it seemed natural that the two of them would continue their friendship. After dating for about a year they married.

Loretta seemed uneasy talking about Phillip. She said, "We seemed compatible at first. But soon I began to see a pattern of being very nice then switching to being angry and controlling. He even made me resign from my job even though I had only one year left before I was eligible for retirement." Loretta looked away and shook her head. "It didn't seem to matter to him that I had worked there for fourteen years. He said that he wanted a wife, not a breadwinner. He also made me sell my house and immediately started asking for money."

Over the next eight years, the couple spent a large amount of Loretta's money but Phillip would not allow Loretta to see his paycheck. When she eventually discovered that he was holding out several hundred dollars a month for himself in a private account, he destroyed the records.

In 1970 Loretta was diagnosed with leukemia. The doctors told her that her prognosis was poor and that she should avoid stress. However, her marital relationship continued to deteriorate and life for Loretta became more stressful and eventually unbearable. She explained, "His cheating, lying, and stealing became more prevalent. His disposition became nastier. I considered divorce but didn't think I had the strength to go through with it because my blood condition became worse." Loretta eventually began to respond to medical treatment and showed improvement over the next few years.

When Phillip retired in 1974 the couple bought a house in Arizona with what was left of Loretta's money and a loan from her son. After living in Arizona for about six months, Loretta's son and his four-year-old daughter moved in from Maine. She explained, "My son remarried and his new wife didn't want his daughter living with them. My son asked me to take care of her. I agreed and raised my granddaughter as my own daughter. When she was thirteen we adopted her."

When I redirected Loretta back to her relationship with Phillip, she hesitated then took a deep breath. "Since we moved to Arizona," she said, "Phillip became more moody, jealous, secretive, and possessive." Loretta's eyes filled with tears when I pressed for details. She tried to answer, "I felt like a prisoner in my own home because he would monitor my telephone calls and would seldom let me go anywhere alone. He wouldn't let me have much more than a few dollars, then he would interrogate me about the money I did spend."

I waited for Loretta to launch into a description of horrendous physical abuse typical in such cases, but when she didn't I asked her directly. I was surprised when she denied any form of physical abuse but not surprised when she began to describe severe verbal abuse. She said, "Phillip was always screaming at me about something and calling me dirty names. In his eyes I could never do anything right. He said I was dumb and stupid. He would also insult my granddaughter's intelligence and would tell terrible lies about both of us." As Phillip's verbal attacks escalated, Loretta became increasingly fearful that the emotional abuse would soon become physical. And she became very concerned for her life when she suffered a cardiac arrest in 1981. Phillip refused to call 911.

Loretta tolerated the emotional abuse for another six years

then separated from Phillip and filed for a divorce. Phillip's abuse did not stop. She told me that Phillip broke into her house several times and taunted her with acts of vandalism. "I came home one night and found the ring finger of my favorite figurine broken off. Another time he destroyed a Franklin Mint horse and left the pieces all lined up on a table. I got really scared when I couldn't find my heart medication and glasses. I know he took them."

Loretta got a restraining order on Phillip but he continued to terrorize her at home at night for about a year. Often he would slip into her carport and turn off or rearrange the lights in some strange configuration. Loretta told me she was beginning to feel helpless because the police refused to arrest Phillip. She said, "They said they couldn't do anything because it was a domestic squabble or a community property crime."

I knew this was a familiar response by law enforcement to calls on domestic violence and harassment. It is one of the factors that often leads to an abuse victim's frustration and learned helplessness. They search for help but find none.

After I completed my evaluation, I called Stoneback with my findings. I told him that his initial impression of Loretta's case was correct. In my opinion her lethal actions against her husband were similar to other cases documented in the clinical and research literature about women who struggle with long-term domestic abuse situations. I thought she was a battered woman.

Stoneback waited a moment then said, "But there is no evidence that her husband ever physically abused her, so how can she be a battered woman?"

I reminded him that, according to Lenore Walker, Angela Browne, and others who treat abused women, physical abuse is only one factor leading to battered woman syndrome. The other factors are sexual and psychological abuse. Her husband's history of psychological abuse through intimidation, fear tactics, lies, control, and isolation produced similar responses as seen in physically abused women.

Emotionally abused women like Loretta often develop a long

list of psychological problems such as depression, difficulty in expressing anger, feelings of vulnerability, helplessness, decreased self-esteem, fear, distortions of reality, and diminished decision-making and problem-solving abilities. And these women often remain in or return to the abusive relationship until either they or their abuser are seriously injured or killed.

I told Stoneback I was prepared to offer an opinion in court that Loretta did not consciously plan to murder her husband on that fatal day and that her responses to Phillip were more a tragic result of years of fear, anger, and emotional abuse. But a major problem remained: trying to convince a jury that Loretta's actions with the gun did not portend a premeditated intent to off her husband. After all, she had bought a weapon with enough power to stop a charging rhino, taken target practice, toted the gun to her husband's apartment, and blasted an unarmed Phillip with four well-aimed shots. Then she hit him with another when he shifted in his chair.

While I was secure with my opinion, I knew this case was an example where psychology and the law collide. Abused people, especially women, don't always wait until the abuser is clearly threatening their lives with or without a weapon before they act. They often take protective measures that frequently go wrong and are most always interpreted by the law as premeditated murder. And they usually lose in court. Maybe a plea to a lesser offense should be considered, but even if a plea agreement were offered, it most likely would have the same result for Loretta because of her age—a life sentence in prison. A not guilty verdict was the only real hope for Loretta. Stoneback told me to send a report and get prepared because he was taking Loretta's case before a jury.

Several months passed before I heard from Stoneback again. When he called he informed me that Loretta had decided to hire a private attorney instead of relying on the public defender's office. Stoneback was sending Loretta's file, including my report, to her new attorney, Kirk Reeder, and I should expect a call from Reeder in a few days.

When I met with Reeder in his office we discussed my evaluation of Loretta and my opinion that her actions were related to battered woman syndrome even though she did not report any physical abuse. I added that the abuse by the batterer is generally part of a pattern of obsessional behavior rather than a sudden loss of control and the abuse usually becomes more violent and frequent. Phillip's bizarre actions seemed to reflect a pattern of repeated behavior over time that was carefully designed to threaten and control his wife rather than impulsive acts of direct physical abuse. But his acts appeared to be increasing and more menacing.

I also reiterated my concern that the jury would struggle with the fact that Loretta was packing a gun when she entered her husband's apartment instead of some other more believable self-defense scenario, such as being awakened at night by a murderous Phillip and forced to take immediate action to defend herself. Undaunted, Reeder said he agreed with Stoneback's defense strategy. He asked me to update my evaluation by seeing Loretta again then to get ready for court.

The second interview with Loretta produced no new revelations. Her statements and demeanor were essentially the same. The only exception was her physical condition. She seemed more frail since I last saw her a little over a year before. It seemed obvious to me that the stress of the impending trial was taking its toll on her. Frail or not, Loretta told me she wanted to testify on her own behalf. She appeared certain she could convince the jury that her actions were justified.

I wondered if she could survive what would most certainly be a vigorous and lengthy cross-examination by the prosecution team, but I refrained from advising her of the grave risks inherent in accused murderers taking the stand. I was sure Reeder would cover this topic in great detail.

At trial, county attorney Ruth Madden described Loretta as an angry woman who went to her estranged husband's apartment to steal possessions and murder Phillip. Reeder countered with Loretta's long history of psychological abuse at the hands of her husband and her fear that Phillip's verbal abuse had just turned physical when he lunged at her.

Reeder then offered information Loretta had not shared with me about the shooting. He told the jury that Phillip had actually made contact with Loretta and bloodied her nose before she opened fire. He stressed that Loretta did not premeditate a murder but simply acted reflexively and shot Phillip in self-defense.

Friends of the couple testified Loretta had expressed fear of Phillip but they had never seen Phillip abuse Loretta in any way. And one of Loretta's acquaintances testified that on the day before the slaying, Loretta talked about Phillip hiding assets. According to the acquaintance, Loretta said she was going to take the matter into her own hands if the legal system wasn't going to help her get a fair settlement. The acquaintance also testified that Loretta had recently bought a gun and was taking shooting lessons to learn how to stop an attacker. Other witnesses testified that Loretta dominated Phillip, was disgusted by his cowardice, and carefully planned the murder.

When I took the stand, Reeder established my credentials as an expert in interpersonal violence, pointing out that I treated abuse victims of either gender and that I initiated the study of and was a coauthor of one of the first books published about the sexual abuse of males. After I told the jury I interviewed Loretta on two separate occasions for more than three hours and also administered psychological tests, Reeder asked for a summary of my findings.

I told the jury that Loretta's relationship with her first husband, Gary, seemed loving, appropriate, and functional, except for his involvement with the Mafia, which led to the end of their marriage. I said that her description of Phillip's behavior was consistent with men who attempt to control their wives through verbal abuse and psychological terrorism. I was careful to point out that women do not have to be physically abused to show symptoms of battered woman syndrome. Psychological abuse over time often produces the same result. I went on to explain that Loretta responded to her abuse in a manner fairly typical of battered women: depression, difficulty in expressing anger, feelings of vulnerability, helplessness, decreased self-esteem, fear, distortions of reality, and diminished decision-making and problem-solving abilities.

Reeder asked, "Why didn't Loretta just get out of the relationship like she did with her first husband after she learned about his involvement in the Mafia?" I explained to the jury that the two situations were different. In one, Loretta faced a moral decision and made it. In the other, the abuse created a cloud of control over her that she found difficult to escape. Many abused women show a typical pattern of remaining with the abuser or leaving only to return again despite knowing that at some level they should part permanently. Unfortunately many women stay in abusive situations until either they or their abuser are seriously injured or killed. I also pointed out to the jury that abused women who kill their husbands usually do so when they perceive a threat to their life, usually with a power equalizer such as a gun.

"And what is your opinion in this case?" Reeder asked.

I replied, "In my opinion, Loretta does not appear to have consciously planned to murder her husband. Rather, Loretta fits the characteristics of a psychologically abused woman to the point that she would use lethal self-defense if she perceived her life was threatened."

On cross-examination Madden asked me about a colleague, Dr. Samuel Roundtree. I sensed a trap but answered that I knew Sam. Madden then asked if Roundtree was a respected psychologist in the community. I knew something sinister was coming, but I answered that Roundtree had a good reputation within the psychological community.

In the guise of formulating a long question to impeach my testimony, Madden then essentially "testified" that Roundtree had evaluated Loretta and he did not conclude she was an abused woman. What did I think of that? she asked. This was clearly a wrongful use of hearsay through cross-examination, but it was put before the jury before Reeder could stand and object.

The judge sustained the objection, expunged Madden's comments from the record, and told the jury to disregard her statement about Roundtree's comment. Too late. Not only had the prosecution "testified" about Roundtree's opinion, Madden actually misstated his opinion and never called Roundtree to testify. I found out later that Roundtree believed Loretta probably was an abused woman, but he refused to testify on her behalf because he could not confirm her claims of abuse sufficiently. This was a common problem in cases of an abuser who puts on a good front in public then abuses in the privacy of home — no collateral documentation.

Most defense attorneys advise their clients not to testify on their own behalf. The dangers are many, including a rigorous cross-examination by prosecutors. In spite of the risks, Loretta insisted on telling her story. She took the stand. The jury looked eager to hear from this thin and frail elderly woman who killed her husband. She didn't disappoint them.

Under careful questions by Reeder, Loretta looked at the jury with determined eyes and told them of nearly twenty years of "psychological terror and harassment." As the jury seemed to hang on her every word, Loretta described numerous episodes of terrifying encounters with Phillip, including his penchant for screaming and yelling at her then acting as though he was going to hit her with a karate chop, stopping just short of her face.

Loretta tried to explain away friends' statements that they never saw Phillip act abusively toward her. She told the jury that Phillip would always put on an act whenever they were with anyone, but alone with her he was a different person. She said, "He was a Dr. Jekyll and Mr. Hyde."

When asked to describe Phillip's reaction to the separation, Loretta described repeated episodes of stalking and harassment, in spite of a restraining order. She was certain, she said, that Phillip was also breaking into her house and stealing personal items. Her medications, family portraits, and jewelry were missing. She went on to say that Phillip followed her everywhere and she woke up one morning to find him standing outside her bedroom window. She also told the jury that Phillip hooked up a beach ball and colored lights near her backdoor. The whole arrangement was bizarre and looked like a spaceship. As Phillip continued to taunt and terrify her, she became more and more fearful for her life. Loretta bought a gun. She told friends it was for a "hobby," and she had chosen one certain to stop any intruder. She took lessons to learn how to shoot with accuracy.

A tearful Loretta explained to the jury that she only wanted a divorce and a fair settlement: "I was going to be so glad to get rid of this man, but not this way. I would never harm him. It was the furthest thing from my mind. Anyone who knows me knows I'm a very gentle person."

When Reeder asked Loretta about the shooting, she said she went to Phillip's apartment to give him his passport, pick up some health insurance forms, and retrieve her mother's portrait and jewelry that she knew Phillip had stolen from her house. She took the gun thinking it would frighten Phillip into returning the stolen items. She told the jury, "Phillip was such a terrible coward. I thought just seeing it, he would say 'okay.' Instead, he laughed. He thought it was the funniest thing he had ever seen."

According to Loretta, Phillip's demeanor quickly changed to anger and he demanded the gun. "He looked like the Hulk. Instead of green he was red. His veins were sticking out and you wouldn't believe how his eyes looked. I felt for sure this was it." She went on to tell the jury that Phillip jumped from his chair and lunged toward her. "I didn't have time to aim," she said. "I tried to aim low." Loretta fired four times and Phillip fell back into his chair. When a neighbor arrived she told him to call the police, then shot another round into Phillip "because he shifted in his chair. I didn't know if he was pulling one of his tricks. I thought he was coming at me."

After five days, Loretta's fate was in the hands of the jury. The judge gave instructions on several possible verdicts. At the top of the list was first-degree murder, which meant Loretta premeditated the killing of her husband and intentionally shot him. The next choice was second-degree murder, which meant Loretta did not premeditate killing her husband but she did shoot him. The third choice was manslaughter, which meant Loretta shot her husband during a quarrel or heated passion with provocation by her husband. An additional stipulation that no "cooling off" period between the "heated passion" and the shooting could be part of this choice. That is, to qualify for manslaughter, Loretta could not have waited a few minutes to collect herself after the quarrel before shooting her husband. The shooting must have occurred during the "heated passion" of the moment. Next was negligent homicide, which meant that Loretta didn't see the risk to her husband with her behavior but should have. The jury was also given the choice of finding Loretta insane at the time of the shooting. The final choice was not guilty. The jury instructions also included information about self-defense, meaning that Loretta acted like any reasonable person wold have if she believed she was in immediate danger. Actual danger was not necessary in this case to justify the use of physical force.

Armed with instructions, trial exhibits, and transcripts, the jury marched off to the jury room to deliberate. Within a few hours the jury returned a verdict. They found Loretta guilty of first-degree murder.

When interviewed by the defense counsel following their verdict, some jurors indicated they believed Loretta had been psychologically abused by her husband and feared for her life. They also believed she probably suffered from battered woman syndrome even though she had not been physically abused. Some wanted to acquit. One male juror thought Loretta must have been insane. He said, "Most struggled back and forth with first-degree and second-degree murder with about 75 percent of the jurors leaning toward second-degree murder. Then the foreman pointed out the fifth shot."

Another juror said, "To me the fellow was already dead. The fifth shot was uncalled for, but she took it anyway. I imagine because he jumped or his muscles twitched. I can understand that with a woman. They're not like a man. Fragile."

Finally, they settled on first-degree murder instead of self-defense because Loretta had gone to her husband's apartment with a deadly weapon. They also thought Loretta had suffered some psychological intimidation by her husband's actions that may have caused her to react with the first four shots. Many believed those shots were not premeditated. Loretta had time to "cool off" when the neighbor interrupted. But Loretta had pumped another slug into Phillip when he was, in their view, probably already dead and no real threat to her. The last shot was seen as premeditated by most jurors and eventually a consensus was reached on this vital issue. Loretta was guilty of first-degree murder.

Neither the jury's verdict nor their analysis surprised me. Both reflected the prevailing attitude about battered women and self-defense at that time: No matter how bad the abuse has been you must wait until the abuser is clearly threatening to kill you before you can defend yourself. The abuse yesterday does not count for the killing of today, even if you know today will bring more abuse. A preemptive strike is considered premeditated murder and no amount of "abuse excuse" will help.

But how many women want to wait until they are in danger of losing their life before they act? How certain can they be that the actions they take to defend themselves will be successful? The results of a failed self-defense maneuver could be deadly. If not at that moment, then possibly later.

About three months after Loretta was found guilty, Judge Paul Johnson sentenced Loretta to life in prison. She faced twenty-five calendar years of prison time before she would be eligible to be released on any basis, essentially a death sentence. Through a plea agreement, Loretta was not tried on the first-degree burglary charge.

As expected, Reeder filed an appeal, citing inadequate jury

instructions regarding premeditation. Reeder argued there was no evidence the fifth shot was the one that killed Loretta's husband. In the appeal Reeder wrote, "There is no evidence that the last shot killed Mr. Fontaine. In fact, the evidence would tend to indicate that he was dead or in extremis as a result of one or a combination of the first four shots. He was shot the last time, probably as the result of an involuntary movement on his part which the defendant translated into the possibility he was going to get up and come for her again."

Reeder added that at least one of the jurors was confused about the difference between first- and second-degree murder. He wrote, "One of the first four shots was the fatal one, according to this juror, and he believed Mr. Fontaine was already dead when the fifth shot was fired. This juror is uncomfortable with the verdict of first-degree murder, feels that justice was not served, and that the defendant should not have been found guilty of more than second-degree murder." The appeal process went on for several years before it was denied. It didn't matter much. Loretta had died in prison.

KAREN FRITZ[*]

On a hot August morning, Karen Fritz called the police. "I shot my husband," she said. After police conducted a thorough investigation of the homicide, they filed their reports and discussed the case with prosecutors. While prosecutors believed they had enough evidence, including Karen's confession, to try her on first-degree murder charges, they showed some compassion by offering her a plea agreement stipulating second-degree murder. To avoid facing the death penalty or life in prison without parole, Karen accepted the deal and was sentenced to eighteen years. From her prison cell a few months later, Karen prepared and filed a postconviction relief petition, only to withdraw it a few weeks later. When she reconsidered and filed another petition, the court appointed Glenn Dickson, a private attorney, to assist her. After consulting with Karen, Dickson filed a supplemental petition on her behalf. A couple of months later Dickson called me.

This was not my first murder case with Dickson. I knew he was a very bright young attorney who was detail oriented and worked very hard for his clients, whether they were private pay or court appointed. Karen was in good legal hands and Dickson would demand every ounce of forensic juice he could wring from me. And when I was dry he would wring some more. I started feeling the familiar squeeze when UPS rolled several boxes from Dickson into my office on a hand truck.

Dickson wanted me to evaluate Karen to help the court decide if she had been competent to stand trial and enter into a plea agreement at the time she accepted it. He also wanted an opinion about Karen's state of mind at the time she shot her husband. Did she know the difference between right and wrong? Did she understand the nature and quality of her lethal actions? Enter the elusive insanity defense common to many domestic murders.

Reconstructing a person's competency to stand trial and/or enter into a plea agreement is difficult even shortly after any offense, but it is much more of a problem some three years after a homicide. One of the most important factors leading to an accurate determination of competency so late in the case is finding consistency among the many and varied historical case documents, the clinical research findings relative to the case, and the information from my forensic evaluation of Karen. It would be a long and difficult forensic journey.

The first thing I did was address the issue of Karen's personality characteristics and her responses to stress and perceived threats. My evaluation revealed personality traits quiet similar to those described by forensic psychiatrist Dr. John Weisman, who evaluated Karen three months after she killed her husband. We both saw Karen as a vulnerable and emotionally fragile woman with poor coping skills. Under stress and threats Karen would tend to retreat emotionally and become confused, dependent, fearful, and intimidated. We both saw her as someone with a poor self-image who also appeared to have an increased perception of rejection and abandonment. Dr. Arthur Sealey, a psychologist who evaluated Karen in prison, also described her as an emotionally fragile individual with "a severe problem with low self-esteem" and poor coping skills. Karen's cognitive processes, emotional state, and behavior during the period prior to, during, and immediately following the shooting of her husband were also documented in other file material such as investigative reports.

A methodical reconstruction of this period during my evaluation produced findings consistent with what the law calls diminished capacity. For example, Weisman described Karen as experiencing panic, depersonalization, and reactive depression, and Sealey reported "an extended period of trauma and stress so severe that a virtual psychotic breakdown had occurred by the time of the shooting." Sealey also stated that Karen "was not capable of understanding the significance or meaning of what she was doing. She finally 'snapped' under all the stress and mental and physical abuse and deprivation." Even the police reports documented Karen's agitated state and bizarre thought processes. I found what I was looking for—consistency.

Armed with a reliable description of Karen's personality, I then looked for what role Karen's personality characteristics played in the case. But, again, I needed consistency in Karen's description of her relationship with her husband and her state of mind during the days and moments leading up to the murder, in statements she gave to the police shortly after she shot her husband, and in Weisman's conclusions. I found more consistencies than inconsistencies. Karen described her early relationship with her husband, Ralph, in very positive terms, but it quickly turned sour, a common theme in intimate partner violence. She said Ralph became more argumentative, then he abused her both mentally and physically. He called Karen ugly, refused to engage in sex, and would leave her home alone for extended periods of time. She became extremely fearful of Ralph and would not confront him because she feared he would retaliate with additional abuse.

Ralph was also an obsessive tax evader, which eventually depleted the couple's financial resources to the point of not being able to support themselves. Once Ralph got Karen entangled in the web of deception, she feared she would be found out and immediately imprisoned if she became employed and allowed the normal tax assessment procedures to occur. She also believed her son would be taken from her and placed with a welfare agency. At one point she was convinced that the IRS would "come in shooting up the place and kill me and my son."

Ralph hatched a plot. First, the couple divorced. Then he convinced Karen that she and her son must move to an isolated mountain area in southern Arizona near the Mexican border. He convinced her that this was the only place where she would be safe from the IRS. Karen was terrified about trying to live with her son in such a primitive and dangerous manner, but she didn't see any other more reasonable solutions to her dilemma. But she also knew Ralph had intimidated her into making the decision. She felt trapped between her husband and the IRS on the one hand and the fear that she and her son would die in the wilderness on the other.

On the day before Ralph planned to take Karen and her son into the wilderness, she dutifully packed most of her belongings and secured them in a rental storage locker. That night she couldn't sleep. She tried to fight back her fears, but they eventually won. Dreading the wilderness, the IRS, and the police, she was consumed by irrational thoughts. Desperate, Karen searched for a solution and found one when she finally "realized" that the only way to avoid being abandoned in the wilderness to die was to "stop" Ralph. To stop Ralph meant to shoot him. Killing him would not hurt him, it would *stop* him, her confused mind thought.

Karen obsessed about this irrational thought of stopping but not hurting Ralph until it became her only hope for survival. For her this course of action was a rational solution, strongly suggesting to me a seriously dysfunctional mental condition. Her plan served two purposes important to her physical and psychological well-being: she would be spared from the potential agony of dying in the wilderness with her son and she would not have to feel bad about her behavior because Ralph would not actually be harmed, only "stopped."

When Ralph took Karen and her son to the edge of nowhere, Karen "stopped" him with a slug from a Colt .45. Her immediate response to the shooting remained consistent with her irrational belief. She knew she had shot Ralph but didn't believe she had killed him. Like a lot of women who kill intimate partners, Karen didn't believe he was dead, and she was afraid that Ralph would be very angry. She said, "If he caught me, he would hit me for what I did." She fled to the safety of a friend's home. Once there she felt concern about Ralph because "I didn't want him left out there. He didn't have a ride."

While Karen seemed not to believe that she had actually killed Ralph, she was beginning to realize at some primitive level that she had not just "stopped" Ralph. In this regard Karen demonstrated a basic understanding of right and wrong but a lack of criminal intent. She knew it would be wrong to kill Ralph, but her irrational belief that Ralph would not be harmed, only "stopped," allowed her to act inappropriately without fully understanding that she was indeed murdering him. As a clinical and forensic psychologist I understood the dynamics of Karen's irrational belief system. It made sense to me, but I was grateful I didn't have to explain such a convoluted story to a jury.

The next step on the journey was to compare Karen's behavior with clinical research on women who have killed their spouses. Karen's case was consistent with the research. Her case showed a similar pattern of emotional and/or physical abuse, intimidation, and threats, which subsequently leads to a perception of entrapment and imminent danger for women and sometimes for their children. This pattern was documented in Karen's file material and described to me during my evaluation.

Next, I put the psychological findings to the legal test. While many of the cases involving abused women killing their abusing spouses point more to self-defense strategies than to diminished capacity, Karen's case had characteristics of both. It's true that Ralph was not beating Karen when she shot him, but she believed that she and her young son were in imminent danger. Ralph brought them to a remote area and was going to leave them to fend for themselves without adequate resources to survive. She chose to save her life and the life of her son. Self-defense. It was also clear that her cognitive processes were so impaired that she was unable to arrive at more appropriate solutions to her dilemma than shooting her husband. I saw that her self-defense solution was based upon emotional and cognitive dysfunctions.

Clinical research also suggests that abused women who kill their abusing partners often remain in an emotionally fragile state for several weeks or months following the homicide incident. During this period they are often confused, frightened, and in a state of disbelief. Some exhibit psychotic symptoms, dissociative states, or a post-traumatic disorder. While most are shown to be legally competent to stand trial, their ability to clearly understand the ramifications of the legal decision made during this period is often severely diminished. Many attempt a facade of adequacy when they actually are not capable of assisting counsel in formulating legal strategies on their own behalf.

It was clear to me that collateral documents about Karen's mental state and behavior during the plea negotiations were consistent with research findings and my experience with intimate partner violence cases.

In my opinion, Karen was an emotionally dysfunctional woman who gave the appearance of understanding the meaning of the plea agreement when she actually did not grasp the significance of her decision. Her acceptance was based more on her confused state of mind and continued feelings of intimidation than on a clear understanding of what the plea agreement actually meant in terms of her legal rights. The legal system doesn't wait until a person settles down, especially if she seems outwardly stable. But it is always advisable to provide a person, like Karen, with enough time and resources to deal with the trauma and come to grips with the homicide incident before expecting her to function in a rational manner within the justice system.

The result of following each step along the forensic trail brought me to three conclusions about Karen:

1. At the time she killed her husband, Karen knew the difference between right and wrong but her confused mental condition did not allow her to fully understand the quality and nature of her actions.

2. Karen's mental condition continued to be dysfunctional following the shooting and formal competency examinations should have been requested by former counsel. Instead, only one examiner evaluated Karen, and he did not formally evaluate her mental state and competency to stand trial. But when he concluded that Karen's "state of depersonalization could have rendered the subject incapable of appreciating her very identity or who she was at the time she committed the instant offense," a competency examination should have be requested.

3. While Karen demonstrated a basic understanding of a plea agreement, her emotional fragility and mental confusion following the shooting seem to have rendered her incapable of fully understanding the ramifications of accepting a plea rather than requesting a trial. Again, formal competency examinations would have been key to deciding this issue.

At the court hearing, Judge Spencer Rawlings listened carefully to all witnesses, including me, then took the matter under consideration. Two months later, he announced his decision. He denied Karen's petition. Sometimes the court takes a different journey.

MARY WINKLER

Thirty-three-year-old Mary Carol Winkler took the stand in Selmer, Tennessee, on her own behalf and quietly answered questions posed by her defense attorney. The duo offered the jury a tale of a marriage made in religious heaven but with hellish secrets. Mary, the demure preacher's wife, showed little emotion until she was asked to reveal the clothing her preacher husband made her wear for sexual purposes. The courtroom stood silent as Mary wrapped her small hand around an eight-inch flared heel platform shoe, popular with many working girls walking the street but not a preacher's wife walking to church. Next came an Afro wig.

With her shameful sexual secrets revealed Mary looked at her lap and barely held back tears. She also told the jury that her preacher husband wanted her to wear miniskirts and pressed her to participate in unnatural acts like oral and anal sex. And he showed more than a passing interest in Internet pornography. Apparently, the thirty-one-year-old preacher liked his women on the slutty and kinky side. But the preacher's wife had tired of the game.

On March 22, 2006, after ten years of marriage and three children, Mary took the family shotgun out of its case and blew a hole in Matthew Winkler's back as he slept in their marital bed. The autopsy revealed that at least seventy-seven pellets of birdshot punctured vital organs and broke his spine. As Matthew lay dying in a pool of blood, she whispered, "I'm sorry." Then the preacher's wife threw the shotgun and her three young daughters in the family's minivan and headed for a beach in Alabama. She told the kids that Daddy was hurt but help was on the way. In her purse, Mary had five hundred dollars in cash.

When apprehended a day later, Mary gave a tearful interview

describing a building storm of marital problems over the past few years until she just "snapped." She told an investigator on tape that her husband criticized her for "stupid things" and he had recently threatened her physically. Although she was unclear about the threat, she was clear that he said something that was, to her, life threatening. On the other hand she seemed very protective of her husband and described him as a good man to a fault. Mary also mentioned that she had seen her mother take the same type of criticism by her father, so she "just took it like a mouse" like her mother had. Mary said that she broke out of the mousetrap when she got a job and learned that she could stand up for herself. But nerve and more self-esteem came at a price: "My ugly came out."

Mary cooperated with authorities who brought her back to Tennessee to face a first-degree murder charge. The girls were placed with Matthew's parents, Dan and Diane Winkler. A cousin, Mike Cook, arranged for what the media called a Dixie Dream Team of criminal lawyers from Memphis: Steve Farese and Leslie Ballin.

Back in Selmer, investigators soon discovered another dark secret. The Winkler's checking account was seriously overdrawn. Prosecutors claimed that Mary had fallen prey to an Internet check scheme known as the "Nigerian scam," which promises to transfer large sums of money into a victim's account once the victim sends money to cover processing expenses. According to investigators, Mary had deposited two fraudulent checks into family accounts then shifted some of the money to a second bank. The checks were bouncing and the banks were closing in. Stories varied on how much Matthew knew about the scam, but an angry fight over finances broiled into the night before Mary took the loaded shotgun from the closet the next morning.

Mary was jailed for about five months before her father managed to raise the $750,000 bail by mortgaging his property. An old church friend in McMinnville took Mary into her home. Meanwhile, her defense team worked hard in the court of public opinion, spinning the murder into a sordid tale of unspeakable spousal abuse. It was even intimated that Mary's estrangement from her father was linked to his suspicion that Matthew was abusing Mary and her repeated denials.

After the defense team refused several plea offers from the prosecution, including a decision not to seek the death penalty, prosecutor Walt Freeland went to trial hoping to convict Mary of first-degree murder and put her away for fifty-one years, essentially a life sentence. The defense team worked carefully over a three-day period to select just the right jurors, people who would understand spousal abuse and be sympathetic to Mary. In the end, they seated ten women and two men. At least gender was in Mary's favor, although women tend to be tougher than men on women defendants.

Mary's defense revolved around verbal, emotional, and physical abuse even though Mary initially claimed that her husband only criticized her and used verbal threats. But on the stand Mary described episodes of sexual and physical abuse. She explained that she had been too ashamed and embarrassed to reveal the physical abuse to friends, family, or investigators. "I didn't want anybody to know about Matthew," she said. A couple of witnesses corroborated her story of physical injuries. She also testified that she did not intend to shoot her husband and when the gun went off by accident she panicked. She told the jury, "All I knew was that the stupid gun had went off, and nobody would believe me and they would just take my girls away from me." But would the jury buy the abused-spouse-and-I-didn't-mean-to-do-it defense?

By comparison to other high-profile murder trials, Mary Winkler's was short, crisp, and to the point. No bloody battle among expensive forensic experts or a never-ending parade of witnesses who had dirt to tell. Only ten people testified, including Mary. After three weeks the case was handed to the jury. The judge explained a wide range of options from not guilty to guilty of first-degree murder then sent them off to sort it all out and determine

Mary's fate. After only about eight hours of deliberation the jury, which had been sequestered throughout the trial, notified the court that they had reached a verdict.

As family members and friends filed back into the courtroom many wondered about the short period of deliberation. I knew a quick verdict usually favors the prosecution. But this was Selmer, Tennessee, the heart of the Bible Belt, and Mary was the preacher's wife with three kids. And the preacher was no saint.

Mary stood before a jury of her peers, waiting. The foreperson read the verdict. Mary was not guilty of murder, only voluntary manslaughter. The courtroom was as silent as a private prayer.

Apparently the carefully selected jury resonated with Mary's story of emotional, physical, and sexual abuse rather than the prosecution's allegations that she was a cold, calculating woman who carefully planned the murder of her husband. In Tennessee, voluntary manslaughter is a crime of passion, not a crime of pre-meditation. Justice was done. Or was it? In a postverdict interview with Court TV, the jury foreperson complained that the jury with "ten ladies" and only two men was unbalanced and favored Mary from the start. He revealed that nine of the ten women were ready to vote for an acquittal and let Mary go home to her kids. He and the other two jurors favored harsher verdicts. The voluntary manslaughter verdict was a compromise. It was clear that the foreperson was not satisfied with the verdict and hoped that the injustice would be somewhat rectified by the judge who could still sentence Mary to a maximum sentence in prison. He also said Mary should never have custody of her children.

During a five-hour sentencing hearing, Judge Weber McGraw listened patiently to arguments from the defense for probation, arguments from the prosecution for the maximum sentence, and testimony from friends and family, either praising Mary or damning her as a murderer. The courtroom was gripped as the victim's mother, Diane Winkler, glared at Mary and gave her a thirty-minute lecture on the impact of her unspeakable act. "You broke your girls' hearts," she said. "You have destroyed your husband's character." Then it was Mary's turn.

Wearing a simple print dress and white sweater, Mary stood before Judge McGraw and tried to show remorse and express regret over her actions. "I've lost my freedom. I've lost my children, and I've had my life be put on public display. I think of Matthew every day, and the guilt, and I always miss him and love him," she said. Mary also sent out a call for others caught in a web of relationship abuse. She said, "I hope this situation sheds light on unhealthy relationships, and that others will find the strength and have the courage to seek help before such a tragedy occurs again." Prevention. Prevention. Prevention.

Mary and her defense team waited for Judge McGraw's decision. As a first-time felon, Mary faced a range of three to six years in prison with an outside chance of probation. Judge McGraw sentenced Mary to 210 days in prison, with 60 days to serve in a mental health facility, and 3 years probation. With credit for 143 days as time already served before she was released on bond, Mary would be released soon after her stint in the mental health facility.

In a lot of cases of spousal murder, it is clear that the woman was in imminent danger from an abusive husband. In Mary's case, the primary abuse seemed to be psychological and sexual. But Mary also testified that her husband had once threatened to cut her "into a million pieces" because he thought she was too sassy. Mary seemed to qualify as a battered woman but was that enough to justify killing her husband?

I examined all the information I could find about Mary's background for clues. From the outside looking in Mary seemed to have had a stable and loving childhood within a strongly religious family. Her father, Clark Freeman, earned a good living in real estate and her mother, Mary Nell, was a teacher. The family lived in a modestly affluent neighborhood in Knoxville, Tennessee, and attended Laurel Church of Christ, where Mary's father was a deacon. Although her father seemed dominant and a bit critical of

Mary Nell, no reports of abuse tainted his family. Yet a strong bond between father and daughter seemed to crack several years later when Mary's mother died of cancer. Maybe the abuse, if it existed, was buried deep under religious repression and closely guarded family secrets.

Mary seemed to be a stable child with a dream of becoming a schoolteacher like her mother. Mary was a good student and active in a variety of extracurricular activities. She graduated from South-Doyle High School in 1992 then spent the following academic year at Chris Lipscomb University, a college affiliated with the Churches of Christ, in Nashville. After one year, Mary transferred to Freed-Harmon University, in Henderson, Tennessee, another college affiliated with the Churches of Christ. There she met handsome and charismatic Matthew Winkler. They became college sweethearts. Mary studied elementary education while Matthew had his sights on a career in the ministry. They both were devout in their Bible studies and faith.

The only tragedy in Mary's childhood seemed to be the death of a younger sister, a quadriplegic, when Mary was about eight years old. The void was filled when Mary's parents quickly adopted three girls and two boys from the same family. The death of a sibling and a sudden explosion of children in the family did not seem to affect Mary negatively. No reports of emotional or behavioral problems have surfaced.

Matthew was born into a family with a rich history of fire-and-brimstone evangelism. His grandfather and father were both preachers. His mother, like Mary's mother, was a teacher. Matthew had two brothers. The family moved often because Matthew's father went from one church to another spreading the Gospel, but, in spite of the frequent moves, Matthew seemed to thrive and embraced the family's religious heritage.

In 1996 Mary and Matthew married while still attending college. Her father presided over the ceremony held in the backyard of her family home in Knoxville. The couple quickly went forth and multiplied. In October 1997 their first child was born, a daughter, placing additional strain on their finances. They left college and went to Nashville, where Matthew worked as a youth minister at the Bellevue Church of Christ and completed his degree in Bible studies. A second daughter was born. Matthew then moved his growing family to McMinnville, Tennessee, where he found a job teaching Bible classes at Boyd Christian School. Mary got pregnant again but miscarried.

In January 2005 Matthew realized his dream. He was offered a job as pulpit preacher at Fourth Street Church of Christ in Selmer, Tennessee, a small town of about 4,500 people, thirty churches, and a solid fundamentalist Christian soul. The couple and their two children settled in the small but comfortable parsonage located near the church. Mary assumed the role of the perfect preacher's wife, but she also planned to go back to school to follow her dream of becoming a schoolteacher. Her dream had to wait, though, because she was pregnant again.

In March, Mary gave birth prematurely to their third daughter. Tiny Selmer did not have the medical facilities necessary to care for a premature child, so the baby was cared for in a hospital in Nashville about 150 miles down the road. The frequent trips to Nashville were stressful and expensive. Family finances, always on the brink of a crisis, now became even more of an issue. Then, in 2006, the Nigerians came calling on the Internet.

Mary's background revealed few clues to her lethal acts other than cumulated stress from trying to be the perfect preacher's wife when the man she married turned out not to be perfect. At one point she told investigators, "I loved him dearly, but gosh, he just nailed me in the ground," she said, "and I was real good for quite, quite some time." As I wondered what it meant to be "real good for quite, quite some time," I was reminded that many women come to blame themselves for the abuse and work harder at being a better wife only to find the abuse continues. We know any kind of abuse is a fundamental breach of trust and the abuse is generally part of a pattern of obsessional behavior rather than an expression of sudden loss of control.

A hint of problems in paradise came from college friends who said they saw Mary gradually change from upbeat, vivacious, and attractive to plain, mousy, and emotionally flat during her marriage to Matthew. Her father testified that he saw evidence of abuse and urged his daughter to get help, but she refused. If the abuse was so bad, why didn't she get help, or just leave? Many women do and they become identified as an abused wife, an unspeakable label for most women, especially a preacher's wife, caught in the powerful grip of religious dogma and unrealistic expectations. And leaving doesn't always solve the problem. By looking closely at the years of treating abused women who seek help in women's shelters or therapists' offices, we have come to know that at least half of the women who try to separate from an abusive relationship are subsequently stalked, harassed, or further attacked by the abuser.

While Mary, her family, and her defense team were quite pleased with the court's decision, Mary still faced serious legal problems. Matthew's parents were seeking permanent custody of Mary's three children and they had filed a $2 million wrongful death civil suit against her.

As I take another look at the cases presented in this chapter, social and forensic psychologist Angela Browne's sage words in her 1987 groundbreaking book, *When Battered Women Kill*, scream to be heard again. Here is my summary of her analysis of the battered woman and what goes wrong: The decisions a woman makes in an abusive relationship are based on her perceptions of the pattern of the abuse and possible alternatives. Battered women often spend years trying to understand what went wrong, hoping that once they comprehend it, they can then fix it. Sadly, a woman's attempts to live with a violent and unpredictable mate may eventually result in her committing an act of violence.

NOTES

1. G. T. Hotaling, David Finkelhor, John T. Kirkpatrick, and Murray A. Straus, eds. *Family Abuse and Its Consequences* (Newbury Park, CA: Sage, 1988), pp. 14–36.

2. For excellent reviews of prevalence rates and theoretical concepts related to intimate partner abuse see Angela Browne, *When Battered Women Kill* (New York: Free Press, 1987); Donald G. Dutton, *The Abusive Personality: Violence and Control in Intimate Relationships*, 2nd ed. (New York: Guilford, 2007); Lenore Walker, *The Battered Woman* (New York: Harper & Row, 1979); Lenore Walker, *Battered Woman Syndrome* (New York: Springer, 1984); Lenore Walker, *Abused Women and Survivor Therapy* (Washington, DC: American Psychological Association, 1994).

3. Ann Jones, *Women Who Kill* (New York: Fawcett Columbine Books, 1980), p. 308.

4

A LITTLE BIT LETHAL

Women Who Didn't Mean to Do It

For most of us it is easy enough to imagine that any battered person would eventually want to be rid of an abusive partner. But women do not have to be caught in a web of abuse to eventually become dangerous to others or themselves, and sometimes the results are lethal or a little bit lethal.

Melissa Markley*

Early on a dark November morning, Melissa Markley and her live-in boyfriend, Chris Sandler, drive from their home in Safford, Arizona, to Tucson to take care of some business and pick up supplies for a small going away party they are hosting later in the evening for a friend. They typically carry a loaded gun in their vehicle when they travel out of town and today is no exception. When they get back from Tucson they unload the supplies and Chris takes the gun from the pickup and places it in its usual place in a bedroom closet.

That evening the couple start drinking an hour or so before their friends arrive. After a few hours of barbecuing, eating, and drinking the group decides to take the party to a local bar, the Rusty Spur, where they drink, dance, and have a good time until last call for alcohol. Everybody wants to keep the party going, so they decide to return to the couple's home then go to an after-hours bash at a remote location outside of Safford known appropriately as the "Boondocks."

As the bar is closing Chris goes outside. Melissa waits in the bar talking to one of her friends, Kristine. In the Rusty Spur's parking lot, Chris exchanges angry words with another patron, Carl Catlow, then goes back into the bar. Seeing that Chris is really mad about something, Melissa asks him about what is going on. He won't tell her. Instead he says that they are going home and then he is going to the Boondocks.

When the couple and their friends arrive at the couple's home, Chris goes inside alone for a few minutes then comes back out. He is still mad. He tells Melissa and the group that he is going to the Boondocks. Concerned about another altercation with Catlow, Melissa and her friends attempt to talk Chris out of going to the Boondocks, but Chris tells them he is going anyway and that if they are going they need to get in the truck now, otherwise he is going by himself. Melissa gets in the passenger seat, while two of her friends crawl into the truck bed. Chris gets behind the wheel, starts the truck, and speeds away, leaving a cloud of dust. Melissa's friend Kristine tries to keep up in her own car.

While Chris speeds along the route to the Boondocks, Melissa tries to get him to tell her what happened with Catlow. Chris scowls at Melissa and tells her to quit asking. She keeps at it until he tells her that he is really pissed off at Catlow. Then Chris shouts over the road noise, "Catlow is a real asshole!" Melissa sees headlights rapidly approaching from the rear. The lights come up on the couple's truck then pass on the left. It's Catlow.

When they get to the Boondocks area, Chris stops the truck, jumps out quickly, and heads off, leaving Melissa and her two friends behind. As Melissa and her two friends scramble out of the truck and down a steep embankment, they lose sight of Chris. Then Melissa sees Chris and Catlow walking to the middle of the road and pushing each other. She knows the fight will soon be on and she wants to stop it.

Melissa struggles back up the steep embankment to the truck, reaches into the passenger side window, and grabs the axe handle Chris has always kept stashed behind the seat for protection. Armed with the axe handle, Melissa thinks she might be able to keep them apart. She runs toward the combatants, hoping Catlow will back off when he sees her coming with an axe handle. But by the time she gets about ten feet from them, the fight is on and Catlow already has Chris in a vicious headlock. Melissa waves the axe handle and yells at them to "knock it off." Catlow tightens his grip. When Melissa gets a few feet from them, the axe handle mysteriously disappears, but she jumps in to separate them anyway.

At the moment Melissa grabs Catlow and Chris to push them apart, a shot rips across the Boondocks. Melissa, startled, looks around. At first she doesn't see anything, then she looks at Chris and sees his eyes roll back as he falls to the ground. She also sees an unclear vision of a figure in dark clothes running away. Melissa falls to her knees with Chris. One of her friends tries to move Melissa away but she tries to comfort Chris instead. In the dark, a lot of frantic voices call for help.

When help finally came, it was too late. Chris was dead.

A combination of police and sheriff's investigators tried to piece together what happened. They interviewed everybody at the scene. Accounts of the shooting varied among the various witnesses, including Melissa. Although Melissa tried to give an accurate account of what she thought happened, she was confused and couldn't remember segments of the incident. Essentially, she told investigators that she tried to break up the fight with an axe handle, which she called the "stick," and she denied ever having a gun at the site or shooting her boyfriend. Most witnesses reported one gunshot, while one reported hearing two. Other witnesses did not see her carry the "stick" or a gun into the fracas but saw a gun in her hand after a shot was fired. Melissa was charged with first-degree murder, aggravated assault, and attempted murder.

A few months later I received a call from Melissa's attorney, Elizabeth Cento. She told me from the start that this was an unusual murder case and she needed help understanding her client's state of mind during and immediately following the shooting death of Melissa's boyfriend. She described Melissa's memory loss and inconsistent statements and expressed a belief that Melissa did not shoot her boyfriend. At least not intentionally. This was not my first murder case involving so-called selective memory loss. I knew the territory well. If I accepted the referral I knew I would face some of the most difficult issues in criminal cases: defendants malingering or exaggerating complex mental health symptoms to avoid conviction. Intrigued but also having some misgivings, I made an appointment for Melissa.

At precisely the appointed hour on a chilly January morning, my receptionist told me Melissa had arrived for her evaluation. When I went to the waiting room to fetch Melissa I found a rather tall, nicely dressed young woman chatting with another nicely dressed but somewhat older-looking woman. They could have been sisters. Melissa introduced herself then her mother, who was on that day a source of transportation and comfort for Melissa. I gave both an estimate of how long the evaluation would take and suggested Melissa and her mother could meet for a lunch break regardless. Melissa's mother gave her daughter's hand a squeeze then headed for the parking lot. Melissa followed me to my private office.

We made ourselves comfortable, then I made a few lame jokes in an effort to establish some semblance of rapport before I launched into the warning of limitations on confidentiality all psychologists are required to tell patients prior to conducting any part of an evaluation. It was like reading Miranda rights to a suspect just placed under arrest. Fine for law enforcement, but a hell of a way to begin a relationship with an anxious patient.

Melissa maintained eye contact while I informed her that I was a clinical and forensic psychologist who was asked to evaluate her by her attorney. When I told her that the purpose of the evaluation was to gather information to assist the court in determining her state of mind during the shooting death of her boyfriend, Melissa's eyes started to fill with tears, then she looked at her lap. I waited while she fished in her purse for a tissue, then I explained the procedures I would employ, including review of records, which I had already completed, today's clinical interview, and possible psychological testing.

As Melissa looked at me again, I told her that I would be asking her questions about the alleged offense and her mental state prior to, during, and following this event. She tightened her jaw and nodded. I explained that I would be consulting her attorney and preparing a report to the court, and the content of my evaluation, including her statements to me, would not be confidential. I explained that she did not have to answer my questions or participate in the evaluation, and she could stop the evaluation at any time and leave. When I asked her if she understood the nature of the warning regarding her rights and the limitation of confidentiality, she nodded and said yes. I then asked her if she wanted to continue with the evaluation. She agreed.

Taking her social history was easy. Melissa was cooperative and a good historian. She reported being born and raised in Safford, Arizona. She had one younger brother, and her parents divorced when she was about two years old. Her mother was awarded custody and remarried about a year later.

Melissa described her mother as a hardworking mom who was always there for her children. Melissa told me that her stepfather was "strict and grumpy but did his best." She said that both parents would yell at her sometimes and occasionally spank her, but Melissa never felt that these episodes were excessive or abusive. She said, "I knew when I was doing wrong and deserved the discipline." Melissa smiled as she added, "As I grew up my mother became my best friend." She went on to say that her mother and stepfather were drinkers and while she felt that some of the drinking could have been considered excessive, Melissa didn't mind because her parents were more lenient when they were drinking.

Melissa's story about her biological father was quite different. She said, "When I was between four and five years old my father got into a big fight with my stepfather and knocked his teeth out." She added that she saw her dad a few times when she was thirteen and again after her divorce. Her face drew tight. "He introduced me to meth and other guys who were doing drugs." With more than a bit of nonobjective anger, I wondered about what kind of father would intentionally get his young daughter mixed up with bad guys and drugs.

When we moved into taking a sexual history, Melissa's face grew pale. I knew what was coming. She stated that a step uncle molested her and her brother when she was about five years old. To keep her quiet, "He would threaten me and tell me I was bad." She didn't tell her mother or stepfather about the abuse until she started having severe nightmares at about age six. Even though Melissa's stepfather confronted his brother and reported the abuse to law enforcement authorities, no legal action was taken. The abuse went on intermittently for about another three years.

Getting no protection from law enforcement or family members, Melissa finally stopped the abuse when she, her brother, and a cousin banded together and fought back every time he would try something with any one of them. She said, "We would scream and were not afraid to tell. I think he finally gave up."

But a family member was not the only abuser in Melissa's young life. At about age seven or eight, one of her stepfather's coworkers sexually assaulted her. Melissa immediately reported the abuse to her mother, who confronted the man. The man denied everything and hastily left the area before he could be apprehended.

When I asked Melissa what impact childhood sexual abuse experiences had on her feelings about herself and her sexuality as she grew up, I already knew what I was going to hear. She said, "I was embarrassed about sexuality and I felt dirty." When faced with her own sexuality, Melissa, like most kids who have been sexually abused, struggled with making good decisions about intimate relationships.

At thirteen, Melissa had her first consensual sexual encounter. Her partner was an experienced, much older acquaintance. She said, "I got stoned and was willing but I got really scared and pushed the guy off." Maybe at the last moment Melissa understood the dangers inherent in young girls succumbing to a combination of drugs and the wiles of older men.

She waited for about three years, then began a sexual relationship with a boyfriend she had been dating for about one year. But soon she found out her boyfriend was cheating on her, so she broke up with him.

While still in high school, Melissa got pregnant by and married her next boyfriend. The couple lived in a converted garage next to her parent's house, went to school, and worked. When Melissa graduated high school, her first child was in diapers. She was also one month pregnant with her second child. Melissa showed a low level of knowledge about sexual matters consistent with most sexually abused kids. She said, "I didn't know I could get pregnant while I was breast feeding."

Her marriage lasted about four years, then she got a divorce. She explained, "He wouldn't work on a steady job and would resent watching the children while I was working. I paid the bills and gave him money to do what he wanted. He also pushed me around and hit me a few times." She was granted custody of the couple's two children.

After her divorce, Melissa made another unfortunate decision about intimate relationships. She began a relationship with Patrick, the second man introduced to her by her biological father when she was a teenager. The bad guy with drugs. She soon found herself in a severely abusive relationship with this man, who also fathered her third child. Even though she tried to leave a number of times he would always find a way to stop her, a pattern shown by many abusive men. She said, "He would do the mental thing on me. Every time I tried to leave he would become violent. He even broke my nose and ribs while I was pregnant."

Melissa managed to muster the courage to slip out of the couple's house and move in with her mother in Safford. But not for long. "He threatened me and the children if I didn't come back to him. I did." Eventually, Melissa effected a successful separation from Patrick in spite of his abuse and threats. The court granted Melissa full legal custodial rights to their child.

A few months after leaving Patrick, Melissa met Chris Sandler. The couple dated for a couple of months then began living together with her three children. For the first time Melissa felt she had found a good man, a man who would love her and not hurt her. She said, "He would listen to me. He was not abusive and he didn't think I was stupid or silly. I loved it when he would hold me and give me flowers." During the year they lived together, the couple considered marriage but decided against it because "we didn't need to get married as long as we had the commitment to each other." She added, "He is the only person that I gave my heart and soul to." Sadly, Melissa learned from friends after Chris was killed that he was getting ready to propose. But not all was well with the loving couple. She shook her head back and forth when she admitted, "We drank way too much together. We would drink and wouldn't stop until we were drunk."

Alcohol and drugs were an important part of Melissa's young life. As a teenager she, like a lot of teenagers, began to sneak beer at parties but didn't drink much until she was sixteen years old. Even then she remembers only one episode of being "really drunk and sick." But it was a start and adults helped her along the drug trail. As a teenager, she babysat for a woman who gave her mari-

juana. By the time she was twenty-one she was smoking marijuana, doing "crank" with her biological father, and hanging out
with other users. This got her into a lot of trouble. She said, "My
boyfriend [Patrick] was doing drugs and when I tried to quit and
leave him, he would beat me up and call me a snitch."

When Melissa was driving to her mother's home in an automobile she had recently purchased, the police stopped her. They found
drugs in her car and she was arrested. She claimed the drugs
belonged to her boyfriend, Patrick, but it didn't matter to the police.
Her automobile was confiscated and she received four years' probation. And that was just the beginning. Melissa's ex-husband
sought and successfully gained legal custody of their two children.

Like most people using drugs, especially the highly addictive
drug methamphetamine, Melissa got hooked. But unlike most
drug users, she had the strength to quit. After about two weeks of
sobriety, she became pregnant with her third child. She denied a
history of blackouts either while abusing alcohol or other drugs.
She said, "I would never put myself in a position of not knowing
what I was doing." I wondered if she really knew what she was
doing when Chris was shot.

After I completed my lengthy interviews of Melissa I moved
her to another room and gave instructions on how to complete
three paper-and-pencil evaluation instruments: a personality
inventory, a trauma symptom inventory, and a hostility inventory.

A few days later, I reviewed all of my interview notes and
studied Melissa's responses to the evaluation instruments. Her
scores were consistent with her presentation and the information
she gave in the interview. I was relieved to find no surprises.
Murder cases with selective amnesia are difficult enough without
a bunch of pieces that don't fit together.

With that information fresh in my mind I again tracked
through the collateral documents, especially the investigative
reports, until I felt confident that Melissa's confusion and selective
loss of memory were real. All of the information pointed to an

array of symptoms common to experiencing a traumatic event, one of which is dissociative amnesia. I was also sure her childhood abuse history made her especially vulnerable to developing trauma symptoms. In fact, many childhood trauma victims, like Melissa, show many symptoms of post-traumatic stress without experiencing another traumatic event in adulthood. In Melissa's case, it seemed clear to me that stress symptoms were triggered by the direct exposure to the shooting death of her boyfriend.

I called Elizabeth Cento with my results. She said that my evaluation of Melissa was consistent with what she had observed. Again, no surprises. But she expressed some disappointment that Melissa did not recover more details of the shooting that would point to her innocence. Even so, she asked me to prepare a detailed report. I was surprised to receive a subpoena commanding my attendance and testimony before I completed my report. Justice on the fast track in Graham County.

As I drove through the desert from Tucson to the high country of Safford, I worried that Cento and I did not have much time to prepare for my testimony. She was a very bright and competent lawyer, but I was certain that she, like most trial attorneys, had little experience in court with complex cases of dissociative amnesia. I tried to prepare her with a telephone consult as best I could on such short notice, but I knew my testimony was still going to be quite an adventure. I decided that I would have to take the lead and try to provide as much information as I could with each of her questions on direct examination. But I wasn't sure the judge would allow us that much latitude. Even so, it seemed worthy of a try.

I knew I had to translate the technical information about the traumatic effects of witnessing a shooting death up-close into language any judge and jury could understand. I tried to organize my testimony into bite-size servings. I decided to address three major issues, one at a time. The first involved the reliability of witnesses in general, the second involved the signs and symptoms of dissociative amnesia exhibited by Melissa, and the third was the possibility Melissa was malingering.

On the stand, I planned to tell the jury that the majority of forensic and laboratory research on the accuracy of witness statements suggests several witnesses can observe the same event and subsequently report some consistent but also many inconsistent and contradictory details. I would explain that this finding occurs even when eyewitnesses have nothing to lose or gain by their reports. That is, people don't have to make things up for their own benefit. I could give some examples of studies, like the one exposing surprised "witnesses" to a staged shooting. Afterward the "shooting" witnesses were asked to describe what they had seen and provide a description of the "shooter." Fewer than half of the witnesses were able to recall the event as staged and documented. Many gave conflicting reports about the number of shots fired, the type and color of clothing worn by the shooter, and his physical characteristics. I would conclude by pointing out that eyewitness reports are notoriously unreliable and that it is not unusual for witnesses or participants in an actual traumatic event to disagree on what actually occurred. Just like investigators found with Melissa and other witnesses in this case.

The next bite was going to be more difficult because most people, including many mental health professionals, have difficulty with the complex concept of dissociative amnesia, especially a loss of memory for only parts of an event. I thought I could set the foundation by giving examples of clinical case studies. The most notable case studies have been associated with soldiers with battlefield trauma, persons who have been involved in automobile, train, or plane accidents or natural disasters, and witnesses to life-threatening interpersonal violence. I could use some of the best examples, such as soldiers who take live rounds to save fallen comrades then are later able to recall none or only snippets of their brave acts. Or another example, police officers who remember returning fire at an armed and dangerous suspect: they can remember the suspect falling when hit but cannot recall how long the battle went on or how many shots were fired before the suspect was killed.

The examples would help, but I knew dissociation could not be explained adequately using examples and lay terms only, so I planned to use the necessary technical language softened with as many common words as I could muster. I hoped they would understand that dissociation may happen when an individual experiences a severely emotionally disturbing event and the psyche counters with strong defensive maneuvers in an effort to protect the person from additional psychological distress and injury. In simpler terms, the mind tries to calm the emotional state by ripping the event out of consciousness then building a protective wall around it. I also explored describing dissociation as a clever defensive trick the mind uses to deal with a sudden heightened emotional state triggered by a relatively acute but profoundly disturbing event like seeing someone get killed or killing someone. I could point out the disconnections that occur between the emotional distress and the conscious mind. The conscious mind may go someplace else, such as in a fugue state, or refuse to remember the traumatic event, such as in amnesia. In some extreme cases multiple personalities are developed.

To relate dissociation directly to Melissa I planned to explain to the jury that the memory loss can vary and may encompass all aspects of the traumatic event, including activities subsequent to the episode or amnesia for only certain aspects of the event itself. I would point out that Melissa appeared to be suffering from a subcategory of dissociative amnesia called selective amnesia. That is, she recalled many but not all of the events associated with the tragic shooting of her boyfriend. She also appeared to be confused about some of the details she believed she remembered. For example, how does an axe handle suddenly disappear?

Even if I were successful in getting the jury to understand dissociation and how it related to Melissa, the prosecutor was certain

to make a big fuss about how to tell the difference between dissociation and faking confusion and memory loss to avoid responsibility. The third bite.

I worried that I had to tell the jury that there are neither tests
nor a circumscribed set of procedures that can, with unwavering
confidence, differentiate faked memory loss from dissociative
amnesia. However, I could explain the process experienced clinicians use to extract data from collateral material, clinical interviews, and psychological testing, which assist in making the diagnosis. I could point out with confidence that Melissa's clinical presentation suggested substantial stress emanating from the vagaries
of not knowing exactly what happened to Chris that night and
what role she may have played in the tragedy. She appeared
haunted by the uncertainty. Was she responsible without intent?
Her presentation of historical data as well as her responses to psychological testing all pointed to cooperation and an attempt to present information about herself in an open and honest manner.

I could then explore what Melissa would gain by malingering.
Faking mental health symptoms is often associated with some
form of self-serving motivation, especially in criminal cases. But
Melissa's belief that she was carrying the "stick" when witnesses
saw her carrying neither an axe handle nor a gun does not appear
particularly self-serving. If she was malingering to avoid criminal
responsibility, why admit to carrying any kind of weapon?

Finally, I planned to tell the jury that findings from psychological testing were consistent with Melissa's history and suggested
real not faked symptoms of acute stress followed by the development of post-traumatic stress responses. Post-traumatic stress is a
fertile breeding ground for dissociative amnesia.

When I arrived early at the Graham County courthouse, I sat
in the car for a few minutes rehearsing my plan. Once inside I saw
Cento standing near the appointed courtroom. She wasn't waiting
for me. Cento, barely five feet tall on a good day, and with heels,
was engaged in a heavy discussion with the prosecutor, Edgar

Wright, and a couple of uniformed officers who towered over her like polar bears after a seal. Something was up. I suspected the trial had been postponed at the last minute and my long drive was wasted. I was glad that all my referral sources, including Cento, knew I charged portal to portal and not just for the time I spend on the stand testifying. An early lunch then back to Tucson, I thought. I was wrong.

Cento motioned for me to join the group. She told me the sheriff's department was reconsidering the evidence against Melissa, and Wright was reconsidering the charges. Everybody thought my input would be helpful, so we all marched off to a conference room to deliberate Melissa's fate like jurors.

The major issue was how the gun got in the middle of the fight and into Melissa's hands. While no witnesses saw anybody take a gun into the fight, some were now telling investigators about Chris's penchant for getting into fights and always having a gun nearby in case he needed it. I told them that Melissa had confirmed stories about Chris getting into fights, but she never saw anyone bring out a firearm. I also shared Melissa's report to me that she had been angry at Chris several times because he liked to "play games" with his gun while intoxicated. And the gun was always loaded.

Wright wondered if Chris took the gun into the fight and the two combatants and Melissa were struggling over it when it went off in her hands. I told the group that I had no idea how the gun got in the mix, but Melissa was familiar with guns because her ex-husband had taught her gun safety and how to shoot. I reported that she was able to demonstrate a proper two-handed grasp and the amount of recoil produced by a high-powered handgun. She also could identify the distinctive smell of expended gunpowder.

I then gave the group a quick summary of the dissociation material that I had prepared to tell the jury. When I felt everybody in the room understood, I reported that Melissa still had no memory of getting a gun from the truck or even seeing the gun in the truck or on Chris. And she did not remember feeling a gun recoil in her hands or smelling gunpowder when she heard the shot that killed Chris. I explained that her selective memory could be a result of incidental contact with the weapon, dissociation, or a mixture of both. I finished with: "At the very least, her actions do not seem to follow a plan to murder the only man who treated her with dignity and respect."

I sat back and watched Cento and Wright spar over a possible plea agreement. When the deal was finally struck, Melissa was facing an involuntary manslaughter charge with a recommendation for probation. I suggested probation be made contingent on Melissa's active and successful completion of comprehensive substance abuse counseling programs. They agreed.

As Cento and Wright disappeared into the bowels of the courthouse to find the judge, I shot across the street to Sandy's Old Fashioned Ice Cream Parlor, the retro-deco home of the largest and thickest homemade chocolate malts on the planet.

SILVIA CARMONA[*]

Over the Christmas holidays, Silvia Carmona took her two-year-old daughter, Lydia, and four-year-old son, Ruben, to visit her divorced parents in Nogales, a small town on the Arizona-Mexico border. Her husband, Angel, stayed in California to finish the semester at a community college and look around for a better place for his family to live. Silvia hoped the visit would go well but she knew her strained relationship with her mother would make things difficult. To help reduce the tension she decided to stay at her father's trailer, which he only used as a retreat when he got into arguments with his current wife.

One evening, Silvia's sister, Paula, dropped off Paula's son and Silvia's brother, ten-year-old Cesar, so Silvia could babysit them overnight while Paula went to a party.

When the children got restless because there was little for them to do in the small trailer, Silvia made a trip to her mother's house to get some videos. When she got back to the trailer about thirty minutes later, the children were excited about the videos and soon huddled together in front of the television. About halfway into the second video, Silvia's friend, Eduardo, stopped by to visit. Pretty soon the children complained of being hungry, so Silvia and Eduardo decided to leave the kids with the videos while they went to get some food. They returned with a bag full of goodies in about forty-five minutes.

During the rest of the evening, the children ate snacks and watched television while Silvia sat in a car outside of the trailer talking with Eduardo. After midnight Silvia returned to the trailer alone, found the children asleep, and went to bed.

In the morning, Silvia got up with the children. She tried to put together a breakfast, but her daughter, Lydia, seemed distressed and cranky and needed more attention than usual. When Silvia asked Lydia to tell her what was wrong, Lydia would only point to her vagina and cry. While Silvia tried to find out what had happened, her son, Ruben, ran up to her and said, "Cesar tried to take my clothes off."

Alarmed, Slivia grabbed Cesar as he was heading for the door. He tried to wriggle away and denied he did anything to her children. Silvia persisted until her brother finally admitted to some inappropriate sexual contact with Lydia, including putting a butter knife near her private parts. Cesar got loose and ran into the bathroom.

Silvia grabbed a box of kitchen matches and chased after him. She jerked the door open, lit some matches and toilet paper, and tried to burn Cesar's penis off. When that didn't work she grabbed a knife. Cesar managed to wriggle away and ran for help.

Later, Cesar told the police Silvia burned him but he managed to get away before she got to his penis with the knife. Silvia was arrested and charged with two counts of aggravated assault. Because Silvia seemed confused and emotionally out of control, her attorney motioned for and was granted a mental health examination to determine both Silvia's competency to stand trial and her probable mental condition at the time she attacked her brother. Because of my background in sexual abuse cases, I was chosen as the examiner in the case.

When Silvia arrived at my office she was late for her appointment and seemed agitated and confused. She paced the floor and would often jump from her chair, yelling and waving her arms about, especially when asked to describe her actions with her brother. I felt caught in a whirlwind of high-strung hysteria.

Silvia finally gained some control. She told me she was born in Mexico, but lived in the Nogales, Arizona, area since she was four and was raised by her biological parents in a family of four brothers and three sisters. She was animated again and raised her voice when she told me that her father, a mechanic and small business owner, was an alcoholic who physically and emotionally abused her, her sisters, and her mother. She told me her mother was controlling and overprotective but never abusive. Silvia's parents divorced when she was about seventeen years old.

Silva's voice slowed some. She sat down and told me she was eighteen years old and a virgin when she married Francisco. She smiled as she described the "strong, strong love" in her first marriage, then her face turned sad when she told me that her first child, a daughter, died at childbirth. Silvia divorced her husband shortly after the death of their daughter due to his drinking and jealously, as well as the strong meddling by her mother-in-law and her own family.

Four years later, Silvia met Angel while attending college. I thought she may have made a good choice since she waited until she found someone who was also interested in improving his education. I was only partially correct. Silvia's mood switched back and forth from happy to sad as she extolled the virtues of Angel as a husband in spite of his long-term affair with a woman in Mexico. She said, "He denied he was having an affair but I found a love letter. He finally admitted it after many years. Our relationship is better after the admission. He is showing that he is repenting." But Silvia became tearful when she told me that she lost her beautiful body after giving birth to Lydia and Ruben and that Angel gradually became emotionally distant and finally stopped having sex with her.

Silvia calmed down again as I explored her mental health history. During high school, Silvia received both family and individual counseling due to her father's alcoholism and abusive behavior. She smiled when she told me the sessions were helpful. Following the death of her first daughter, Silvia received counseling from the Catholic Church "to help me through everything."

When Silvia became depressed after the birth of her second daughter, her family physician told her that her condition was "normal" and not to worry about it. In spite of lingering symptoms suggestive of postpartum depression, her physician offered no treatment options.

The rest of Silvia's background was unremarkable. As a student, she earned mostly average grades but did not graduate. She was one semester short of earning a high school diploma even though she was taking college courses that earned credit for a high school diploma as well as an associate's degree. Most of her work experience was part-time employment at various positions while she attended college. She expressed interest in continuing her college studies and becoming a counselor. Other than experimenting with alcohol while in high school she denied using any other type of drugs. She also had no criminal history.

After I finished my evaluation with questions related to competency and state-of-mind issues, I called Silvia's attorney, Robert Collins, with my results. I told him that, in my opinion, Silvia showed only a marginal level of information and understanding of the role and function of courtroom personnel. Although she understood the charges against her, she could not identify the possible penalties associated with those charges and she did not understand plea agreements. Even so, I thought, with a little help from her attorney, she was capable of developing a rational and factual understanding of criminal proceedings and assisting in her own defense. I told him that, overall, Silvia appeared competent to stand trial once these deficits were corrected.

Collins said that he had been working with her on some of these issues and thought she could improve if she would control her emotions better. He wondered how mentally ill she was.

I told him Silvia neither reported a history of psychosis nor appeared psychotic in my office or during the time she attacked her brother. She also appeared to know the difference between right and wrong. On the other hand, Silvia was quite animated and showed strong emotional swings throughout most of the evaluation. I explained that Silvia's description of her interaction with her brother, Cesar, was heavily punctuated with crying, screaming, outbursts of anger, and dramatic demonstrations of her actions.

Based upon her description of the instant offense and her wild behavior during the interview, I believed that she was severely emotionally distraught and unable to control herself when she went after her brother. Her actions during the instant offense suggested excessive emotionality, loss of control, and self-dramatization often associated with histrionic personality types. I pointed out that histrionic personality types are prone to overreact to personal crises, but they typically do not pose a high risk for criminal behavior. I suggested that the court might consider probation with counseling rather than incarceration. He agreed and was hoping to work out a suitable plea agreement for Silvia.

My report was accepted by the court without follow-up testimony. The prosecutor offered Silvia a plea agreement for a misdemeanor assault. She would not face any jail time if she agreed to participate in counseling. She agreed.

JUDY MASTERS*

Judy Masters, an attractive thirty-year-old wearing fashionable clothes, was escorted into my office by her counselor from a residential treatment facility. Judy appeared a little nervous but engaged easily. She told me she was born and raised in Minnesota along with her three older brothers. Her father, barely sixty, died of a heart attack when she was a toddler.

Judy smiled when she told me her mother was an "intelligent, artistic, strong, and independent woman who raised three kids by herself." The smile disappeared when she said, "My mother was also a crazy drunk who made life miserable for us." She went on to explain that her mother physically abused Judy's brothers and emotionally abused her. Judy had few friends as a child because "I had to stay home and take care of the house and sober my mother up." At twelve, Judy was raped by one of her brothers. She added that her brothers were drug addicts.

In spite of the sorrow and chaos in her young life, Judy was a good student and graduated high school with honors. I waited for her to tell me she went on to college, but instead she told me she didn't go because she was pregnant and ended up marrying the seventeen-year-old father of her child. She subsequently miscarried but gave birth to a daughter about a year later. Her first marriage lasted about two years. She said the marriage failed because she "went home to mama."

About one year later, Judy married a second time, which also lasted about two years. "He was a mama's boy and was on drugs. He also gave me gonorrhea when I was pregnant with my second daughter." I started to worry about her choices in partners. My concern was justified.

Six months after Judy's second divorce, she married for the third time. "My two kids needed a father," she said. The stepfather of her two kids soon gave her a son. Keeping with the two-years record, she divorced her third husband when she found out he was addicted to cocaine. She agreed to allow her husband to have custody of their son because she already had two daughters to raise. Judy's face drew tight as she told me she regretted the decision because "he took off with him and I have not seen my son since."

I knew what was coming next. Judy married for the fourth time. This time the marriage broke a record and lasted three years but produced no children. Her selection process did not change much. Her fourth husband was an alcoholic who mentally and physically abused her.

Judy admitted she was an alcoholic and had difficulties caring for her two children. Down on her luck and drunk, Judy contacted her second husband, the drug-addicted mama's boy who gave her gonorrhea, and asked for help. He agreed to help if she would allow him to adopt both of her children. Desperate, Judy agreed and was awarded visitation privileges. After about one year "he took off with the kids and I don't know where they are. So I just stayed drunk. I began drinking and drugging and hitchhiking across the country."

Judy maintained a transient lifestyle until she finally got tired of hitchhiking. Her plan, she said, was to "drink myself to death." After she nearly succeeded one night, she changed her mind and contacted Alcoholics Anonymous instead. When she was placed in a halfway house in Alabama she met and fell in love with Grace, a fifty-something lesbian.

Judy told me this was the first open lesbian relationship she acknowledged, but she had been a "closet lesbian" since she was twenty years old. "My marriages were fronts," she said. "I was in love with my brother's wives and had sexual relationships with them. With Grace I decided to come out with my sexuality and we got an apartment together." Judy thought the relationship was ideal. "I was sober. I had AA. And I had a partner. It was a perfect fairy tale."

The fairy tale of love soon changed to a familiar nightmare of abuse. Grace became extremely possessive and abusive. When the couple moved from Alabama to Arizona because Grace needed a dry climate for her arthritis, Judy hoped the move would also help the relationship. It didn't. Tears flowed down Judy's red cheeks as she told me, "Once we got to Arizona, Grace really began to take over. She made me cut my hair so I would look more butch and she told me what I could and could not wear. Grace is a big woman and she has a black belt in karate. I saw her bust boards with her fists. I was afraid of her."

Judy was in turmoil and knew she was about to fall off the wagon. She contacted AA for help but became more depressed and began to drink again. Her relationship with Grace got even worse. Judy described harrowing episodes of being "beat to hell" and having her hair torn out by the roots. Judy became more confused and depressed with each episode.

Finally she told Grace she was leaving and called her family for assistance in securing transportation home. Grace intervened. "She grabbed the phone and told my family not to do it because I was sick. She told them that she was going to take care of me. We fought all day over my wanting to leave." Feelings of desperation returned. Judy got really drunk then decided suicide was the only way out. She went to the kitchen for knives but Grace followed her and took them away.

Later, when Judy convinced Grace she wasn't going to leave and wasn't going to kill herself, Grace left the apartment to attend a meeting. Judy seized the opportunity. But instead of leaving, Judy set the bedroom ablaze then waited in the living room to be overcome by smoke. She had been drinking all day and passed out on the couch as she sat waiting to die. The couple's frightened cat thwarted her plan when it jumped on her face and woke her up.

Aroused from her drunken stupor, Judy realized the danger for others in the apartment building. She staggered outside, banged on doors, and warned the other apartment dwellers. Once everybody seemed safe Judy had a strong urge "to run back into the fire and die, but I didn't." When the fire department and police arrived, Judy told them her sad tale. She was charged with arson, property damage, and causing substantial risk of imminent death.

When I explored the failed suicide by fire with Judy, she admitted she had a long history of depression and failed suicide attempts. She told me that she normally felt the depression coming on and became more suicidal with alcohol because it gave her the courage to do it. Previous attempts failed because "somebody has always saved me." That time it was her cat.

In my report I explained to the court that the case was not a typical case of arson, where somebody ignites a structure for the purpose of destroying the structure and/or killing someone else. In my opinion, this was a case of attempted suicide by a seriously dysfunctional young woman in a desperate situation. I explained Judy had a propensity toward selecting other dysfunctional and potentially abusive individuals for partners. This self-defeating behavior often leads to depression and subsequent suicide attempts when the relationships, predictably, turn sour. While I thought Judy was dangerous, I believed the danger was primarily to herself and secondary only to anyone else.

I recommended that she continue treatment in a residential treatment program like the one she was in. She needed help with a number of issues included depression, dependency, self-image, interpersonal relationships, sexuality, and substance abuse. I also explained that treatment was more likely to be long rather than short term because individuals like Judy with a history of childhood and partner abuse often lack adequate psychological resources to establish a stable lifestyle without help.

Judy, like many other victims of childhood abuse, grew up with chronic feelings of insecurity, inadequacy, and inferiority. And many women like Judy often find themselves repeatedly stuck in the cycle of abuse by others because they exhibit passive-dependent characteristics and appear unable to take a dominant role in interpersonal relationships. They become easy prey for more-powerful personalities. Alcohol and substance abuse are also common factors that often exacerbate ruminations about wanting to die and impulsive suicide attempts.

HELEN JORDAN*

I watched while two armed corrections officers escorted a petite woman in her midtwenties into my examination room. Like a dangerous desperado, she was secured tightly by handcuffs and leg-shackles. She made her way carefully with tiny shuffles in jail-issued slides. Once Helen was seated at the examination table, I made eye contact with the guards. Both nodded and removed the handcuffs. They were veterans of my examination room and quite familiar with my routine request. No words were necessary. They also knew fresh coffee waited for them in the observation area and, after securing one of Helen's ankles to one of the table's steel legs, they quickly headed in that direction. As they shut the examination room door, one shot a warning, "Now you be good, Helen." Helen looked up with tears in her eyes. She didn't understand jail-house humor. This was her first arrest.

As Helen dabbed her eyes with a tissue she looked depressed and miserable. I wanted to forego the dreaded warning of limitations of confidentiality but knew breaching protocol could create more problems for her down the road. She had more than enough legal problems already, with multiple counts of child abuse, which had left her four-year-old son seriously injured. To my surprise she handled the information well and gave consent without a fuss.

I began the evaluation by asking Helen to provide information about her childhood. She started by telling me she was the middle child of three born to her biological parents. She also had six older half sisters by her mother's previous marriage who had been farmed out to other relatives because her father would not "accept" her mother's children. Helen's mother was forced to choose between Helen's father and her own kids.

Her mother's attitude about her other children wasn't much better. Helen began to cry when she told me, "My mother treated me more like a stepchild. She put me at the very least. I was hardly included in family activities. I felt not wanted and lonely." Helen also reported that her mother would whip her with a belt "when I had done something wrong and other times when she just decided that it was my fault and I would get the beatings."

Helen's sad face turned angry and sadder when she said her father, a retired miner, molested her when she was about five years old. As Helen sobbed she told me that she went to her mother for protection and disclosed the sexual abuse. I privately predicted her mother's response. "She didn't believe me. I felt that my mother didn't really love me because she didn't do anything about it," Helen sobbed. Her father continued to sexually abuse Helen for about two years then suddenly stopped. But Helen lived in fear that the abuse would begin again at any time.

Helen's childhood fear was justified. But this time the abuse came from somewhere else. Shortly after Helen's seventh birthday, she was molested by a brother-in-law. When she tried to fight him off, he told her, "It's okay because your mother is a bitch and all you kids are bitches and deserve to be molested." Knowing her mother would do nothing, Helen felt the only thing she could do was tell her father, an unlikely protector. Helen was surprised when her father got angry and got into a fight with her brother-in-law.

When I asked Helen if her father reported the abuse to authorities, I already knew the answer. He didn't. Her father might fight his rival but he certainly would not risk Helen disclosing the sexual abuse. But a fight was not enough to stop it.

Helen's brother-in-law continued to molest her for another three years. Finally, when she was ten, Helen told her sister, the wife of Helen's molester. At first her sister didn't want to believe Helen, but then she told Helen she had heard from another sister that her husband was molesting another child in the family. Again, no one bothered to report the abuse to authorities.

After two decades of evaluating and treating cases of sexual abuse, I must admit very little surprises me anymore. But then Helen told me a twist that gave me pause. When Helen was twenty-one years old her sister, the wife of the molester, died. Shortly after the funeral, the brother-in-law who molested her as a child approached Helen and said, "I always loved you and I stayed in the family waiting for you to get older so I could marry you." I could hardly wait for the rest. Helen went on, "After my sister died, Child Protective Services asked me to take care of my sister's children because my brother-in-law was molesting one of the girls. We took care of them by moving them from family to family." I couldn't help but think that this was the tactic used by Helen's mother to dispose of Helen's half siblings when Helen's father rejected them.

In addition to all the sexual abuse in this family, Helen told me both her parents abused alcohol and the family was always in turmoil with Helen caught often in the middle. "They were always drinking, arguing, and fighting," she said. "A lot of times my mother would throw my father out of the house, and she always made sure that I went with him. We would go to my uncle's house for a couple of days then come home. When I was about eleven years old, mother left and took us with her. We hid out for about six months before we saw my father again."

Based upon Helen's chaotic and abusive background I was not surprised when she told me she got pregnant at about age fifteen and later became a single mother with six children by six different men. In each case, she began a relationship with someone "because I was looking for that love that I never had." She also indicated that she was always looking for men to care for her as a person and "not just that they want something from me."

She thought she found this elusive love with Roger, the last man she partnered with, but Helen's family wouldn't accept him because he did drugs. "He told me he loves me and the kids, but I left him because of family pressure." Ironically, the longest relationship, two years, with any man was with Roger, who did not father any of Helen's children. Most of her children's fathers were emotionally and/or physically abusive toward the children and/or Helen.

Taking a drug history revealed that Helen abused cocaine, heroin, and marijuana before she got pregnant with her first child. She said the father of her first child introduced her to drugs. She stopped using until after she gave birth and gave the child to one of her sisters to raise. Helen then returned to her drug routine, then stopped again when she became pregnant with her second child. She looked me in the eyes and gave a very strong statement that she was no longer abusing drugs.

Knowing Helen had been charged with child abuse, I asked her how she was with her kids. She hung her head down as she told me about her first referral to Child Protective Services a couple of years previous because "I was using the belt on the kids." She looked up and continued, "But not really hard." Hard or not, her caseworker was concerned enough to place Helen in a six-week parent-training program. Helen said the program was helpful but indicated that she needed additional training beyond what was available at the time. She also admitted that she could use counseling to help her with problems of "anger, depression, and stress."

I then asked Helen about the allegations of child abuse and the injuries to her son. She explained that she tried to use the techniques she learned in the parent-training program, but they didn't seem to work very well with her four-year-old, a rambunctious boy who was always getting into everything. Her smooth face twisted into a mask of frustration. "Ben was always touching things. I tried other forms of discipline, but he continued to do it. Everyday I would hear of Ben touching this and Ben touching that. When my sister told me that Ben and the other boy, Robert, had broken a lightbulb, I spanked both of them." She made eye contact. "But not real hard. Just enough to let them know what they did was wrong."

Helen waited for a response from me that didn't come, then continued, "Later I found baby powder and mascara all over the place.

The baby had black all over her and Ben's hands were covered with mascara." Helen looked away and her hands rolled into tight fists. "I began feeling really frustrated and hurt. I was really mad at Ben. I just couldn't understand why he kept on doing this to me."

Then one of Helen's old fears came back. "I started to worry that Ben may have molested the baby. I didn't know what to do with him. I wanted to teach Ben a lesson. For him not to touch things and not to turn into somebody like what I went through — turning into somebody like my father and my brother-in-law."

Helen said she lost control. She grabbed Ben and dragged him into the kitchen. He struggled in vain as she held her young son's hands over the flames of a cooking stove. When Ben's screams and the smell of burning flesh finally cut through Helen's anger, she let him go. Helen said, "At the end, when I heard him scream, and scream, and scream, I realized that he was really hurt."

When I called Helen's attorney I told him Helen was the product of a long history of child sexual, physical, and emotional abuse. As a result she struggled with a fairly typical cluster of emotional problems often demonstrated by victims of child abuse, including a poor self-concept, poor judgment in interpersonal relationships, an elevated level of anger and hostility, poor control over emotions, and strong dependency needs. Substance abuse and unsatisfying sexual relationships are also common symptoms. Abused children, like Helen, often produce children for their own emotional needs without clearly recognizing or understanding the needs of the children. When confronted with the harsh reality of a child's needs and occasional misbehavior, these parents often feel betrayed and are at high risk of losing control of strong, angry feelings directed at the child. The result is often serious injury to the child, or even death.

Helen's attorney reminded me the prosecution was aware of the national studies that show most abused children do not grow up to abuse their own children. They would press this issue in court. I countered by reminding him that the same studies also show that being abused as a child is a significant factor in many subsequent child abuse cases. I told him I would handle the attack by pointing out that most parents who abuse and/or neglect their children do so as a function of emotional problems created by the childhood abuse, not because they have a criminal disposition. In my opinion Helen did not show criminal intent even though she committed a serious crime. A lot of abuse victims, like Helen, are not often totally aware of their dangerous actions until something brings them back from their anger.

I told him I would tell the court that Helen appeared to have lost control of her anger and attempted to "teach her son a lesson" by putting his hands over an open flame. I also thought that Helen experienced a brief period of dissociation while holding her son's hands over the flame during which she lost contact with the harmfulness of her actions. This period of dissociation seems to have been broken and control was regained when Ben's screams signaled that she had gone beyond a lesson and was, in fact, putting her son's well-being in jeopardy.

What did I recommend? he asked. First, I warned that Helen was at high risk for future inappropriate expressions of anger unless she worked hard at resolving her serious emotional problems and established effective anger management skills. Then I offered hope by telling him that abusive parents can respond well to a directed therapeutic regimen consisting of parent-training programs, anger management training, stress management, individual counseling with a focus on personal child abuse issues, and self-help groups such as Parents Anonymous. I would also recommend adjunct therapy programs addressing issues of substance abuse or other addictive behaviors.

To ensure the safety of her children I would recommend that Helen not be permitted unsupervised contact with her children until she demonstrated significant positive changes in stress and anger management skills, as well as effective and appropriate parenting strategies. And I thought that probation, if granted, should be made contingent on Helen's participation in all of my treatment recommendations until her caseworker determined Helen's risk to abuse her children was reduced to the lowest level possible. The court accepted my recommendations.

Helen was sentenced to five years' probation contingent on her participation and completion of a series of parent education programs, including attending Parents Anonymous meetings.

KAREN MONTANA*

Fresh out of a shelter for the homeless, Karen Montana was staying with an acquaintance, Robert, when another acquaintance inexplicably left two young children in Karen's care. Karen did not supervise the children carefully and they damaged the house. When Robert discovered the damage he disciplined the kids then went to his bedroom for a nap. Karen interpreted the discipline as physical abuse and got upset. She sent the kids outside then went to another bedroom where she threw bedding and paper in a corner then set the pile on fire. She waited until the blaze was going strong then she left the house quietly. Robert awoke to billowing smoke and a raging fire. He called 911 then grabbed a small kitchen fire extinguisher and fought in vain to save his home. By the time firefighters arrived the house was fully engulfed. Other than minor injuries Robert was unhurt. He lost his home but not his life. When the police caught up to Karen she confessed that she set the house on fire hoping to kill Robert because he abused the kids. She was charged with attempted first-degree murder and arson of an occupied structure.

Karen's court-appointed public defender soon discovered Karen had a history of chronic mental illness. Concerned about Karen's ability to stand trial and assist him with her defense, he asked the court for a competency evaluation. I was on the list of court-approved examiners and was chosen as one of two evaluators.

While a sad and depressed nineteen-year-old Karen sat across the table from me and attempted to answer every question I asked, her responses were mostly concrete and attenuated. Spontaneous statements were infrequent and flat. I made a note to check for receptive and expressive language deficits, then waited for the answer to my question about hallucinations.

Karen looked at me with a blank stare. "I sometimes hear voices," she said. When I asked what the voices said, Karen told me she couldn't tell because today the voices were "mumbled." She indicated that she normally heard the voices more clearly but her "pills" helped in subduing and eventually controlling them. I checked her medical summary and found she had a history of psychiatric hospitalizations and prescribed psychotropic medications. Since her arrest and incarceration for attempted murder, medical personnel at the jail had prescribed a regimen of two antipsychotics, haloperidol and trazodone, to be administered before bedtime. Strong medicine, but she did not seem overmedicated or unable to participate in the evaluation.

In spite of Karen's obvious mental problems her memory was reasonably intact and she was a good personal historian. Other than where she was born, Karen's information was fairly consistent with the file material provided by her public defender. With little change in emotion, Karen told me about her mother's long history of violent behavior, substance abuse, and criminal arrests. At the end of her story about her mother, Karen said, "She sold her body for drugs." Her biological father, also a substance abuser with a criminal record, was killed when the car he was in was demolished by a train. Karen thought she was about eight years old when she and her sisters were molested by one of her mother's friends or tricks. When Karen's mother found out about the sexual abuse, she killed and dismembered the man in front of Karen. Karen's mother was sent to prison for the gruesome murder, leaving Karen an orphan.

Throughout the rest of Karen's childhood she was placed with a variety of relatives, where she was sexually and physically abused by a parade of family members and their friends. Karen hoped she had seen the last of the abuse when she was finally placed in a foster home. She was wrong. The abuse was the same, only the cast of characters changed. Karen's last hope was adoption, but she knew no one would want a sexually abused young girl with a history of learning disabilities, low intellectual functioning, and severe emotional problems. She was correct.

Karen told me that as hopes for her adoption were abandoned, she was placed in a number of programs to help her eventually live on her own. She thought she learned a lot in the programs but the records showed something quite different. As one case manager wrote, "Karen is a family of one. She does not have a clue as to what it takes to live on her own." Another wrote, "Karen is an unbonded child who had no one to bond with. She never had a period of her life with normalcy. She was always exposed to continual crises."

In spite of the challenges, Karen tried to live on her own in a group home after her eighteenth birthday, but she ran away several times. When I asked Karen why she didn't stay in the group home, she said simply, "Because I didn't like it." Until her arrest, Karen had lived in various shelters or with anybody who would take her in.

Even though questions used to evaluate competency are fairly straightforward, I eased into them carefully. I found that Karen was able to provide basic answers to questions regarding court personnel, proceedings, and plea bargains, but she often seemed confused and gave conflicting answers.

When we explored the serious allegations that she tried to commit murder by arson, Karen said she understood the charges against her and the possible penalties if found guilty. She discussed her actions openly and did not waiver from information she provided to police, including her confession. She gave me no reason to challenge her account.

Although competency examinations cost a flat fee set by the court and are intended to be brief and to the point, I decided Karen's case needed much more careful consideration. Karen was one of society's "throwaway kids," and I knew, at age nineteen, she was on the verge of being thrown away again. This time into prison for a very long time.

I spent several extra hours interviewing and testing Karen, consulting with previous evaluators and counselors, and studying police reports, her voluminous Child Protective Services records, and medical reports. Once I formed my opinion, not only about her competency to stand trial but also recommendations for an appropriate disposition of the case, I wrote and submitted a detailed report to the judge. The report went far beyond the usual two-page letter about competency issues that most examiners submit. Flat fee be damned.

I addressed the issues of Karen's competency to stand trial with concerns that Karen showed serious deficits in those abilities usually considered when assessing a defendant's competency to stand trial. Even so, it was my opinion that Karen demonstrated the bare minimum level of abilities necessary to understand the nature of legal proceedings and to assist in the preparation of the defense. However, I concurred with the second evaluator's opinion that Karen may experience difficulties in understanding legal proceedings overall and particularly "if the nature of the hearings are complex."

I suggested that the court may find it necessary to reduce language and proceedings to their simplest form. Then I expressed concern that Karen may not be able to maintain her current minimal level of understanding over time. I pointed out that Karen's case material documented serious problems with comprehension, abstract reasoning, and retention of important facts. I had serious concerns that Karen would have difficulty in applying learning skills to unique situations such as complex legal proceedings. As one of her treating psychiatrists warned in a discharge summary,

"I am not absolutely sure that on repeat mental status exam tomorrow I might not get some different answers."

As I addressed issues of her mental status at the time of the alleged offense, I was again careful to document Karen's history of chronic mental illness and low intellectual functioning. I explained that most of her past behavioral problems, including setting other fires and a variety of inappropriate behaviors, have been linked to intellectual deficits as well as post-traumatic stress, depression, and psychotic processes, such as auditory hallucinations in the form of voices instructing her to harm herself or others. I argued that with such a well-documented history of multiple psychiatric diagnoses, it would be erroneous to believe that Karen was not suffering from a mental disease or defect during the time of the instant offense.

To drive the point home I reported that many of Karen's psychiatric symptoms had been successfully controlled in the past with psychotropic medications, but records showed that Karen did not have access to her medications for a period of several days before she tried to kill Robert. I learned that staff at Karen's last group home feared she would use the medications to commit suicide so they kept them from her. Like most chronic psychiatric patients, without proper medications Karen's mental condition deteriorated. Most notably, she became agitated and depressed, a dangerous combination of symptoms often leading to suicidal thoughts and attempts.

Without her medications, Karen self-medicated with alcohol and marijuana, which only made her psychiatric symptoms worse. Then, the voices came back.

I knew the prosecutor would go after Karen with allegations of malingering so I addressed this issue carefully. I again pointed to my extensive review of material related to Karen's psychiatric history, none of which provided any evidence that she was prone to faking symptoms of mental illness. In fact, one of her former therapists reported to me that Karen would often exude an optimistic and positive manner even when her life was in turmoil. And Karen's presentation during my evaluation certainly did not suggest an attempt to exaggerate symptoms associated with her well-documented history of mental illness and low intellectual functioning.

I emphasized in my report that a careful consideration of all the information obtained through my evaluation brought me to the opinion that Karen was suffering from a mental disease or defect at the time of the offense that effectively prevented her from understanding, at the time of the offense, that her actions were wrong. I added it was also my opinion that acute voluntary intoxication may have been a factor, but I couldn't ascertain with any certainty the level at which intoxication contributed to Karen's actions.

Since I declared that Karen was suffering from a mental disease or defect at the time of the offense, I was required by law to identify the disease. I again noted that Karen had a history of multiple psychiatric symptoms and her diagnoses had varied over time. I offered my opinion about the most accurate diagnoses of Karen's mental status during the time she attempted to kill Robert by arson. She was suffering from depression, schizophrenia, borderline personality disorder, mild mental retardation, and an overlay of alcohol and cannabis intoxication. This was a heady mix of multiple mental disorders. This was Karen.

While not required in a competency evaluation, I prepared a recommendation that urged against sending a severely mentally ill young woman to prison for most of her life. To provide a strong foundation for this, I again pulled statements from Karen's extensive psychiatric and Child Protective Services records. I pointed out that case managers and mental health experts consistently rated Karen's intellectual and emotional problems as chronic and severe. For years, they recommended some form of residential treatment program for Karen but failed to find a proper placement for a mentally ill young girl within what I saw as an underfunded and neglected mental health system. I offered my opinion that Karen did not, at this time, possess the emotional and intellectual resources to develop independent living skills and she still posed a danger to herself and others.

I concurred with Karen's case managers and treatment professionals and recommended a long-term placement at a residential facility for the chronically mentally ill until such time as treatment staff determined she could be released into an outpatient treatment program. Perhaps, as an adult, a place for Karen could be found.

LISA MARIE NOWAK[1]

On the Fourth of July 2006, I watched the countdown on television for the launch of the Space Shuttle *Discovery*. The words *Ignition!* and *We have liftoff* always spark my childhood dream to be blasted off into space and, as the *Star Trek* anthem promised for decades, "Go where no man has gone before!"

My dream ended early when I learned that a boy who couldn't tell the difference between green and blue and needed strong correction for astigmatism had no chance of growing up to be a man who could pilot fighter planes, commercial planes, or any other kind of high-performance aircraft. But I managed to keep a sliver of the dream alive by earning a restricted private pilot license and catching a ride in the copilot seat of just about any kind of vintage aircraft that came along. And, of course, I followed the space program, read Tom Wolfe's *The Right Stuff*, and can quote lines from the movie. (Tom Wolfe was one of my favorite authors before he wrote *The Right Stuff*.)

As I watched *Discovery* lift from its pad with the unmistakable burst that overpowers the senses, I somehow knew how those aboard must have felt. They all had followed their dreams and were, at that moment, living them. I was especially excited for astronaut Lisa Nowak, who was the shuttle's robotic specialist.

US Navy Captain Lisa Nowak had followed the space program as a child and dreamed of someday becoming one of the first women astronauts. Now, as I watched, this married forty-three-year-old mother of a teenage boy and twin five-year-old daughters was roaring through space toward the International Space Station.

Ten days later *Discovery* made a perfect landing, ending a highly successful space flight. In the fall Nowak went back to her hometown as a hero. She stirred dreams in other young girls with her tales of space science and adventures. Truly a model up to whom any child could look. She had made it. Or so it seemed.

On February 5, 2007, I was listening to the news on PBS as I was cleaning the last of the residue from the Super Bowl party the day before. I host a Super Bowl party each year for my poker buddies and their significant others. This one was special. I was born and raised in the rolling farm lands between Indianapolis and Chicago and grew up a Bears fan, then divided my loyalty when the Colts moved from Baltimore to Indianapolis. With the Bears and Colts in the Super Bowl, one of my teams was going to win no matter what.

As I stacked items to be put back in storage until next year, the PBS announcer said something about an astronaut that shifted my attention right away. At first I didn't quite understand what I thought I was hearing. Something about a female astronaut arrested at the Orlando International Airport after she attacked someone. I was shocked when the assailant was named. It was Lisa Nowak.

Over the next few days I followed the story and tried to be objective but, honestly, I was dismayed and disappointed. In a lot of ways my space dream rode with *Discovery* and its crew, just like it did with the other missions. I had already felt a terrible loss when one shuttle exploded on launch and another, *Columbia*, fell back to earth in charred bits and pieces.

I guess I shouldn't hang my hat on the stars. I just couldn't understand how someone could give up a dream that I held so dear but could never achieve. Then I put my feelings aside and fired up my forensic side. Maybe I could understand what happened to astronaut Nowak.

Lisa was born and raised in the Washington, DC, area. When she was a child she was enthralled with the *Apollo* moon landings and dreamed of someday becoming a pilot and flying in space.

After graduating from Charles W. Woodward High School in 1981, Lisa was accepted into the US Naval Academy, where she earned a bachelor's of science degree in aerospace engineering and her commission in the US Navy in 1985. Lisa became a naval flight officer in 1987, then received a master's in science degree in aeronautical engineering and a degree in aeronautical and astronautical engineering in 1992 from the prestigious US Naval Postgraduate School in Monterey, California. She met Richard T. Nowak while she attended the Naval Academy. They married in 1988. A son was born in 1992 and the couple had twin daughters in 2001.

Next in Lisa's professional sights was Aerospace Engineering Duty, including the rigors of the US Naval Test Pilot School, where she earned her wings as a navigator. She logged over fifteen hundred hours of flight in more than thirty different aircraft, relentlessly pursuing her childhood dream of becoming an astronaut.

In 1996 her dream came true. Lisa entered the elite NASA Astronaut Corps and worked diligently to qualify as a mission specialist in robotics. Although slated for mission STS-118, schedule changes delayed her first flight into space until mission STS-121 on July 4, 2006.

Lisa was the first Italian American woman to go into space and she made the most of the opportunity. As a mission flight engineer, Lisa skillfully operated the space shuttle's robotic arm during several spacewalks at the International Space Station. Back on earth, Nowak added a new aircraft and twelve days, eighteen hours, and thirty-six minutes of spaceflight to her bulging logbook. But her most memorable trip was just months away.

On February 4, 2007, Lisa Nowak slipped into her car and headed for Florida. Compared to the time and miles she had traveled in space as an astronaut, the nine hundred highway miles between Houston and Orlando would seem like forever. She had been careful to pack all of the items she would need for the trip and diligently thought through her course of action for when she would meet her rival.

On February 5, 2007, Lisa arrived at the Orlando International Airport. She pulled on a black wig, grabbed a black duffle bag full of weapons, went to the baggage claim area, and waited. When US Air Force Captain Colleen Shipman retrieved her bags, Lisa donned a hooded tan trench coat and followed Shipman to a satellite parking area. As Shipman approached her car, Lisa rushed forward. But Shipman got in quickly and locked the door. Thwarted by her target, Lisa tried to yank the door open and slapped at the window in frustration.

Then Lisa tried a different ploy: she started to cry and asked for a ride. The plan sort of worked. Shipman dropped the window a couple of inches, just enough for Lisa to use her can of pepper spray. But then Shipman quickly drove off to the parking lot booth for help.

It took just a few minutes for police to respond. When they arrived they found Lisa throwing her duffle bag in a trash bin at a parking shuttle bus stop. She was detained and the bag was retrieved. According to police reports, Lisa's duffle contained three weapons, all new and unused: a steel mallet, an eight-inch folding buck knife with a serrated blade, and a loaded BB gun that resembled a 9mm automatic handgun.

A search of her car revealed detailed directions for Houston to Orlando International Airport, maps of the airport terminal interior, schedules of shuttle buses serving the terminal and parking lots, and a handwritten map showing the way from the airport to Shipman's house. Lisa knew not only how to find her way around space but on earth as well. She also knew how to prepare for her confrontation with Shipman. The police found latex gloves, ammunition for the BB gun, black gloves, rubber tubing, her computer, and a handwritten list of items including food and other items.

Initial reports from the police indicated Lisa had worn diapers on the trip so she wouldn't have to stop to use restrooms along the way. Lisa has since disputed the report, but diapers were found in the car, some used according to police reports.

Lisa was placed under arrest for attempted kidnapping, attempted vehicle burglary with battery, destruction of evidence, and battery. At her arraignment the next day, two fellow astronauts appeared on Lisa's behalf. The judge ordered Lisa released on fifteen thousand dollars' bail under the condition she wear a GPS tracking device and not contact Shipman.

The prosecutor, who argued that Lisa was a dangerous woman and should not be released on bail, was not happy, and before Lisa could be released, she was charged with attempted first-degree murder with a weapon, a life felony in the state of Florida. At Lisa's second arraignment, the prosecution again recommended no bail, but the judge just added ten thousand dollars to the original bail amount and affirmed his previous order to release Lisa with a monitoring device and that she have no contact with Shipman. Lisa made bail, strapped on the GPS ankle device, and headed back to Houston on a plane.

Back in Houston, Lisa was placed on a thirty-day leave by NASA and underwent medical and psychiatric evaluations at the Johnson Space Center. On March 7, 2007, she was dismissed by NASA and reassigned to the US Navy. Grounded.

Investigators soon learned that Lisa began a secret two-year affair with recently divorced astronaut William Oefelein in 2004. Although Lisa has described her relationship with Oefelein as less than romantic, she was clearly threatened by Oefelein's interest in Shipman. And Oefelein was gradually shifting his interest in Nowak to Shipman, an engineer at Patrick Air Force Base in Florida, toward the end of 2006. In January 2007 Lisa separated from her husband and children.

When investigators interviewed Oefelein, he told them he had broken off his relationship with Lisa even though he had lunch with her at his apartment at least once in January and they still trained together for a bicycle race. Cell phone records showed that Nowak and Oefelein talked to each other at least a hundred times during December and January.

On the day before Valentine's Day 2007, Lisa entered a written plea of not guilty to all charges, including attempted murder and attempted kidnapping. About two weeks later, the prosecution came back with three formal charges: attempted kidnapping with intent to inflict bodily harm or terrorize, burglary of a conveyance with a weapon, and battery. Absent were charges associated with attempted murder.

On March 22, 2007, Lisa's attorney, Donald Lykkebak, entered a plea of not guilty to the kidnapping charges and requested a jury trial. The trial date was set but subsequently postponed. On August 12, Lisa asked to have her ankle GPS bracelet removed. On August 28, 2007, the trial judge unsealed a court document revealing that Lisa's attorney planned to pursue an insanity defense, claiming Lisa suffered from depression, obsessive-compulsive disorder, insomnia, and a brief psychotic disorder with marked stressors. Oh, crazy astronauts.

NOTE

1. For a comprehensive examination of the Lisa Marie Nowak case, see Diane Fanning, *Out There* (New York: St. Martin's, 2007).

Britney Spears, a former Mouseketeer who rocketed to pop stardom before she turned twenty, is a frequent target of the paparazzi and is ridiculed often for her bad girl behavior. *AP photo.*

Mug shot of Susan Smith, whose wild love life and deep emotional problems led her to kill her two young boys by drowning. *AP photo.*

Aileen Wuornos, who has achieved cult status in the United States as a female serial killer, was convicted and executed for the murder of seven men. *AP photo.*

Astronaut Lisa Marie Nowak, who was captured by police in an airport parking lot after accosting a woman she believed was her rival in a love triangle with another astronaut. *Courtesy of NASA.*

Mary Winkler was convicted of voluntary manslaughter in the death of her minister husband, Matthew, in the small town of Selmer, Tennessee. *AP photo.*

Debra Beasley LaFave, a Florida teacher who pleaded guilty to lewd and lascivious behavior with a fourteen-year-old male student. *AP photo.*

5

ROCK-A-BYE BABY

MURDEROUS MOTHERS

For nearly a mile, the blue minivan weaved recklessly across the road then came to an abrupt stop on the gravel shoulder. The driver, a petite woman in her twenties, got out of the van and went to the rear passenger door. She slid the door open and pulled a distressed baby from an infant car seat. With the crying baby dangling from her outstretched arms, Sally stumbled through a culvert toward a farmer's field. A fence topped with barbed wire protected the farmer's crops from trespassers. When Sally reached the fence, she tossed the baby on top of the barbed wire, then raked the infant across the steel barbs repeatedly. A startled farmer in the middle of the field looked up as the baby's head tumbled to the ground then disappeared among his prize-winning melons.

As I sat in a Parent's Anonymous meeting listening to Sally's sad story, I was simultaneously repelled by the facts and yet compelled to listen in hopes of learning more about what could have pushed a young mother to the point of killing her only child in such a horrific manner. Yet, hers was but one of many stories of mothers who kill their children. Researchers have found that children under the age of ten are murdered in the United States at a rate of about two per day, and approximately one child per day is killed before the child's first birthday. Studies show that most children are killed by their biological parents or a male acquaintance of the mother. Only 3 percent of children die at the hands of a stranger. Biological mothers accounted for approximately 30 percent of the child homicides between 1976 and 2000. This translates into an astonishing annual rate pushing three hundred, or a mother killing one child about every day and a half.[1] But these mothers often do not kill just one of their children.

BERTA ESTRADA

When Alejandra Estrada's sister, Berta, didn't show up for her early morning shift at Wendy's, Alejandra thought that she had just overslept, so she went to her sister's trailer near Hudson Oaks, Texas, to wake her. The job was important. Berta had four young children and finances were tight. Alejandra knocked several times at Berta's front door but no one, not even the kids, answered. Concerned, Alejandra forced her way into the trailer, where she faced a gruesome scene. Eight-month-old Evelyn Frayre, five-year-old Maria Estrada, three-year-old Yaneth Frayre, and twenty-one-month-old Magaly Frayre dangled by their necks side by side like laundry hung from a clothesline. The children's mother, Berta, hanged at one end of the makeshift gallows, cleverly constructed with bedding and clothing. Only the baby survived.

Investigators found no evidence of outside foul play so they ruled the massacre a murder-suicide. Berta Estrada had joined the company of other well-known murderous mothers such as Andrea Yates and Susan Smith. She was also the eighth mother in Texas who killed her kids in a time span of about six years. One, Dee Etta Perez, lived just a scant mile away from Berta. Dee also killed herself after she drugged and shot her three children.

Family members described Berta, a twenty-five-year-old immigrant from Tamaulipas, Mexico, as a loving and caring mother. But she was under a lot of pressure to support her four children on about nine hundred dollars a month. Berta had recently left her common-law husband after he raped and strangled her then threatened to kill her with a knife. Berta sought help and protection at a nearby battered women's shelter. When she left the shelter she moved into a mobile home with her children. A friend reported that Berta seemed depressed and complained about her situation a few weeks before the murder-suicide but did not threaten to kill the kids or herself.

No one seems to know for sure why Berta killed her kids then herself. She didn't leave a note. But in a June 11, 2007, *Newsweek* article, a well-known child welfare expert, Dr. Richard Gelles, offered his opinion about the case.[2] He suggested three possibilities: lingering postpartum depression, revenge for the abuse by her common-law husband, or a twisted way of protecting the children such as taking the children to heaven with her.

Postpartum depression and seeking the protection of heaven may have also been factors in the highly publicized case of a mother who drowned her five children in a bathtub.

ANDREA YATES[3]

At 9:48 on an already steamy Houston morning in June 2001, Andrea Yates called 911.

"I need a police officer," she told the operator.

"What's the problem?" the operator wanted to know.

"I just need him to come," Andrea answered.

Following protocol to determine the nature of the emergency before sending officers into harm's way, the operator pressed. "I need to know why they are coming." She added, "Is your husband there?"

"No," Andrea answered.

"What's the problem?" the operator persisted.

"I need him to come," Andrea repeated.

"I need to know why they are coming," the operator countered.

Andrea's irregular breathing and noise as she fumbled the phone led the operator to ask, "Are you having a disturbance? Are you ill, or what?"

"Yes, I'm ill."

"What kind of medical problems?"

When Andrea didn't answer, the operator asked, "You need an ambulance?"

"No, I need a police officer," Andrea answered.

Still thinking the emergency may be medical, the operator repeated, "Do you need an ambulance?"

Andrea's labored voice said, "No," then, "Yes, send an ambulance." After that nothing but static.

The operator again talked through the static but got no response. She persisted, "Is someone burglarizing your home?"

"No," Andrea finally replied.

"What is it?" the concerned operator asked firmly.

No answer.

The operator tried again, "What kind of medical problems are you having?"

Still no answer. Then came another request from Andrea for a police officer.

The operator confirmed Andrea's location then asked, "Are you there alone?"

"Yes," Andrea answered. Then more static and silence.

When the sound of distressed breathing returned, the operator asked, "Andrea Yates?"

"Yes."

"Is your husband there?"

"No. I'm sick," Andrea said.

"How are you sick?" Andrea's response was unintelligible. The operator pressed again, "Andrea Yates, is your husband there?"

"No."

"Why do you need a policeman, ma'am?"

"I just need him to be here."

"For what?"

Andrea repeated her answer then silence and static returned.

Becoming increasingly concerned that Andrea was being threatened by someone, the operator asked, "You're sure you're not alone?"

Andrea tried to reassure the operator she was not alone, "My kids are here."

"How old are the children?"

"Seven, five, three, two, and six months."

"You have five children?" the surprised operator asked.

"Yes."

"Okay. We'll send an officer."

"Thank you," Andrea said, then hung up.

Eight minutes later, Andrea dialed her husband's cell phone. "You need to come home," she said in a determined voice.

"What's wrong?" Rusty Yates asked.

"It's time," was her cryptic answer.

"What do you mean?" Rusty asked.

"It's time," she repeated.

Rusty rushed from his sixth-floor Shuttle Vehicle Engineering Office at National Aeronautics and Space Administration's Building One. On the way he called his mother, who was staying at a nearby motel, and told her to get to the house as soon as possible. In his car, Rusty dialed Andrea. She answered.

"Is anybody hurt?" he asked.

"Yes."

"Who?"

"The kids."

"Which ones?"

"All of them."

When Officer David Knapp arrived at the Yates's modest three-

bedroom brick home on Beachcomber, he found a wet and emotionally distraught Andrea who told him, "I just killed my kids."
She showed Knapp the way to the master bedroom, where he
found four children lying side by side on a mattress and box
springs as though they had been tucked in for a good night's sleep.
The telltale froth of trauma escaped from four tiny noses. In a
guest bathroom with blue walls, a fifth child floated in a shallow
white bathtub full of water and fecal matter.

At Harris County Police Headquarters, Sergeant Eric Mehl
asked questions, listened carefully, and took notes as Andrea
described how she methodically drowned each of her five children—Noah, John, Paul, Luke, and Mary—one at a time. Then
Mehl punched the record button on his audiotape machine and
asked the questions again. When the taped interview was over,
Andrea asked, "When is my trial?"

The next morning Andrea, dressed in a bright orange Harris
County Jail jumpsuit, stood quietly before Judge Belinda Hill. Her
court-appointed attorney, Bob Scott, stood between Andrea and
prosecutors Kaylynn Williford and Joseph Owmby. Williford presented the facts of the case to Judge Hill, emphasizing that Andrea
had intentionally and knowingly drowned her five children.
Andrea was officially charged with a single count of capital
murder involving John and Noah together. Texas law allows for a
charge of capital murder when two or more people in the same
criminal episode and a child under the age of six are murdered.
Decisions about additional charges related to the other children
and the death penalty were pending. Andrea pled not guilty.

Later, Andrea's mother and three brothers contacted their
family lawyer John O'Sullivan for advice about Andrea's legal rep-
resentation. Upon O'Sullivan's recommendation, Andrea's family
hired Houston attorney George Parnham, who quickly sprang into
action on Andrea's behalf. After filing the necessary legal papers
he interviewed Andrea in jail, pulled his partner, Wendell Odom,
into the case, and began to prepare a defense based upon Andrea's

two-year-long losing battle with mental illness. Andrea Yates was not only not guilty, she was insane.

The Harris County District Attorney's Office was also busy planning the prosecution's strategy. On August 9, 2001, Assistant District Attorney Owmby filed a Notice of the State's Intent to Seek Death as a Penalty in the Andrea Yates case. The stakes just got higher and the jury pool smaller. By asking for death, the prosecutors gained the advantage of narrowing the jury pool to only those people who are willing to impose the death penalty, even though they denied that seeking the death penalty was a ploy to get a more prosecution-friendly jury. But first, another jury would struggle with issues of Andrea's competency to stand trial.

In Texas, the standard for insanity is whether the accused knew his or her acts were wrong at the time of the crime, a throwback to a nineteenth-century right-from-wrong test originated in England. Even more modern versions of the McNaughton Rule, as it is still called in most states, pose a challenge to the jury's understanding of mental health issues and legal definitions of insanity.

Dr. Gerald Harris, a University of Houston psychologist retained by the defense to evaluate Andrea, gave compelling testimony that Andrea was seriously mentally ill, should receive further treatment in jail, then should be reevaluated for competency in ninety days. In support of his opinion, Harris pointed out that it was impossible for Andrea to defend herself in court when she strongly believed that her death would get rid of Satan. Parnham amplified the point with an impassioned challenge to the jury. "Show me one person in this courtroom who ever said, 'I am Satan and I deserve to be punished, and George W. Bush will see that it's done.' Show me one person." He turned to Andrea. "There is only one. She's sitting there." The jury deliberated for nearly nine hours before declaring Andrea competent to stand trial.

Awash in a media circus and curiosity seekers, Andrea's trial began. She pled not guilty to two indictments alleging that she used a deadly weapon, namely water, to drown three of her children, Mary, Noah, and John. In his opening statement, Owmby emphasized the evidence in the case, pointing to premeditated murder. He countered the impending insanity defense by saying Andrea had been found sane and that experts would testify that she knew what she was doing when she overpowered her children and held their heads underwater until they were dead. Parnham outlined Andrea's struggle with mental illness and promised testimony from a stream of mental health experts to document her insanity. The battle of the experts was about to begin.

Each side went for the heaviest hitter they could find. Dr. Phillip Resnick evaluated Andrea for the defense. The prosecution hired Dr. Park Dietz.

Resnick is the director of the division of Forensic Psychiatry at Case Western Reserve University School of Medicine in Cleveland and a recognized expert in parents who kill their children as well as defendants who fake mental illnesses. He had been a consultant for the government on the Unabomber case and the Oklahoma City bombing case.

Dietz sported very impressive academic credentials of his own, including work at Cornell, Johns Hopkins University School of Medicine, and University of Pennsylvania in Philadelphia. He was assistant professor at Harvard Medical School before becoming the medical director of the Forensic Psychiatry Clinic and medical director of the Institute of Law, Psychiatry, and Public Policy at the University of Virginia. His publishing credentials included an article on the prevention of filicidal drowning of children. He left his university positions in favor of a private practice, where he specialized in forensic case work, stalking, and prevention of violent crime. He had conducted hundreds of high-profile sanity evaluations, including those of criminals such as John Hinckley, Jeffrey Dahmer, and the Unabomber.

Both experts sported a long list of consulting clients, including the FBI. This was not the first time Resnick and Dietz were on opposite sides of a case. Sometimes they agreed (Jeffrey Dahmer) and sometimes they disagreed (John du Pont).

Resnick testified that he had spent nearly four hours evaluating Andrea on July 14, 2001, twenty-four days after she drowned her children, and he had spent a little over three hours with her on November 3, 2001. He pared down the July 14 interview to a representative fourteen-minute videotape, which was shown to the jury. As a disheveled and moribund Andrea tried to answer Resnick's crisp and concise questions about her relationship with her children and why she killed them, her twisted delusional system unfolded like pages of the Old Testament: Andrea believed she and her children were not righteous in God's eyes and she had to kill her children in order to save their souls from Satan. After explaining how a psychotic delusion works, Resnick looked at the jury and drove the point home. "Mrs. Yates had a choice to make: to allow her children to end up burning in hell for eternity or to take their lives on earth." He gave his opinion that Andrea knew the difference between right and wrong but that killing her children was right according to the dictates of her psychotic delusional system. She was legally insane when she drowned her children.

On cross-examination, Owmby tried to crack Resnick by asking him to present evidence supporting his opinion. Resnick pointed to statements given to Dr. Melissa Ferguson, who treated Andrea in jail shortly after Andrea killed her children. In part, Andrea had said that she was prepared to go to hell and that her children would also burn in hell because she was not raising them according to God's will. Owmby was not satisfied and pressed for more. How about Andrea's statements before she was put in jail? Resnick was ready. He told the jury that Andrea believed that if she spoke of harming her children out loud, Satan would hear her and then make it happen. Resnick stuck by his opinion and offered a diagnosis: schizoaffective disorder.

As a rebuttal expert witness the prosecution called Dietz, who had interviewed Andrea four times in November 2001, four and half months after she killed her children. He, like Resnick, had prepared videotaped segments of the interviews. He captivated the jury with an impressive description and analysis of Andrea's life stressors and medical history leading up to the murder of her children. He used the videotape segments to punctuate his compelling argument that Andrea was a mentally ill person but her psychosis was brought on by the stress of killing her children and being incarcerated. How about Satan? The jury watched the final videotaped segment prepared by Dietz.

"At the time, you didn't feel you were struggling against Satan?" Dietz asked Andrea.

"No."

"You felt he had taken over?"

"He was nearby. Early on, I didn't think he was in me."

"When did you first think he was in you?"

"When I was arrested."

Dietz pressed, "So you didn't feel that he was in you while you were drowning the children. It was afterwards."

"I felt his presence."

"When?"

"When I was doing it."

Dietz pressed Andrea for the ultimate answer to Satan's role in the murder of her children. "His presence, or that he was in you?"

As I watched the videotape, I knew that Dietz had just set a trap.

"His presence," Andrea answered not knowing Satan had to be inside you, not near you, to be declared insane. Never mind that Satan was present while you commit a horrendous crime and enters you only after you are arrested. I wondered if this was just another trick by Satan to punish Andrea further.

When Owmby asked Dietz if he was able to form an opinion relative to Andrea's sanity at the time she killed her children, I was surprised Dietz declined to offer an opinion but stated with certainty that Andrea knew her actions were legally, morally, and spiritually wrong at the time she drowned each of her children. He added, "Mrs. Yates may have believed the killings were in the best interest of the children and that the ends, saving the children, justified the means, which was to wrongly and illegally kill them."

During cross-examination Parnham and Dietz sparred vigorously, but Dietz held firm to his opinion. As part of the exchange Dietz, a technical advisor to the hugely popular television program *Law & Order*, testified that Andrea might have gotten the idea of drowning her kids from a show about a woman with postpartum depression who drowned her children in a bathtub and was found insane. No one disputed that Andrea had watched *Law & Order* a lot before she killed the kids, but Suzanne O'Malley, an investigative reporter and a former scriptwriter for the show, sat in the courtroom thinking Dietz was mistaken.[4]

O'Malley followed up her suspicions and found that she was correct. Dietz had made a serious mistake. As the prosecutor's key expert witness, the esteemed Dr. Dietz had given false testimony to the jury: no episode of *Law & Order* as described by Dietz had been produced, filmed, or aired with a plot similar to Yates's case. And the prosecutors had used that testimony in an attempt to impeach a defense rebuttal witness, Dr. Lucy Purear, to establish a motive during closing arguments. Dietz's error was grounds for a mistrial, but the case went to the jury before the defense could find an executive from the show willing to testify that Dietz's claim was false.

After lunch on Tuesday, March 12, the jury began deliberations. Although it is always difficult to predict what a jury is going to do, everyone was surprised when the foreman announced, after a little over three hours, that the jury had reached a verdict. As everybody reassembled in the courtroom to hear the verdict, most wondered how a jury could carefully consider nearly three weeks of testimony in such a short time. Andrea's family and legal team worried that the jury had asked only for a copy of the Texas insanity statute, Andrea's taped confession, and the 911 audiotape. Their worries were justified. The jury found Andrea Yates guilty of capital murder.

Two days later, the penalty phase of the trial began. By then the defense had arranged for Dick Wolf, series creator and a producer for *Law & Order*, to testify about Dietz's egregious error. But, at the last moment, some kind of deal was worked out among the attorneys. Wolf never testified. The next day, before the jury was called in, Parnham made a motion for a mistrial based upon "false evidence." He also urged Judge Hill to declare a mistrial for the verdict already in and the punishment still to come. Hill denied the motions but allowed Parnham to present a stipulation to the jury that Dietz's earlier testimony be revoked and that the record would be corrected to reflect that no episode of the *Law & Order* television series as described by Dietz was ever produced. Armed with the stipulation, Parnham stood before the jury and aggressively attacked Dietz's false testimony and the false premise leading to the prosecutors' allegations of premeditation.

The jury had only two choices: Order Andrea to be strapped to a gurney and killed with a lethal injection, or have her locked up in a Texas prison cell for the rest of her life. Parnham made a passionate plea to let Andrea live. Williford countered with a strong argument that Andrea deserved to die because she was a mother who betrayed her five small children. Owmby, still stinging from the Dietz debacle, told the jury that either decision, life in prison or the death penalty, would be the right thing to do.

On March 15, 2002, after a thirty-five minute deliberation, the jury recommended a life sentence. Two days later, Judge Hill followed the jury's recommendation and sentenced Andrea to life in the Texas Department of Criminal Justice–Institutional Division.

Within days after Andrea's sentencing, her defense team filed a notice to appeal Andrea's conviction and sentencing. About six months later, after much wrangling and considerable financial expense, the defense team finally received all the necessary documents for their appeal, including a twelve-thousand-page transcript of Andrea's trial, the same material the jury took only a few hours to consider. A little over a year later, the Texas First Appeals Court heard oral arguments from the defense team and the prosecutors. Three weeks later, on January 6, 2005, the justices concluded that Dietz's false testimony could have affected the judgment of the jury and the substantial rights of Andrea. They found "... the trial court abused its discretion in denying appellant's motion for a mistrial." The prosecution appealed the decision. On November 9, 2005, the Texas Court of Appeals upheld the First Appeals Court's reversal. Andrea was entitled to a new trial.

Andrea was retried in the summer of 2006. Over several weeks, a new jury of Andrea's peers heard mostly old evidence from the same cast of characters from the 2002 trial. This time Dietz was careful not to mention any episodes of *Law & Order*, but he reaffirmed his previous opinion that Andrea was not legally insane when she drowned her five kids in a bathtub. The defense team maintained its position that Andrea was so psychotic from postpartum depression that she killed her children to save them from Satan.

The jury in 2002 deliberated less than four hours before finding Andrea guilty of murder. Four years later the new jury, split evenly between men and women, deliberated for about thirteen hours over three days. They found Andrea not guilty by reason of insanity. Andrea was taken to a maximum-security state mental hospital to be held until hospital personnel deem she is no longer a threat to herself or others, instead of life in a prison cell. Even so, Andrea's release is not likely to be anytime soon, if ever.

I followed Andrea's court proceedings on television as much as my busy practice and the incessant chatter of Court TV's talking heads would allow. I also read everything I could find about the case. As snippets about Andrea's social and medical history were revealed by a parade of family members, friends, religious leaders, and medical personnel, I felt an urge to scream, "Of course she killed her kids! Why didn't anybody see it coming?"

Of course I know that it is easier to be a Monday morning psychologist after the tragic game than when it is being played. And I also know that family members and friends seldom have the knowledge or expertise to diagnose the early stages of a serious and potentially lethal mental illness. But what about the medical professionals? Surely they should have known. Unfortunately, many mental health professionals are not as knowledgeable about the delicate balance between the biochemical factors in mood disorders and subsequent pregnancy and childbirth as they should be. Fewer still are experienced enough with this deadly dance of toxic biochemicals to diagnose and prescribe the proper psychopharmacological antidote. Specialized knowledge often comes at an expense that a lot of "mangled care" (managed care) for-profit companies are reluctant to pay.

Lengthy stays at hospitals drain financial bonuses from CEOs and profits from shareholders. In my experience, a favorite tactic by HMOs to limit psychiatric hospitalizations is to use the magic term "stable." Once a patient is declared "stable," she is discharged. And the word "stable" often pops up on a patient's medical chart at about the time she has reached the limit of her coverage. With seriously disturbed suicidal patients this practice is deadly because stable does not mean the patient is no longer a danger to herself or others.

When one of my patients attempted suicide I had him hospitalized. His HMO did not cover hospitalization at the hospital where I had admission privileges, so I arranged for one of the HMO psychiatrists to admit my patient to his HMO-approved hospital. I was given temporary privileges to see my patient in the hospital but was not considered the treating physician. His HMO coverage was for three days. On the third day he was declared stable. I attended the case conference and protested the decision to discharge him. My sessions with him at the hospital revealed he was clearly still very much suicidal. My protestations were ignored and my patient was discharged.

In spite of surrounding my patient with a cadre of family and friends, he managed to make another serious attempt within a couple of days. We packed him up and sent him back to the hospital. After another three days, the magic word "stable" appeared again in his chart and plans for his discharge were made.

I again protested his discharge because my patient was already making plans to kill himself and, this time, he assured me, he would be successful. I informed the treating psychiatrist and the hospital medical director that I was documenting that a discharge was tantamount to a death sentence for my patient and that his family and I would hold the medical director, the treating psychiatrist, the hospital, and the HMO responsible for his death.

The medical director contacted the HMO and it was decided that a malpractice suit of that magnitude would cost much more than extra days of hospitalization. For HMOs, money talks. My patient stayed in the HMO hospital until I determined that he was truly no longer a danger to himself and others.

Ironically, working as a team for the patient instead of against him moved my patient's condition along nicely; he improved and he was ready for discharge in about ten days. From there we moved forward with a successful outpatient treatment program. Today, he is a "stable" professional with a bright future instead of being memorialized by a headstone in some dreary cemetery.

Unfortunately, the five headstones of Angela's children remind all of us that ignoring warning signs for whatever reason often leads to tragic consequences. Let's look at some of the warning signs.

Andrea was the youngest of five children raised by loving but demanding parents, especially her father, who seemed to always push for more from Andrea without giving her the positive feedback most children need to form a firm self-image. The family was raised Catholic. Her parents pushed for success and Andrea complied. She excelled at sports and academics, earning the honor of high school valedictorian. After high school Andrea earned her BSN degree at the University of Texas School of Nursing at Houston, then went to work as a registered nurse at the University of Texas's M. D. Anderson Cancer Center of Houston.

Classmates and friends have described Andrea as shy and studious. She didn't date much in high school and she didn't socialize much outside of work as a young adult. Andrea was also opposed to sex before marriage, an issue for a couple of failed relationships before she met her husband-to-be, Russell "Rusty" Yates.

Rusty, like Andrea, had excelled at sports and academics in high school, but unlike Andrea, Rusty had an active social life and was known to drink too much. Rusty's father was a Nazarene preacher who raised Rusty in the Nazarene and Methodist traditions. Rusty attended Auburn University, then became an engineer for NASA in Houston.

During the summer of 1989 Rusty and Andrea had a chance meeting of little consequence at the swimming pool of the apartment complex where they both lived. In the fall, shortly after Rusty's twenty-fourth birthday, they met again and began dating. Even though Andrea believed cohabitation was wrong, she and Rusty started living together in 1992. Rusty and Andrea married on April 17, 1993, and set out, by most accounts, to have as many children as God would allow. The good news for the couple was God was generous and allowed Andrea to have four children and only one miscarriage in just under six years. The bad news was that Andrea's already compromised hormonal system suffered repeated salvos with each pregnancy and little time to recover. The other bad news was that a seriously mentally ill woman was now a stay-at-home mother charged with the proper care and feeding of four very young children, including home schooling them in a converted Greyhound bus.

Some warning signs appeared early on. As a teenager, Andrea seemed prone to mood swings. When she felt down, she seemed to just "disappear," one of her former classmates said. When up, Andrea would accomplish great things. Most teenagers have mood swings, but Andrea's seemed more extreme than most and could have been the symptoms of an emerging mood disorder previously called manic depression but known now as bipolar disorder. She also experienced a bout with depression following a failed relationship when she was in her early twenties.

Just four months after the birth of her fourth child, Luke, Andrea took an overdose of trazodone, an antidepressant prescribed for her father who was suffering from Alzheimer's disease. At the time, Andrea, Rusty, and their four children were living in the converted bus in Hitchcock, Texas. Andrea was hospitalized for the first time. Her diagnosis was major depressive disorder, single episode, severe. At Methodist Hospital, Dr. James Flack prescribed Zoloft, an antidepressant. Andrea's condition did not improve but she was discharged because of insurance restrictions. After about seven days, the magic word — "stable" — appeared in Andrea's discharge summary. She was released with a month's supply of a medication that wasn't working and referrals for outpatient treatment, which included meeting with psychiatrist Dr. Eileen Starbranch.

Following Andrea's discharge, an alert social worker, Norma Tauriac, sensed danger. She called Child Protective Services and described the family's living conditions and other safety concerns for the children. CPS investigated but did not find a "substantial risk of abuse or neglect" and declined to intervene. I wondered what it was about four young children crammed in a converted bus with a seriously dysfunctional mother and a father who could not provide close supervision they didn't understand.

When Andrea wouldn't feed Luke, showed very little interest in the other children, isolated herself from the family, and showed numerous self-inflicted scratches, Rusty took her to see Dr. Starbranch, who prescribed the antipsychotic Zyprex. Some reports indicate that Andrea was routinely noncompliant with prescriptions and may have flushed the Zyprex down the toilet. A few weeks later, Andrea tried to kill herself again. This time she tried to slit her throat with a knife. Starbranch admitted Andrea to Memorial Spring Shadows Glen Hospital, noting that Andrea was mute, suicidal, and psychotic.

Andrea's previous diagnosis of major depressive disorder, severe, changed from single episode to recurrent with psychotic features. Apparently Andrea's grasp of reality was slipping. The hospital staff also had questions about other psychotic processes such as audio and visual hallucinations associated with hurting somebody, so a "rule out" diagnosis of schizophrenia, catatonic type, was added. In one of its most serious forms, catatonia often requires careful supervision to avoid self-harm or harming others.

Starbranch considered electroconvulsive shock therapy (ECT), but Rusty and Andrea objected. Alternatively, Starbranch prescribed an injectable form of Haldol/Deconate, an effective high-potency antipsychotic sometimes used on patients with mania. Starbranch also prescribed the antidepressants Effexor XR and Wellbutrin. This time the medications and hospital care seemed to work. After nearly three weeks Andrea was discharged to a partial hospitalization program, where she attended programs in the day and spent the nights at home, now a three-bedroom house in Clear Lake, Texas. Starbranch continued to monitor Andrea's medications, assuring her compliance.

Andrea seemed to improve, then the couple made a fatal mistake. They decided to ditch the medications and have another baby. They ignored Starbranch's repeated strong warnings of severe negative consequences. On November 30, 2000, Andrea gave birth to her fifth child, Mary.

Now this severely disturbed mother of four young children had a newborn under her care. To add to her woes Andrea's father died in March 2001, four months after Mary was born. Andrea slipped into a serious depression. After consulting with Starbranch and making an appointment for Andrea, Andrea's brother and Rusty took her to Devereux Hospital, where she was admitted by Dr. Ellen Allbritton with an additional diagnosis of postpartum depression. She was discharged in about two weeks. "Stable" again, I wondered.

Less than a month later Andrea was hospitalized for the fourth time. Andrea resisted a voluntary admission to Devereux but agreed to sign herself in after Dr. Mohammed Saeed filed to have her committed to a state hospital. This time Andrea's stay in the hospital was for ten days, followed by a week as a day patient. The diagnoses were essentially the same as the previous hospitalizations. At Devereux, Andrea was treated with Haldol until Saeed discontinued it. He never prescribed any other antipsychotic medication. A little over two weeks later, an unmedicated Andrea Yates drowned her five children in the bathtub.

Complicating Andrea's medical problems was the couple's relationship with Michael Woroniecki, a charismatic preacher who often espoused messages of fire and brimstone. Rusty met Woroniecki, his wife, Rachel, and their six children through religious youth groups in college. While Woroniecki denied any responsibility for the death of Andrea's children, Andrea was strongly influenced by his religious rhetoric and his criticism of her parenting skills.

Andrea began to believe that she was a bad mother and that the children were not developing right and doing the things God likes. Her explanations for her actions often drifted into a reference to the Gospel of Mark, often quoted by Woroniecki, about the temptations to sin and how to avoid being cast into hell. Taken literally, bad mothers and bad children were destined to hell unless they were cleansed. Andrea's troubled mind, with a little help from Saint Mark, devised a plan to save the children.

In a sad twist of fate, the leading expert on infanticide, Dr. Margaret G. Spinelli, who was gearing up to testify for the defense, broke her neck and had to back out. A leading expert in neurohormonal mechanisms, perinatal psychiatrist Dr. Deborah Sichel, offered to help the defense for no fee and was consulted, but she was never called to testify. Later, Spinelli told investigative reporter Suzanne O'Malley that most new postpartum psychosis diagnoses were bipolar.[5] Sichel said she was certain that Andrea had symptoms of a typical bipolar disorder as a teenager, and the illness evolved into a more serious form in adulthood. Sichel went on to state that the Yates tragedy was completely preventable had Andrea been correctly diagnosed and properly medicated. She pointed out that Andrea's social history and medical records reflect a misdiagnosis of depression with psychotic features but never the correct diagnosis of bipolar disorder. The tragic result of such misdiagnoses is the wrong treatment. Andrea was treated mostly with antidepressants. In Sichel's opinion, antidepressants *without a mood stabilizer* often exacerbate the illness and may increase the mania. The treatment of choice for bipolar disorders is the lithium family of drugs, not "rocket fuel," a term coined by noted psychiatrist Dr. Stephen M. Stahl for the combination of Remeron and Effexor. Stahl notes that rocket fuel is powerful as an antidepressant but can be catastrophic for bipolar or psychotic disorders. As a diagnostic rule of thumb, if patients stabilize on lithium, chances are they are bipolar.

Records show that Andrea's prescribed antidepressant and antipsychotic medications included injectable Haldol, which seemed to work, Effexor and Wellbutrin, which, in combination with Haldol, may have helped, and Zoloft and Zyprexa, which didn't. Nothing from the lithium family of drugs. But bungled medical care is not the only possible cause for a mother to kill her children.

SUSAN SMITH

A burgundy Mazda four-door sedan pushed through the quiet of a soft South Carolina night, kicking up dust on one country road after another, then stopped abruptly on a bridge over the cool waters of Broad River. Susan Smith got out of the car. She walked to a railing, the tears in her eyes fell to the murky water below. She could end her pain now with just a little effort. Up and over and it would be finished. But she turned away from a watery end and returned to the precious cargo strapped safely in the backseat of her car: fourteen-month-old Alex and three-year-old Michael.

Susan got back in the driver's seat and headed off the bridge and into the night. Again the sedan followed country roads, leading this way and that but arriving at no place in particular until it slipped by John D. Long Lake, a popular recreational area for fishermen and families. The sedan slowed then pulled into the parking area. Susan got out and walked to the back of the car. Inside, her sons were asleep, cozy in their car seats. A boat ramp caught her eye and a plan to end her suffering started hammering in her head. She got back in the driver's seat, then released the hand brake. As the sedan rolled slowly toward the water's edge, Susan yanked the hand brake back. She got out again and walked to the rear of the car, then got back in the driver's seat and released the hand brake for a second time. When the sedan reached the lake, Susan jumped out. As she ran up the boat ramp, the sedan with her two little boys drifted lazily toward the dam, then slipped slowly into the dark waters of John D. Long Lake. Susan held her hands over her ears to silence the screams.

After reporting that a black man had hijacked her car and taken her children, Susan pleaded tearfully on national television for the safe return of her beloved sons. I saw a number of Susan's appearances on national television. Each time, the depth of Susan's anguish tore at my heart. I believed that Susan was genuinely grieving over the loss of her children, but I worried that her story of abduction by a stranger was fabricated. Call it intuition or call it clinical and forensic experience, I believed she killed her kids and was broiling in the agony of her acts.

Union County Sheriff Howard Wells mounted an extensive investigation of the case, including several interviews of Susan, who denied repeatedly that she killed her sons. On November 3, 1994, nine days after the disappearance of Alex and Michael, Susan finally confessed.

Forensic psychologist Geoffrey McKee was one of several

mental health experts who evaluated Susan either for the prosecution or the defense. His account of Susan's social history leading up to drowning her children is compelling. McKee reports that Susan's life, from the earliest years, was filled with instability and uncertainty.[6] Clinical psychologist George Rekers at the Hall Psychiatric Institute, which provided court-ordered mental health evaluations of Susan Smith, offers insight into the complex life of a victim turned victimizer.[7] Susan's mother, Linda Russell, documents a chaotic and unstable family life,[8] and Susan's husband, David Smith, reveals a severely troubled marriage.[9] A walk through Susan's childhood, adolescence, and early adulthood, as seen by those close to her, those who evaluated her, and court documents, traces a trail from childhood insecurity to the tragic death of innocent children.

Susan was the third child born into a ten-year marriage full of turmoil and tragedy. At age three her parents separated for the first time. Susan stayed with her mother but was traumatized by the absence of her father, Harry. She had a strong emotional attachment to him. Susan was relieved when her parents reconciled and he moved back into the house. But it didn't last. Within a few months Susan's father was gone again. And more trauma was on the way.

About seven months later, Harry came back, but not to move in. He was armed with a shotgun and threatened to kill Susan's mother and himself. He left without shooting anyone, but Susan's parents separated for good and filed for divorce. When Susan was six years old the divorce was final and her father threatened her mother again, then he shot himself. Although Linda never told Susan how her father died, the loss was devastating to a young girl who refused to believe her father was dead. When a cousin told Susan about the suicide, the loss became even more unbearable.

One suicide in a child's family is more than enough to disrupt a healthy view on life, but what about two? A few months after Harry's suicide, Linda's mother, despondent over the death of

Linda's father, attempted to kill herself by overdosing on prescription pills. And the message for a young traumatized girl? As McKee wrote: "Suicide as a means of resolving grief, depression, and loss was a family lesson that young Susan was learning well."[10] By age ten, most children are thinking about fun and friends. Susan was thinking about killing herself.

Less than two years after Harry shot himself, Linda started dating Beverly Russell, a prominent businessman in Union with family political connections. Talks about marriage left both of them uncertain. Then, shortly before Christmas 1979, Bev proposed and the couple eloped without telling Susan, who was then about eight years old, and her brothers, Michael and Scott. According to Susan's mother, Susan's sense of insecurity seemed to increase after Bev moved in and the children were told of the marriage. Susan seemed constantly to seek reassurance from her mother and other family members that they loved her.

By the time an anxious and unhappy Susan turned thirteen, she was not only thinking about suicide but she also had developed a plan to take more than ten aspirin a day until she died. Susan disclosed her plan to her stepsister and wrote a suicide note to a teacher. Linda was surprised by Susan's actions but took her threats serious enough to suicide-proof the house. However, the family resisted seeking professional help for Susan until the school requested that Susan receive counseling at school. Tired of Susan's sullen attitude, Linda also threatened to put Susan into a halfway house.

For a while Susan seemed to improve, but in the ninth grade she told a teacher that she continued to obsess about killing herself. Linda was consulted and reluctantly agreed to allow Susan to see a school counselor on a weekly basis. The counselor subsequently urged Linda to have Susan evaluated by a research program for depressed adolescents. Linda refused.

Susan appeared to make progress with the counseling at school. She seemed less depressed and more involved in after-school activities. But more trouble for Susan was brewing. Susan disclosed to the same teacher she first told about her suicidal plans that Bev, her stepfather, was molesting her. The teacher told Susan's counselor, who discussed it with Susan then urged her to tell her mother.

Now here's the tricky part. If an adult molests a child, who is responsible? Who needs protection? When Susan disclosed the sexual abuse to her mother, Linda confronted Bev, who confessed and promised never to do it again. A promise always works because child molesters always keep their promises, correct? Linda also confronted Susan as an accomplice because she failed to stop her stepfather by leaving the room when he started to molest her. I wondered when abused stepchildren gained as much power as an abusing stepparent. So up to this point the message for Susan was Bev won't do it again, but if he does, just leave the room.

For some inexplicable reason no one notified law enforcement or social services, but Linda arranged therapy for Bev and Susan to meet individually with a licensed psychologist. After several months of therapy sessions, Susan terminated the treatment. Bev broke his promise and went after Susan again, this time fondling her in her bedroom while she pretended to be asleep. How do you walk out of your own bedroom when your stepfather is fondling you in bed? Susan didn't, but she did tell her school counselor who, this time, notified the proper authorities.

After a social services and law enforcement investigation, Bev was faced with serious criminal charges, but Susan would have to testify. Susan asked her mother for advice. Linda told Susan she had to decide for herself what to do, but Linda didn't want Bev prosecuted and jailed. Susan, the girl who was desperate for love, didn't disappoint her mother. When the criminal charges were dropped, Bev agreed to leave the house, and everybody went into counseling with the same psychologist. A good solution to a difficult family problem, correct? No harm, no foul. Not quite. After several months of seemingly successful therapy, Bev moved back into the house. And back into Susan's bedroom. But this time a sixteen-year-old Susan acquiesced. Nobody got it right. And nobody saw the rest coming.

In fairly rapid succession, Susan lost her virginity when she succumbed to the advances of an older married man who was the manager of a grocery store where she had taken a part-time job. She became pregnant, had an abortion, and started a concurrent sexual relationship with the assistant manager at the same grocery store. Susan was not yet seventeen.

When Susan told her first lover about the second, her first lover, the manager of the grocery store, went ballistic. When Susan tried to calm him down, he refused to talk to her. Now she was afraid that she would lose both lovers. She needed a solution to her problem—a suicide attempt. As she did when she was in the eighth grade, Susan overdosed on painkillers. This time she told her mother and her stepfather about her predicament and the overdose. They got her to a hospital right away. Following successful emergency treatment, Susan was hospitalized in intensive care and received a week of inpatient psychiatric care.

Susan's life was relatively calm for a few months after she got out of the hospital. Then she began dating David, another employee at the grocery store where she worked. It didn't seem to matter to either one of them that David was engaged. And it didn't seem to matter that they seldom used condoms. Susan became pregnant and told David. David told his fiancée, who broke off the engagement. David and Susan decided against an abortion and decided to get married right away. For her wedding day, Susan chose March 15, 1991, her biological father's birthday. For a church they chose the same church where the funeral of David's older brother, Danny, had been held a couple of weeks earlier. Danny had died when an operation to treat Crohn's disease went badly.

The first year of Susan's marriage to David was tumultuous. Almost right away, attempted suicide in the family reared its ugly head again. This time, David wondered where his father was and sent Susan to find him. She did. He was lying on the floor of his bedroom barely conscious. Depressed over Danny's death and the breakup of his marriage, Susan's father-in-law overdosed.

When Susan's first son, Michael, was born on October 10, 1991, he had a congenital misalignment of his foot. To correct the problem Michael was fitted with a brace. The newborn was inconsolable. Susan and David argued more than most newlyweds and David became physically abusive. They separated for the first time when Michael was about six months old.

Susan found love elsewhere. She renewed her relationship with the assistant manager at the grocery store. When David found Susan and her lover in a car late one night, he dragged the man out of the car and beat him up. Susan continued the sexual relationship with her former lover and was discovered again by David, this time at her lover's house. Again, David beat the man. They were separated, so why should David care? Separated or not, Susan and David resumed their sexual relationship. Multiple men. Multiple love. She got pregnant again. Multiple children.

Susan and David decided to save their marriage. They reconciled and moved into a modest home partly financed by Susan's mother and stepfather. A real home for them and their children was just what they needed to establish a stable and happy family. But it didn't help. Soon David and Susan were squabbling again and Susan discovered that David was having an affair with a young woman recently hired at his grocery store. About three weeks after Susan gave birth to her second son, Alex, by cesarean section, she and David separated again.

A few months later, Susan got a job in the bookkeeping department of Conso Products and began an affair with the boss's son Tom Findlay, who was considered the most eligible bachelor in town. They saw each other and had sex frequently. Susan thought she had, at last, found the deep, enduring love she needed.

A week after David discovered Susan's affair with Tom, David moved back into the house. Like previous attempts at reconciliation, this one didn't work. Within a month, and on David's birthday, Susan asked for a divorce. They agreed that they should go their separate ways and that the divorce would be amicable.

They got half of it right. Susan renewed her relationship with Tom, and David started seeing his young woman again. But Susan couldn't seem to avoid acrimony in her life and filed for divorce on grounds of adultery. David was angered, felt betrayed, and countered with documented claims of Susan's adulterous affair with Tom.

On October 15, 1994, Tom invited Susan and a few coworkers and friends to his house for a party. The alcohol flowed freely and soon Tom, Susan, and most of the other guests ditched their clothes and headed for the hot tub. According to McKee's account, Susan may have been surprised when Tom asked her to kiss a man seated next to her, but she did it.[11] For most people, this odd request from a lover would have been a red flag indicating something was amiss with Tom's love and devotion to Susan. Maybe she was too drunk to figure it out or her desperate need for lasting love clouded her judgment, but she complied with Tom's request. Later she appropriately had strong regrets about her actions but still didn't seem to understand that Tom's request was inappropriate. Instead, she feared that her actions somehow would upset her relationship with Tom. It seemed that Susan had made another poor decision about intimate relationships. It didn't take very long to find out.

A few days after the hot tub incident, Tom gave Susan a long "Dear Jane" letter. He explained that he wasn't ready for marriage or children and hoped they could remain friends. Susan's response was predictable. She felt worthless, abandoned, panicky, and suicidal. All was lost. To make matters worse, two days later, David confronted Susan about Tom, saying he had a copy of Tom's letter. They had a heated argument about the divorce and their respective adulterous affairs.

Susan was desperate for Tom's love and wasn't about to give him up without a fight. On October 23, 1994, she called Tom, hoping to convince him to reconsider. In the process she told Tom about Bev and the sexual abuse. If she was looking for compassion, she was looking in the wrong place. Tom was revolted by the disclosure and held firm to his decision to break off their intimate relationship. The next day Susan tried to find Tom, hoping that a face-to-face meeting might persuade him to take her back. She couldn't find him. Desperation and panic filled her entire being.

On October 25, 1994, Susan started the day full of anxiety and fear. She was desperate to talk to Tom. When Susan finally reached Tom in the afternoon at work, he softened some and agreed to talk with her. Susan poured her heart out to him, even revealing that she was having an affair with Tom's father. Tom's face filled with disbelief, then disgust, then he walked away. Susan was crushed. She told a supervisor she was going home but she went to Tom's office instead. Tom tried to comfort Susan but did not tell her what she was desperate to hear: he loved her and wanted her back. An inconsolable Susan left, hinting that he might never see her again.

After Susan picked up her sons from daycare, she told a friend that she had just played a joke on Tom by telling him she had an affair with his father, but Tom was not amused. She asked her friend to call Tom and verify the joke. Her friend refused but agreed to watch her children while Susan went back to Tom's office to smooth things over.

Tom was surprised when Susan walked into his office with her two children and her friend. Susan told Tom that she was just playing a silly joke on him with her story about an affair with his father. Susan turned to her friend hoping she would corroborate Susan's story. Her friend said she knew nothing about Susan's sex life and left the room. Tom confronted Susan about her motivation for telling him about her affair with his father. Susan revealed that it was a way she could find out how much Tom loved her. Tom refused to talk about it in front of her children and asked her to leave.

Susan managed to get her children home and feed them in spite of waves of anxiety and panic. She roamed the house sobbing uncontrollably until the children recognized their mother's pain and joined the chorus of anguished wails of despair. In a panic she called a friend at Tom's favorite bar hoping to find out if Tom was there lamenting the breakup. Maybe his sorrow would bring them back together again. Her friend was no help. She told Susan that Tom had not mentioned Susan at all then hung up.

Susan loaded up her kids and headed for Tom's hangout. When she saw his car in the parking lot, she knew Tom's love was lost forever. His life moved on while hers had ended. Susan drove off into the night with Alex and Michael strapped safely in their car seats. The muddy water of John D. Long Lake waited.

In South Carolina a person charged with murder has four possible pleas: guilty, guilty but mentally ill, not guilty, and not guilty by reason of insanity. Since Susan's confession seemed valid and irrefutable, a not-guilty plea was eliminated right away. Susan's defense team indicated that Susan would either enter a guilty but mentally ill or a not guilty by reason of insanity plea sometime before the trial was scheduled to begin.

But she confessed, so why not plead guilty, avoid a trial, and let the judge sentence Susan? Because South Carolina is a death penalty state—death by electrocution. Even the guilty but mentally ill plea carried a possibility of death because the judge could sentence Susan to death once she was no longer declared mentally ill. Stay mentally ill and live, get well and die. South Carolina also has a life sentence with the automatic possibility of parole at fifteen years.

It seemed clear to me that Susan's attorneys were planning a defense of mental illness, not so much to find Susan not guilty but to mitigate the sentence in the event that she was found guilty. After delaying their decision the defense team entered a plea of not guilty by reason of insanity.

I knew finding Susan legally insane was a long shot but it gave the defense team the opportunity to present strong evidence about Susan's struggle with mental health issues. Even though they certainly planned to convince a jury to find her not guilty, their overall plan was to persuade the jury to recommend life instead of death if they found Susan guilty. And they thought they had a better chance of convincing a jury than a judge that Susan should be sentenced to life instead of death.

With a media circus jamming every nook and cranny in tiny Union, the judge banned cameras in the courtroom and ordered a gag rule. Inside the stately courthouse, the prosecution presented a picture of an evil, manipulative, and selfish woman who killed her children to win over a spurned lover. With the blessing of the boys' father, David Smith, the prosecution announced it was seeking the death penalty. The defense countered with a picture of a depressed woman who set out to kill herself and killed her children instead. The underlying defense strategy in Susan's case was mental illness and insanity. Only a crazy woman or a cold hard criminal would kill two innocent young boys. Susan had no history of criminal behavior but she had a history of mental health problems. She was a mentally ill young woman who snapped, the defense argued.

Both sides called in their mental health experts to evaluate Susan. The media expected another bloody battle of the experts, but the battle ended before a shot was fired. Virtually all forensic psychologists and psychiatrists for the prosecution and the defense arrived at the same opinion: Susan was certainly clinically depressed and suicidal, but she knew that her acts were legally and morally wrong. In other words, Susan was mentally ill but legally sane at the time she sent her two boys to the bottom of John D. Long Lake.

The jury didn't buy the bungled suicide gambit offered by the defense and found Susan guilty of two counts of murder. With insanity and guilt issues resolved, the players turned to deciding Susan's punishment. How should society penalize people who commit such horrendous crimes against their own children? Not surprising, the prosecution continued to press for execution and the defense pleaded for lifetime incarceration.

Each side brought in numerous witnesses who revealed and opined on Susan's sad history of family depression and suicide, repeated episodes of childhood sexual abuse by her stepfather, and her ongoing battle with depression and suicide attempts. The mental health defense saved Susan's life. The jury voted unanimously to send Susan to the South Carolina Department of Corrections for the rest of her life. She was twenty-three years old. With automatic eligibility for parole in thirty years, Susan could be released when she is fifty-three. Cynics believed that the jury wanted Susan to live with her guilt for the rest of her live. Death was too good for her.

When Susan turned from her Mazda as it slipped into the water, she, and only she, was responsible for the deaths of her innocent children. But Susan wasn't born a killer. How did she evolve from a very bright, innocent child who dreamed of going to college into a promiscuous and emotionally unstable young adult unable to keep herself and her children from harm's way? An analysis of her childhood experiences reveals a fertile breeding ground for anxiety, depression, fear of abandonment, unstable self-image, sexual acting out, and poor coping skills. According to forensic evaluators in this case, Susan's genetic makeup and her childhood experiences shaped her nicely into an extremely depressed woman with a dependent personality disorder (DPD) as well as a borderline personality disorder (BPD).

The essential element of DPD is a pervasive and excessive need to be taken care of that leads to submissive and clinging behavior and fears of separation, beginning by early adulthood.[12] Among other characteristics of DPD, Susan had a history of going to excessive lengths to obtain nurturance and support from others, feeling uncomfortable or helpless when alone, urgently seeing another relationship as a source of care and support when a relationship ends, and being preoccupied with fears of being left to care for herself alone. Dr. Seymour Halleck, one of the forensic experts who evaluated Susan, testified that Susan "has as severe a dependent personality disorder as I have ever seen."

Although McKee categorized Susan as a Psychotic/Depressed Mother, Impulsive Type, on his Maternal Filicide Risk Matrix, many mothers with this categorization have borderline personality disorder or traits. McKee points out that the diagnosis of borderline personality disorder takes five criteria out of nine to be met and Susan far exceeded that cutoff.[13] Susan's history is replete with BPD diagnosable criteria such as frantic efforts to avoid real or imagined abandonment, a pattern of unstable and intense interpersonal relationships, unstable self-image, self-damaging impulsivity, recurrent suicidal behavior, unstable moods, chronic feelings of emptiness, and frequent displays of temper.

It is interesting to note that a careful look at Susan's biological father's emotional problems strongly suggests that he, too, may have had BPD. Statistically, BPD is diagnosed mostly in females but is about five times more common among first-degree biological relatives of those with the disorder, such as Susan's father, than it is in the general population.

A mother may kill her children for many different reasons and under a wide range of circumstances, and high-profile cases such as Andrea Yates and Susan Smith are just two examples. For Andrea, a history of depression, bungled psychiatric care, religiosity, and extremely poor judgment regarding family planning appear to have provided the foundation for the mental deterioration of a loving mother and the tragic deaths of five beautiful children.

For Susan, a probable genetic predisposition for depression, combined with childhood abandonment and trauma, may have produced a young adult with a pervasive pattern of instability in emotional functioning, self-image, and interpersonal relationships. When her marked impulsivity and recurrent fear of being abandoned and unloved kicked in, she and/or the children seemed doomed. This time it was the children.

Documentation of high-profile and "ordinary" cases in the research and clinical literature suggests several categories of murderous mothers. Major examples are detached mothers who never form an adequate emotional bond with their children; mothers pressured to deny or reject pregnancy; mothers who are overcome by serious mental illnesses, especially postpartum depression/psychosis; mothers with a need to retaliate against something or someone; and mothers who use children for exploitative and self-serving reasons such as financial gain.[14]

Geoffrey McKee developed a tool, the Maternal Filicide Risk Matrix, to help identify mothers who are at risk to abuse or murder their children.[15] The risk and protective factors range over a time period from prepregnancy through postinfancy and fall within three major categories: Individual, Family of Origin, and Situational. A quick look at McKee's most salient points may help all of us recognize the major risk factors involved in mothers who murder their children.

INDIVIDUAL RISK AND PROTECTIVE FACTORS

It should come as no surprise that the mother's age is a risk factor. Preteens and teenagers are at higher risk for maternal filicide than mothers twenty-one years and older. Intellectual deficits and less than a high school education are risk factors, but average or above-average intellectual abilities and a college education lowers the risk. Mothers who suffer from emotional problems such as postpartum mood disorder, psychosis, substance abuse, or suicide attempts are at a much higher risk than mothers with no mental disorder diagnoses. A mother's own childhood trauma experiences, such as physical or sexual abuse or the loss of her own mother, play an important part in subsequent responses to a child, including murder. No prior trauma reduces the risk significantly. A host of other factors related to the mother's negative attitude about the pregnancy, such as no prenatal care and problems with the birth, contribute to the risk, while planned pregnancy, prenatal care, and an overall positive attitude about the pregnancy reduce the risk.

FAMILY OF ORIGIN

A mother is at a higher risk if one or both of her parents have a history of mental illness or substance abuse, frequent separations or divorce, abandonment, child or spouse abuse, and financial instability than if her parents bond well, are sufficient providers, and give a nonviolent and stable approach to marriage and parenting.

SITUATIONAL

The risk factors in this category have a familiar ring to them: single parent, sole caretaker or abusive partners who are substance abusers, poor financial status, mothers under the age of seventeen with more than two children, a baby the youngest in her care, other children in her care, sibling abuse, difficult child or children, and prior abuse of children. Mothers with supportive, helpful partners and relatives, along with a reasonably healthy child, have a lower risk of murdering their children.

NOTES

1. For excellent reviews of prevalence rates and theoretical concepts presented in this chapter, see Geoffrey R. McKee, *Why Mothers Kill: A Forensic Psychologist's Casebook* (New York: Oxford University Press, 2006); Lita Linzer Schwartz and Natalie K. Isser, *Child Homicide: Parents Who Kill* (Boca Raton, FL: CRC Press, 2007).

2. Gretel C. Kovach, "A Mother's Darkest Day," *Newsweek*, June 11, 2007, p. 52.

3. For a comprehensive examination of the Andrea Yates case, see Suzanne O'Malley, *The Unspeakable Crime of Andrea Yates: "Are You There Alone?"* (New York: Pocket Star Books, 2005).

4. Ibid.

5. Ibid., pp. 316–26.

6. McKee, *Why Mothers Kill*, pp. 156–74.

7. George Rekers, *Susan Smith: Victim or Murderer* (Lakewood, CO: Glenbridge Publishing, 1996).

8. Linda Russell, *My Daughter Susan Smith* (Brentwood, TN: Authors Book Nook, 2000).

9. David Smith, *Beyond Reason: My Life with Susan Smith* (New York: Kensington Books, 1995).

10. McKee, *Why Mothers Kill*, p. 160.

11. Ibid., pp. 158–59.

12. American Psychiatric Association, *Diagnostic and Statistical Manual of Mental Disorders: DSM-IV-TR* (Washington, DC: American Psychiatric Association, 2000), pp. 721–25.

13. McKee, *Why Mothers Kill*, pp. 164–70.

14. For a review, see Schwartz and Isser, *Child Homicide: Parents Who Kill.*

15. McKee, *Why Mothers Kill*, pp. 34–53.

6

THE TABOO BREAKERS

MOTHERS WHO MOLEST CHILDREN

Although the study of women who molest children is still relatively new, some preliminary statistics are startling. According to the Bureau of Justice Statistics, sex offenses by females (except forcible rape and prostitution) increased by nearly 11 percent between 1985 and 1994.[1] Psychologist Craig Allen estimated that slightly more than three million children have been sexually abused by females in the United States, and that was over a decade ago.[2] Studies of clinical and nonclinical populations of male and female sexual abuse victims indicate that 5 to 60 percent were abused by a female.[3] It is a noticeably wide margin and a good indicator of the problems of gathering reliable data on female perpetrators, but as the idea that females sexually abuse children becomes more widely accepted, the data should become more precise. L. M. McCarty found that 52 percent of female sexual offenders molested females and 35 percent molested males.[4]

By far the majority of women who molest children are also mothers. Sometimes the victims are the children playing with the mother's children. Lisa Lynette Clark, a forty-one-year-old Georgia mother, was indicted for child molestation only one day after she married her teenage son's fifteen-year-old friend. She told authorities that she became romantically involved with the teenager, which eventually led to a sexual relationship. When she found out that she was pregnant, she took the boy to a retired probate judge to be married under a 1962 Georgia law that allows someone under the age of fifteen years to marry if the bride is pregnant. One day later the teen's parents found out about the marriage and protested to authorities. Clark was arrested on several charges associated with sexual conduct with a minor. She eventually pled guilty to one charge of statutory rape and was sentenced to nine months in jail. Clark was prohibited from seeing the boy until he turned seventeen, prohibited from any contact with children other than her own, required to register as a sex offender, and ordered to serve four years on probation. Clark gave birth to the baby in prison and the child was placed with foster parents. Later, Clark received an additional two-year prison sentence for helping the teen, who had been convicted of burglary and was on probation, flee to Ohio. The 1962 marriage law has since been changed to eliminate the pregnant bride stipulation; teens must now have the permission of a parent or legal guardian and a judge.

Some mothers are not content to just watch their daughters have fun with their friends but are driven to revisit adolescence and become part of the social group. In Colorado, forty-one-year-old Silvia Johnson worked hard at being cool and fitting in with her daughter's popular social circle. The teenage boys gave her attention. She gave them drugs, alcohol, and sex. Just like any cool mom. She was sentenced to thirty years in prison. Real cool.

A lot of diverse theories, ranging from biological to mental disorders, have been proposed to explain why women molest children. From my clinical and forensic experience with female sexual offenders, the typology proposed by J. Matthews, R. Mathews, and K. Spelt seems to hold the most promise.[5] They describe five categories of female child molesters:

- *Teacher/Lover* — women who view themselves as being involved in a romantic relationship with a child or adolescent
- *Predisposed* — women who have a history of being sexually abused as a child, usually by a parent or other close family member
- *Male-Coerced* — women who are dependent individuals locked into an abusive relationship with a partner who is a perpetrator
- *Experimenter/Exploiter* — usually an adolescent girl in a caretaking role of younger children
- *Psychologically Disturbed* — mentally disturbed women who often are psychotic

In spite of the increase in studies of female offenders, research on mother-son incest and mother-daughter incest struggles to keep pace. Although incidence data are hard to come by, those working in the field know that incestuous mothers are not as rare as most people believe.

Accepting that women can molest children flies in the face of all we think we know and believe about our mothers, sisters, and other women. To accept this means we must embrace the notion that some women, including our own mothers, are not only sexual but their sexuality also may be deviant. Failing to acknowledge the problem of female sexual offenders serves to perpetuate it. With the growing number of stories in the press about women behaving badly, more people are accepting the notion that some women, especially teachers, may molest adolescent boys. But are there really monsters out there in mother's clothing?

The victims who speak out in clinical counselor Beverly Ogilvie's book, *Mother-Daughter Incest*, think so.[6] They describe emotionally unstable mothers who violated intimate boundaries for their own twisted needs, devastating their daughters' lives, much like the following mothers from my case files.

VIRGINIA LION*

I was preparing for my testimony in a double-homicide case when my secretary dropped the day's mail on my desk. Among the many pieces, I recognized the return address on an oversized mailing envelope—a new case I was expecting from the public defender's office. The file was small compared to most files I receive, which are stuffed into a number of boxes and often fill a filing cabinet drawer or two or more. But this case was not about a long history of criminal behavior and numerous heinous crimes. It was about a mother, Virginia Lion, who had no previous criminal history but was charged with sexually exploiting and molesting her youngest children, an eleven-year-old son, Alan, and a thirteen-year-old daughter, Becky.

Virginia did not have the resources to hire a private attorney, so her case was assigned to an energetic young public defender, Bill Myers. When Myers first contacted me about the case he made a strong argument that Virginia was insane. After all, how could a mother molest her children, write letters with graphic details of her sexual involvement with the children, photograph the sexual acts, then send the letters and photographs to a boyfriend in prison if she was not insane? A sane man might do this, he thought, but a sane mother?

According to Myers, all I needed to do was confirm his impression with an evaluation. But behind all the bluster, I knew Myers was backed into a corner and had only one possible defense in this case—insanity—because the prosecution had a mountain of seemingly irrefutable hard evidence that Virginia molested her children—the photographs. Virginia did it and everybody, including her defense team, knew she did it. Insane or not, Virginia was facing some serious mandatory prison time if she was found guilty on any of the charges.

Even though I had doubts about the defense strategy Myers was cooking up, I agreed to evaluate Virginia because the case was so unusual. Seldom do women document and distribute evidence of their criminal sexual behavior with children. But I was not looking forward to reading the letters and seeing the photographs.

I had been exposed to numerous descriptions and photographs of grizzly crime scenes and autopsies over the years. And, sure, I had developed the protective emotional objectivity most forensic investigators must have to continue working in this area. But seeing the sexual exploitation of children was different. Here, frozen in time, were acts that I knew would haunt these children for the rest of their lives. And someone who was supposed to cherish and protect her children, not molest and sexually exploit them, committed the crimes.

Cases involving children are the hardest for me, and those about sexual abuse are the hardest of all. Visual evidence of sexual abuse is the worst. Often, after working on several child sexual abuse cases in a row, I would find myself yearning for a simple murder or dismemberment case for relief. I tossed the unopened envelope on top of my review pile and went on with my murder case, hoping to delay the inevitable.

A couple of weeks later, armed Cochise County corrections officers escorted Virginia to my office for the psychological evaluation. She wore a jail-issued orange jumpsuit and was trussed with ankle and wrist restraints according to regulations. I asked them to remove her handcuffs to make her more comfortable. I also needed her to be able to handle any testing materials I wanted to administer. The officers complied, sat Virginia at a table in the center of my interview room, shackled her to one of the table's steel legs, then went to an observation cubicle where they could drink coffee and watch their prisoner through one-way windows.

I sat across the table from Virginia and wondered how this forty-one-year-old mother of five had evolved into a child molester. Was she a pedophile, as the prosecutor alleged in file material? Everybody knows pedophilia in females is rare, but it may not be as rare as we think. Virginia had been a truck driver and had been all across the country, but no others charges in other states had been filed. Still, I worried that the prosecutor's hunch written in the material could be correct and that Virginia may have molested an unknown number of kids in her travels. After all, she had been arrested for these charges while working at a local adult theater and bookstore—not the kind of place pedophiles often hang out, nor a place where mothers usually work.

I also worried that Virginia could have molested many children other than her own because she was "crazy," as her attorney alleged. One thing was certain, though: I knew that my colleague had a bunch of kids in play therapy in the next room and felt relieved that Virginia was shackled to the table. Secretly, so was I.

For the record, I made a mental note that she was overweight, but well groomed in spite of the garish orange jumpsuit. She seemed to know who she was, where she was, and why she was in my office. When I looked into Virginia's eyes, she looked back steadily. Yes, she understood the charges against her and the roles of the major players in the criminal justice system. I could also see that, at some primitive level, she understood the difference between right and wrong. And no, she didn't claim to hear strange voices or be possessed by aliens, the devil, or God. So much for claiming insanity.

Sitting across the table, Virginia simply looked depressed as she told her story of being raised on a farm in a small rural community in the Midwest. The middle child of five girls, she felt rejected by both her parents, especially her father, who favored and molested an older sister. She said, "I saw dad patting Kathy on her butt and pinching her near her boobs. He didn't do that to anybody else because he didn't love us."

She added, "I always got punished more than the other kids. One time my father put me in my room and nailed the window shut overnight." As she described numerous other episodes of physical abuse and rejection, my gut told me that, as a little girl, Virginia might have welcomed inappropriate sexual advances by her father because they would have reassured her that she was accepted and loved. I hoped my gut was wrong. Young children should not yearn for sexual molestation as the only way to get love from parents then feel rejected and unloved when it doesn't come.

By the time Virginia was twelve years old, she was experimenting sexually with a same-age girlfriend and her friend's somewhat older brother. After Virginia had intercourse with the brother, she had sex with every boy she dated. Softly, she offered that she has always enjoyed consensual sex. Then Virginia's softness turned to anger as she spat out, "I also had sex to get back at my father."

Given Virginia's childhood history, I was not surprised when she seemed confused about appropriate expressions of love and sex, often linking the two as if they were the same. Her gaze was clear and unashamed when she announced, "My parents never told me nothing about sex, but my children won't be blind to sex." I felt my gut begin to twist as I absorbed the meaning behind her words.

As a teenager, Virginia was on a seemingly desperate quest to find the love and acceptance she hadn't found as a child at home. She had a problem, though; Virginia had never seen a good example of an accepting and loving relationship. Even so, at nineteen Virginia thought she had found the love of her life and married for the first time, even while she was pregnant with her first child, a son, by another man.

When the relationship turned ugly, she stayed in it and had two daughters by her husband. After enduring three years of physical and emotional abuse, she got a divorce. She said, "He abused the kids, wouldn't work, was overly demanding for sex, and committed adultery with a lot of women."

After the divorce, Virginia went on another quest for love and quickly made another poor decision about relationships. This time, she married an alcoholic. After six years of abuse and two more children, Alan and Becky, Virginia divorced her second husband.

Virginia waited nearly six years before she married again. This time she hit the abuse jackpot. She chose a man who not only abused her but also physically abused all of her children and molested her daughters. On at least one occasion, Virginia's third husband tied her to a chair and forced her to watch the molestations. She was also forced to participate in sexual acts with her husband and other women he would bring home.

Virginia told me she was always afraid her husband would kill her and her children, but whenever she would run away with the kids, "he would always find us and it would start over again." She got a divorce from her third husband after about one year. He was eventually convicted of child molestation and sent to prison.

Virginia's misadventures with men continued. Shortly after her third husband was sent to prison, Virginia began corresponding with John, a man languishing in a prison cell in Indiana. Even before Virginia told me, I sensed that she must have fallen in love with John through letters before meeting him behind bars when her truck route took her nearby. They made plans to marry after his release from prison in a couple of years, but John was apprehended after an ill-fated escape attempt and sentenced to six more years.

Undaunted, Virginia committed herself to the relationship with John as a marriage. She wrote and telephoned often and visited John in prison whenever she could. Virginia told me she believed that Alan and Becky were beginning to relate to John as a father and they were looking forward to his release so they could be a family. Her other three children were grown by this time and lived on their own.

Wearily, Virginia put her head down and began to sob as she described how hard she had worked to establish a family unit with John and her two remaining children. Then she mentioned the photographs. I steeled myself and pulled them from the file.

While we looked at the photos, Virginia spoke as though it wasn't out of the ordinary to send sexually explicit pictures of her children to a man in prison. The first were typical snapshots of her and her children, photographs most anyone would feel comfortable sharing with friends and kin, or even those in prison. Later photos included shots of Virginia and the kids posing in the nude with full exposure of their genitals.

Later still, I saw the camera had been passed around, as Virginia engaged in various sex acts with each child separately and Alan and Becky engaged in sexual activities with each other. She said, "The kids had no objections to me sending the pictures because they saw John as their dad. I was just including him as part of the family and it would make him love me more."

I was hardly surprised when Virginia was unable to explain how sending sexually explicit photographs of her children to a man in prison would create more love for her. She didn't have a clue. Here was a woman who lacked a serious understanding of the nature of interpersonal relationships, sexuality, and love.

Even worse, she didn't seem to understand that taking these photographs was criminal and potentially harmful to her children. She never even imagined that the photos themselves might be subject to screening and interception by prison authorities. For Virginia these concepts, basic to most of us, were forever shrouded in a fog of her own childhood abuse and neglect.

After I spent several hours interviewing Virginia, I administered an intelligence test and a personality inventory. Testing confirmed many of my initial hypotheses about Virginia. Her scores showed overall low intellectual abilities with serious deficits in the ability to perceive social situations accurately and to respond in appropriate and meaningful ways in interpersonal relationships.

She showed mental confusion, low self-esteem, low self-confidence, strong dependency needs, and high social anxiety. She also seemed to have serious problems in expressing her emotions in adaptive ways. None of this was a good recipe for establishing stable interpersonal relationships, but Virginia was far from being insane.

I called Myers to give him the bad news and a little good news. First the good news. I told him Virginia did not appear to have a compulsive, longstanding need to engage in sexual activity with children. In other words, I thought the prosecutor was wrong. In my opinion, Virginia was not a dangerous pedophile with an insatiable need to seek out children in any setting for personal sexual pleasure.

Then I gave Myers the bad news — Virginia was not legally insane. After listening patiently to his desperate argument that I must be wrong because no mother could have done what Virginia had done without being "crazy," I offered an alternative explanation for her criminal acts. Virginia suffered from serious intellectual deficits and an equally serious emotional dysfunction associated with interpersonal relationships, poor judgment, and confusion about sexuality and love.

I diagnosed her with a combination of depression (without psychosis) and borderline personality disorder (primary diagnosis). Then, I told Myers that therapists who treat borderlines report most are women and many have a history of childhood abuse and neglect, like Virginia. Also, most borderlines, like Virginia, show a pervasive pattern of poor self-image and unstable and intense interpersonal relationships.

Many of these unfortunate souls make frantic efforts to avoid real or imagined abandonment and over-idealize interpersonal relationships. They then devalue a relationship when someone fails to meet their needs. For example, many borderlines may first believe that a desired individual is the greatest of the great and will always meet all of their emotional needs. When the individual ultimately fails to live up to these impossible expectations, the borderline relegates the person to the worst of the worst.

There's no middle ground for most borderlines. In addition, they tend to react to relationship stresses with poor judgment and intense displays of unhappiness, irritability, anxiety, panic, or despair. Many, also like Virginia, engage in impulsive self-damaging behavior, including reckless and inappropriate sexual behavior.

In spite of my failure to find Virginia legally insane as Myers had hoped, he asked me to write a report and give my testimony at trial. I expected that he would try, on direct examination, to glean anything he could from my testimony to support his defense strategy. Myers was an excellent defense attorney and he was determined to defend Virginia with anything he could no matter how weak.

I also knew that Deputy County Attorney Sharon Archer, a top-notch prosecutor, would find my testimony helpful in debunking the insanity defense. Either way, I expected to get hammered by both sides.

When Virginia was arrested, Alan and Becky tried to defend their mother by telling police they willingly participated in the sexual acts. All this changed during the trial. The two children decided not to defend her and testified that they did not want to have sex with their mother, or with each other. They also revealed that some of the molestations occurred while Virginia was talking on the telephone with John, and that Virginia had used "sexual instruments" on Becky. When Archer asked Becky if she loved her mother, Becky replied, "I guess that's kind of hard to say."

When I took the stand, Myers organized his questioning around Virginia's childhood abuse history, her subsequent mental impairment, and how all that explained her difficulties with men and her sexual acts with her children. Then he tried to lead me into stating that her mental impairment was serious enough to qualify as insanity under Arizona law.

I again explained to the jury how I thought that Virginia's serious mental impairment related to her criminal behavior, but I stopped short of rendering an opinion that she was legally insane. After a few more unsuccessful attempts by Myers to draw the magic word from my lips, he passed me off to the prosecution.

Archer cut to the chase. She had me review my findings again just to make sure the jury understood it was my opinion that Virginia was mentally impaired, but not insane, when she molested her children. She backed off some on the pedophilia allegations but insisted that Virginia fit the profile of a predatory child molester.

Archer didn't bother to wallop me vigorously as she had in previous cases. She didn't have to. This time she had all the hard evidence she needed — the photographs.

On the last day of the trial, Virginia took the stand. She revealed information she had not shared with me. She testified that she was jealous of her older daughters and was afraid men would find them more attractive than she. She also admitted she was afraid John would reject her if she did not take sexually explicit photos of herself and her children and send them to him. Although she expressed remorse, she showed little understanding of her inappropriate sexual behavior.

The jury deliberated a scant three hours before finding Virginia guilty of ten counts of sexual exploitation of a minor, five counts of sexual conduct with a minor, and two counts of sexual abuse.

Prior to her sentencing, Virginia wrote a letter to the presiding judge, Arthur King. She tried to explain her behavior: "I didn't stop to think that it was wrong — only that I was proving to him that I loved him like he wanted me to. I expected to get a loving husband and father for my kids."

These words officially stamped Virginia as a perfect example of a woman with serious deficits in establishing proper boundaries for herself and her children. They also underscored her inability to see the differences between love and exploitation in interpersonal relationships.

While most mothers would sense the impending danger and flee immediately to protect themselves and their children, Virginia rushed headlong into danger, pushing her children ahead of her in the hopes that she would find love for herself and her children in the embrace of a man she could not recognize — despite all the signs — as a predator.

In a presentence report by the probation department, Virginia admitted that John had requested the photographs of her and her children engaged in various sexual acts. She also said that she refused at first but cooperated when John threatened to end their relationship.

My report was included as part of the presentence report. The press highlighted my detailed descriptions of Virginia's serious intellectual weaknesses, her poor judgment in interpersonal relationships, her even poorer judgment regarding sex education for her children, her confusion about sexuality, and her serious emotional dysfunction. They omitted my diagnoses — depression and borderline personality disorder.

Archer dismissed me and my report by telling the press, "I did not put much stock in that evaluation because Morris is not an expert in predicting future behavior."

When Judge King sentenced Virginia to over five hundred years behind bars, I was astonished. She received more years of imprisonment than in any case I had worked on in my entire career as a clinical and forensic psychologist. While King made no comment during sentencing, he later made a statement to the press about the "insanity" of some of Arizona's mandatory sentencing laws, which require criminals to serve sentences longer than their life span.

Apparently, Virginia was not insane but state lawmakers were when they replaced judicial decision about punishment involving sex crimes with mandatory sentencing dictated by the law. The judge also took a swipe at the criminal justice system for spending so much money on incarceration and none on psychiatric help, which he clearly understood Virginia needed. I couldn't have agreed more.

JOYCE CUMBERLAND*

When my nine o'clock evaluation appointment didn't show by quarter after, I checked with my receptionist. She reminded me that Ms. Cumberland's attorney called two days ago to confirm the appointment and no one had called to cancel. As we discussed the most efficient way of tracking down the elusive Ms. Cumberland, I noticed two cars pull into the parking lot. I recognized one of the two women who got out of the cars. She was Pam, a paralegal at the legal defender's office. Pam went to the other woman, put a friendly hand on her shoulder, and guided her into my waiting room.

Inside, Pam introduced me to Joyce Cumberland, then apologized for being late. She explained that Joyce was unable to locate my office on her own and called Pam for help. I wondered why Joyce didn't instead call me for directions but I told both of them that lots of people get lost trying to find my office. I reassured them that the evaluation could go on as planned even though we were getting a late start. Pam and Joyce chatted briefly, then Pam left an anxious Joyce with a hug and a smile of encouragement. I joked with Joyce about lost travelers as I guided her to the examination room.

I tried to make Joyce as comfortable as possible then eased into the warning of limitations of confidentiality. I knew Joyce would have difficulties understanding the warning. Her psychiatric records documented a long history of serious mental illness as far back as age fifteen when she ran away from home. She was now thirty-five and still struggling with emotional problems. We worked at it until I felt she understood the situation and felt comfortable to give an acceptable informed consent to proceed with the evaluation. But I knew this was only a tiny step on a long and difficult journey. I asked Joyce to please excuse me for a moment. I went to my receptionist and instructed her to reschedule my afternoon clinical cases to other days. Joyce was going to need time. Lots of time.

During the initial stages of the interview I was encouraged when Joyce seemed willing to participate. But then she became increasingly agitated and angry, in spite of my softest clinical approach. At one point she jumped from her chair and screamed at me at the top of her voice to stop asking the same questions about the charges against her. Then Joyce stormed out of the examining room, slamming the door shut with such force that plaster blew off the wall above the door. By the time I got to the hallway she had rushed through the waiting room full of startled children and out of the office building.

I found Joyce sitting on a curb in the parking lot smoking a cigarette. I sat with her on the curb and suggested we could negotiate terms for the evaluation. Eventually she offered that she would respond to written questions. I agreed. After she reassured me she would come back in after she finished another cigarette, I returned to the examining room to write questions. On the way I instructed my receptionist to keep an eye on Joyce.

Joyce came back in a short time later. She seemed a bit calmer, tried a weak smile, and said, "Sorry." When I presented the first of the written questions, Joyce toyed with the paper then suggested that it would be better if I read the questions to her and she would respond by writing her answers. I knew this procedure would be very time consuming but was willing to try almost anything to pull Joyce into a cooperative and productive evaluation. I asked the first question. Joyce began to write but soon she just doodled on the paper while she answered my questions verbally.

Even though Joyce offered answers to most of my questions she remained very guarded and she would often fly into angry tirades about the nature of a question, or about me, her daughter, her attorney, or just about anybody else in her life. At one point, Joyce called herself "an angry teenager" and hid her head between her folded arms on the table. She often returned to this oppositional juvenile position after lashing out at me.

Between fiery bursts of anger and frequent threats to leave, I was able to glean a few details about Joyce's background. I learned that she was born and raised in England, which explained an accent I mistook for Australian. She reluctantly revealed a history of emotional, physical, and sexual abuse as a child and a rape as a young adult.

Her first marriage, to a US military man based in England, ended in divorce because he beat her. Joyce lost or relinquished custody of the couple's two children, Sam, age eleven, Sara, age ten, as well as Jane, her fifteen-year-old daughter born prior to meeting her first husband. Jane, however, had lived with Joyce and her present husband, William, on a number of occasions. Joyce had been married to William, also a US military man, for approximately two years.

When I asked Joyce to address the allegations that she and her husband molested her fifteen-year-old daughter, Joyce denied any sexual activity ever occurred then launched a rambling and often inconsistent diatribe about her parenting skills, her daughter's incorrigibility, and her husband's sexual interest in her daughter Jane. Joyce even described a completely different scenario for the trio during the time period Jane said the sexual molestations happened. At another point in the interview she told me that her daughter was not even in town during the time period in question.

Attempts to have Joyce reconcile the differences in her statements produced angry and unproductive responses. When I pointed out that her husband told police that he had molested Jane, and that Joyce was also involved, Joyce adamantly denied that she or her husband engaged in any form of sexual behavior with her daughter. She claimed the allegations were lies by her daughter who "trashed the place." After another angry outburst about the allegations, Joyce repeated, "Quit asking me the same questions. I know what my charges are!" She then added that she was charged with "spoiling my child."

When I consulted Joyce's attorney, I told him Joyce was mostly uncooperative and I was unable to evaluate her state of mind during the instant offense because she denied the allegations and refused to talk about her charges. I also told him that she was unable to provide a coherent description of how she could assist him in planning a strategy for her defense. She seemed emotionally unable to address this issue and even demeaned her attorney by calling him a string of derogatory names. I explained that repeated efforts on my part to engage Joyce in a rational discussion about this matter were met with strong resistance and angry outbursts. She also indicated that she had not discussed her case with him and implied that she had no plans to do so.

Joyce's attorney confirmed that she had been totally uncooperative. He told me that repeated attempts by him and his staff to arrange appointments for Joyce had been unsuccessful. He also reported that Joyce would not discuss her case with him and a legal assistant, even when they went to Joyce's home.

I expressed concern that Joyce may appear competent with regard to an adequate understanding of the criminal justice system, but she seems incapable of understanding the severity of the charges against her and assisting her legal counsel on her own behalf. I told her attorney that Joyce would be extremely resistant to any suggestions of wrongdoing, especially child molestation, and the need for legal counsel.

We discussed her mental health issues. I pointed out that file documents indicated at least three psychiatric hospitalizations over the past seven years. Mental health treatment records also documented at least one suicide attempt and a variety of diagnoses consistent with a history of childhood abuse, including major depression, bipolar mood disorder, post-traumatic stress disorder, borderline personality disorder, and a personality disorder with borderline, identity, and histrionic features. I revealed that Joyce told me she was currently in counseling, but she would offer no details about the counselor or the therapy. She also reported she has been "off" prescribed medications for several months even though file material documented favorable results with psychotropic medications. Her condition may have deteriorated as a result.

I told him that based upon file records and my examination, I was convinced Joyce was in desperate need of a comprehensive treatment program. Since it seemed unlikely to me that she would cooperate with mental health treatment recommendations on an outpatient basis, I was going to urge the court to consider placing Joyce in an inpatient treatment facility that offered a full milieu of treatment modalities including psychotropic medications.

Even though I knew Joyce's emotional problems were severe and chronic, I hoped that an inpatient remediation process would be sufficient to allow her to recognize the seriousness of her current legal situation and to assist counsel in the preparation of a defense. I also knew it was unlikely that her mental health problems would be substantially relieved in a short period of time. Clinical studies suggest that long-term rather than short-term therapy is needed for the type of affective and personality disorders displayed by victims of childhood abuse such as Joyce. The judge followed my recommendations and sent Joyce to an inpatient restoration program.

About three months later, Joyce arrived promptly for a follow-up evaluation arranged by her attorney. Joyce's presentation on follow-up was considerably different than the first time I saw her. She greeted me warmly and asked about the damage to the plaster. Although she appeared depressed, she did not display the intense anger and uncooperative manner seen during her initial evaluation. She was cooperative with me and answered my questions without difficulty. She also offered information on her own without waiting for questions from me.

When I asked Joyce how she managed so much progress in such a short period of time, she told me she received little to no therapy while in the competency restoration facility but she was frightened enough by the experience to realize she needed to deal with her anger and begin cooperating with her attorney. When she managed to convince the staff at the facility that she was "motivated enough to behave in a manner that is conducive to resolving her case," she was released.

During the follow-up evaluation Joyce appeared to have a basic understanding of the process of a trial and the various roles of court participants. And to my delight, she also appeared to understand the charges against her, as well as the need for her to assist her attorney in planning a defense strategy.

I was pleased to hear that she was cooperating with her attorney and that they had been working hard on issues related to her defense. They were negotiating a possible plea agreement involving probation now that she was accepting responsibility for her role in the molestation of her daughter.

As most victims of mother-daughter incest are quick to point out, abuse at the hands of a biological mother represents a profound betrayal of trust and the impact of the abuse has immediate as well as significant long-term negative consequences. But what about mother-son incest? In his own words, here is just one son's story that begins at home but goes far beyond.

ANDREW RICHARDS[*]

I was born in the early 1930s. My father lost everything during the Great Depression and the family never recovered. We were very poor and survived on welfare for many years. My father absented himself from the family much of the time, and he tended to be sadistic. I soon learned that my survival depended on my mother. But her protection came at a cost. She demanded absolute conformance to her desires. I was expected to read her mind and never show any hesitancy with complying. Both parents were given to simple and superstitious thinking.

My mother indicated that she was sexually abused as a child. I remember her as lonely and depressed. When I was a small child she seduced me into becoming her lover. We slept together until I was fifteen.

She was very convincing in presenting our relationship as something beautiful, and one that others would not understand. I was told our relationship was something that God approved of. She said that we could touch each other any way we wanted to because I came from her body, and so we were really one and the same. Thus I felt no shame or guilt, and never suspected that our relationship was inappropriate. She started to abuse me from the time I was a toddler until age fifteen, at which time I decided to try to become "normal." Because of my decision she became so very depressed that she was nearly bedridden for years.

My mother engaged in all the adult-type variations of lovemaking with me, including many aberrant sexual activities. She molested me almost daily and dressed me as a girl as often as possible. She sewed many feminine clothes for me. She would fuss over me dressed as a girl and say that I made a prettier girl than my older sister, whom both parents neglected shamefully. My mother often administered enemas "so I wouldn't get impacted." At times she restrained me so she could watch my reaction to intense overstimulation.

Increasingly, as I grew out of my toddler years, I was passed around to female relatives for "their enjoyment." By that time I was very compliant and enjoyed the sensual/sexual attention. My mother was the youngest of six girls (no males). Her older sisters had only female children. Her first cousins were a family of seven girls. My father's first cousins were a family of five girls. These females were part of our close-knit clan. All of these females, having no brothers, enjoyed activities such as dressing me up as a girl and playing girl tea-time games, bathing me, giving me enemas, and other inappropriate touching. All of this was done in a gentle, pampering manner, resulting in positive sensual feelings on my part. I developed a very positive attitude toward females and was comfortable around them — dressed or undressed. Of note is that there are pictures of my father at twelve years of age dressed in a fancy white dress with shoulder length curls of his own hair.

Eventually my father delivered me into a child sex abuse ring that existed in the rural community that he grew up in. I was probably about seven years old. My relatives were part of that ring. I would be shuttled to different people, again, for "their enjoyment." I was often confused and homesick, especially missing my mother. Yet I eventually became so compliant that my parents could put me on the train by myself to that community and I did not protest. I had a sense my father was financially compensated for "pimping me," so I felt I was helping to feed my family. My sister was not delivered into that community and I never knew what was happening to her when I was gone.

Near that rural community there was a large Catholic institution that included a seminary and a large convent . . .

To be continued in chapter 8.

Notes

1. Bureau of Justice Statistics, "Sex Offenses and Offenders: An Analysis of Data on Rape and Sexual Assault," Washington, DC: US Department of Justice, 1997.

2. Craig Allen, *Women and Men Who Sexually Abuse Children* (Orwell, VT: Safer Society Press, 1991).

3. For a review see Barbara K. Schwartz and Henry R. Cellini, *The Sex Offender: Corrections, Treatment and Legal Practice* (Kingston, NJ: Civic Research Institute, 1995), p. 5-1-5-22.

4. L. M. McCarthy, "Mother-Child Incest: Characteristics of the Offender," *Child Welfare* 65 (1986): 447–58.

5. J. Matthews, R. Mathews, and K. Speltz, "Female Sexual Offenders: A Typology," In *Family Sexual Abuse*, ed. M. Q. Patton (Newbury Park, CA: Sage Publications, 1991), pp. 199–219.

6. Beverly A. Ogilvie, *Mother-Daughter Incest: A Guide for Helping Professionals* (Binghampton, NY: Haworth Press, 2004).

7

THE HIDDEN CURRICULUM

WOMEN TEACHERS WHO
SEXUALLY ABUSE STUDENTS

On a crisp September morning a long time ago, I tore out of the house wearing brand-new duds and headed north. My heart pumped hard as I ran, hopped, and skipped the four blocks to Meridian Grade School. When I reached the last intersection, I was stopped by a couple of older students standing guard. They had stern faces and wore strange contraptions that looked like a white belt fastened around the waist and across the chest and back diagonally. The early morning sun flashed hard against their silver badges, pinned against white at heart level. I liked the military-style red hats.

Over their outstretched arms I saw my goal. Three stories of brick and Indiana limestone surrounded with a playground full of swings, slides, and monkey gyms. And basketball hoops. Lots of basketball hoops. As I waited in the crushing crowd of other students, I realized that the shortest way to the school was not crossing the street blocked by the guards. The quickest way across was to cut straight through the middle of the intersection corner to corner. Why wait?

I shot across the intersection in a flash, only to be collared on the other side by another white-belted, stern-faced student who immediately called out for backup. A man wearing a dark, double-breasted suit arrived and quickly dragged me off into the school and into an office behind a huge wooden door with a long name and another word I couldn't see clearly.

Double-breasted asked my name. When I told him, he grunted, shook his head, and ordered me to sit. His stern eyes and firm voice convinced me he meant business. Double-breasted disappeared behind another door then reappeared a short time later. He grabbed my arm and pulled me into the other office.

Behind a desk as big as a baseball field, another man glared at me with eyes as crazed as the rabid dog that terrorized our neighborhood that summer until old Mr. Orr blasted him to kingdom come with a twenty-gauge shotgun. I didn't have a twenty-gauge and I had to pee.

The man with crazed eyes stood, wagged a long finger at me, and launched a barrage of condemnations so fast and furious I never understood all that he was saying until he finished with a promise to tell my parents about my transgression. I didn't understand the transgression but I certainly understood the consequences of the promise.

Double-breasted dragged me out of the office and down a long hall through clumps of giggling students headed the other way. I prayed he was taking me to a bathroom. He wasn't.

As we stumbled up a flight of wooden stairs, I caught a glimpse of a tall woman guiding a little girl into a room, then the door closed. We headed in that direction. Double-breasted yanked the door open and shoved me in. As I struggled to keep my balance, all the kids in the classroom started to laugh but were quickly silenced when the tall woman turned slowly from a blackboard, then waved a white stick of chalk in cadence with slow shakes of her head.

Double-breasted called the woman Mrs. Johnson and told her that I had broken school rules by disobeying the safety patrol. I would need to be watched closely as I certainly was going to be a troublemaker like my brother before me. He told her that it was a sad, sad day that he had to take a student to the principal for discipline on the very first day of school. Double-breasted left mumbling something about how bad kids were getting these days.

While small faces watched over big desks, Mrs. Johnson came to me. I hunched over. When she reached down I flinched and started blubbering that I couldn't wait to get to school because I knew books would be here and I wanted to learn everything I could and I didn't know anything about a safety patrol and I was really sorry that I made the principal mad on my very first day of school and I didn't like my older brother either and . . . she pulled me in close. The warmth of her soft body wrapped me up like a baby blanket. My nostrils filled with the fresh fragrance of her long blond hair as it cascaded over my face. "I know," she whispered. "Now hurry to the bathroom."

At that moment I fell in love with my first-grade teacher. Each day Mrs. Johnson's classroom was a joy of learning and love. But it didn't last. Shortly after I gave her the best and biggest valentine she ever had, Mrs. Johnson gathered the class about her and told us she was leaving. She was going to have a baby. A baby! I felt dizzy! I felt betrayed! I cried for weeks! Mrs. Johnson was my very first teacher and my very first real love. I got over it.

Teachers have a powerful influence over their students' lives and some teachers, unlike Mrs. Johnson, behave badly. An Associated Press investigation of sexual abuse in schools found more than 2,500 educators had their credentials revoked, denied, or sanctioned from 2001 through 2005 due to state actions in sexual misconduct cases.[1] The US Department of Education reported that about 20 percent of students surveyed had experienced verbal or physical sexual misconduct by a female teacher or aide. Most of the students were boys. And in many cases, especially when the teacher is a woman and the student is a boy, the abuse is treated with misplaced fascination and in a salacious manner.[2]

MARY KAY LETOURNEAU

A night watchman at one of the many marinas that dotted the watery landscape around Des Moines, Washington, noticed an unfamiliar minivan in the parking lot. He became suspicious and called the police. When the police arrived they flipped on their flashing lights and approached the car cautiously. One of the officers approached the driver's side window while the other maintained some distance on the passenger side.

The first officer was surprised to see a pretty face framed with rumpled blond hair. Next to her somebody tried to hide under a sleeping bag. "What's going on here?" the officer asked.

The pretty face identified herself as Mary Kay Letourneau, a schoolteacher who was watching a student because his mother was working late.

"How old is the boy?" one of the officers asked.

"Eighteen," she lied.

The police took the boy aside. "What's your name?" they asked.

"Vili Fualaau," the curly haired boy with a dark complexion answered.

"How old are you?" they asked.

"Fourteen," the boy lied, but missed his teacher's lie by four years.

Unable to sort out the matter to their satisfaction at the scene, the police took Mrs. Letourneau and Vili to a police station. When the police phoned Vili's mother, Soona Fualaau, she reassured them that her son's teacher was trustworthy and Vili was in no danger with her. She gave the police permission to let the pair leave together.

A few days later the thirty-four-year-old schoolteacher and her thirteen-year-old sixth-grade student finished the lesson they had started in her minivan. They had sexual intercourse for the first time, setting off a chain of events that would shock and captivate the public.

Over the past several years, a lot of details about Mary Kay have surfaced, some of them more accurate than others. One of the best sources, other than official documents, is the well-researched book *If Loving You Is Wrong* by Greg Olsen.[3] What follows is a summary of the most accurate information I could find.

Mary Kay was born on January 30, 1962, in Tustin, California, to devout Roman Catholic parents. Her father, John Schmitz, was a college professor and her mother, Mary, was a homemaker. She was the first daughter of four children and quickly became her father's favorite; she became more attached to him than her mother. The family's home was in Southern California's Orange County, a hotbed for conservative politics. Her father was a member of the ultraconservative John Birch Society.

When Mary Kay was about two years old, her father threw his hat into the political ring and ran for a seat in the California state legislature. The handsome and outspoken candidate often took his pretty, brown-eyed, blond daughter with him on the campaign trail. His opponent was no match for the pair and her father won by a landslide. The family left sunny Southern California for the temperamental political climate of Sacramento, where three more children were born in fairly rapid succession.

As a state legislator, her father quickly moved up the political ladder. He ran a strong campaign for a seat in the US House of Representatives in 1970 and won. Freshman Congressman John Schmitz packed up his wife and four kids and moved the family to Washington, DC, where he hit his stride as an outspoken conservative. Marching to the same beat, Mary Kay's mother was also active in conservative political issues, including campaigning successfully against the Equal Rights Amendment.

Right-wingers took notice of the dynamic duo and Mary Kay's father became the presidential candidate of the ultraconservative American Independent Party. Schmitz did better than expected by political experts by winning about 1 percent of the popular vote. No longer a congressman and not yet president, Schmitz moved his family back to California. This time they moved into a lavish home in an exclusive area of Corona del Mar.

Mary Kay's adolescence was a page out of a "California Girl" dream. She was pretty, popular, and a party girl. After graduating high school she enrolled and partied at a nearby college but still lived at home. And home was about to be rocked.

Mary Kay was nineteen when the story broke. Her father, the paragon of traditional morals and family values, the devout Catholic, was a hypocrite and a fraud. While he told the world how to live a virtuous family life, he was living a secret life not full of virtue, but of deception and abuse. He had carried on a secret sexual affair with a former student, Carla Stuckle, for years and fathered two children with her. The children were rejected and abandoned by Mary Kay's father and possibly abused and neglected by their mother, a diabetic who received no financial assistance from Schmitz and worked two jobs to support the children.

The case came to light when Carla was suspected of abusing Schmitz's first child with her, a son, when she took the boy to the hospital because his penis was injured by a hair that had been tangled around it for quite some time. The doctor performed microsurgery to remove the hair and repair the injury but suspected that the hair had been purposely tied around the penis. Investigators pressed Carla for information about the injury as well as the identity of the father. At first she refused to talk about the boy's father, but when she was told she would not be allowed to take her son from the hospital until she told them what they wanted to know, she revealed her secret love affair with Schmitz. Investigators were astonished.

When they contacted Schmitz, he admitted that he was the father of the boy but denied any knowledge of the hair. He also said that he would assume no financial responsibility for the children. Mary Kay came to the defense of her father. She assigned fault to her mother, whom she considered a cold person who didn't try to meet the emotional needs of her beloved father.

The scandal also affected Mary Kay's mother, who may have known about her husband's dalliance for years. Her life as a conservative political commentator was over. Mary Kay's mother and father separated and most everybody expected the couple would divorce. They didn't. Against all odds they somehow managed to reconcile. Maybe Mary Kay's mother wasn't as cold as Mary Kay believed. And there is more.

Carla was never charged with child abuse so she kept custody of the children until she died in 1994 from complications of diabetes. Mary Kay's father, the fallen champion of family values, still wanted no part of his second family and turned his back on his illegitimate thirteen-year-old son and eleven-year-old daughter. Mary Kay's mother may have tried to come to the rescue, however, because one of her longtime friends, psychic Jeane Dixon, agreed to take care of the children. The kids stayed with Dixon until she died in 1997. Still without anyone who truly wanted them and with no resources, Schmitz's love children ended up in an orphanage.

Some reports indicated that Mary Kay showed some early concerns for her half siblings who had essentially been abandoned by her father. Mostly, however, she concerned herself with having a good time at her new college, Arizona State University, and not attending too much to the family scandal.

Mary Kay met Steve Letourneau while attending Arizona State University. She may have been depressed and on the rebound from losing the first "love of her life," a man she had hoped to marry. Mary Kay's attraction to Steve was immediate even though some of her friends thought Steve was only an average-looking guy and was going to need some work. By the time Mary Kay realized that Steve, who was gregarious and fun loving, was also rather immature and probably not very bright, it was too late. She was pregnant.

Mary Kay was uncertain about marriage with Steve, but consistent with her conservative background, she was totally opposed to having an abortion. She was considering the life of a single mother, then she started to miscarry. From her hospital bed, Mary Kay called her mother with the bad news about being an unwed mother and the impending miscarriage. Her mother quickly took control. She told the doctors not to perform any procedures that might abort a second child just in case her daughter might be carrying twins. Her mother was right. Mary Kay miscarried one twin but the other remained.

Still pregnant, Mary Kay had some tough decisions to make. Steve had offered to marry her but she still had serious concerns about his character, and she wasn't sure she really loved him. She sought her parents' advice. They advised her to marry Steve.

At age twenty-two Mary Kay married Steve. Within a few months their first child, Steven Jr., was born. Leaving college and the parties in sunny Tempe behind, the couple moved to Steve's hometown, Anchorage, Alaska, where their troubled marriage struggled to survive. Mary Kay's fears about Steve's character were realized. He took a low-paying job as a baggage handler for Alaska Airlines and started a series of extramarital affairs. After about a year in Alaska, Steve was transferred to Seattle, where some of his relatives lived.

In spite of constant arguments about financial matters and Steve's blatant extramarital affairs, the couple stayed together and had three more children. By most accounts Mary Kay was drawn to being a mother. She loved everything associated with being pregnant and appeared to be a gifted mother. She also showed a strong interest in teaching other children and took evening courses at Seattle University in order to finish her degree and become a teacher.

Shortly after she graduated in 1989, Mary Kay started her ill-fated teaching career at Shorewood Elementary School in a Seattle suburb. Her first assignment? Teaching second grade. Sitting in the class was a young American Samoan boy with artistic talent, Vili Fualaau.

Mary Kay seemed to have a gift for teaching. The kids loved

her. Administrators and other teachers praised her. She also took a special interest in children, especially disadvantaged kids, who seemed to be gifted. It seemed that she was determined to help these children overcome their disadvantages, develop their respective talents, and succeed. On the other hand, Mary Kay was soft on discipline and her classes were often as chaotic as her private life.

By all accounts Mary Kay struggled to meet the demands of four children at home and a teaching career. She found no comfort in her marriage. Her home was cluttered. Her marriage was in shambles. And her expensive tastes in just about everything and the couple's collective low income led to them filing bankruptcy after ten years of marriage.

Ignoring all the signs that having another child in such a troubled relationship was not a good decision, Mary Kay became pregnant again. In 1995 she had a miscarriage, a tragic blow to someone who loved kids, lots of kids, around her. Added to her grief was the news that her beloved father was diagnosed with terminal cancer. She looked for but found no emotional support from her husband. Yet she found some joy in a promotion at school where she would now be teaching both fifth and sixth grades. But trouble seemed to follow Mary Kay.

Sitting in one of her classes was Vili, now twelve years old, a student who impressed her as a second grader. She took a special interest in him, so much so that other teachers began to worry Mary Kay was not exercising good judgment about the relationship and was failing to maintain appropriate boundaries. No one intervened.

Mary Kay's interest in Vili was dismissed as a dedicated teacher putting forth the extra effort to nurture a needy but gifted student. After all, Vili certainly qualified as a needy student. Vili's father was an avowed womanizer who was in prison for armed robbery, his mother struggled to make ends meet working a low-pay job at a bakery, and the family lived in one of most impoverished areas of Seattle.

During the summer Mary Kay and Vili were almost constant companions. They took community college and art classes together. He and his older brother were often hanging around her house. All of this attention to Vili did not escape her husband's eye. He complained that she had enough to do just taking care of their own kids without adding Vili and his brother into the mix. He also complained that the house was always a mess. Then there was the issue that she might be permitting Vili and his brother to smoke and drink in the house.

One night Steve came home and Vili was there. Steve argued with Mary Kay in front of Vili, who decided he better leave. Mary Kay went after him in her minivan and found him near a marina.

In the fall, Mary Kay told a friend that she had, at last, found her one and only true love. It wasn't Steve. Later, Mary Kay told the same friend that she was pregnant. It wasn't Steve's although she had sex with him to cover up the pregnancy by her real one and only true love. But there was a problem. The child would most likely not be fair skinned and blond like Steve, but dark skinned with black hair.

Steve was apparently smarter than Mary Kay thought and soon figured out her deception. He responded by becoming increasingly abusive. According to Mary Kay, at one point, an enraged Steve tried to induce a miscarriage by hitting her in the stomach repeatedly. When that didn't work he told her to get an abortion. She refused. Even her ultraconservative, anti-abortion mother urged her to terminate the pregnancy. She refused again. Nobody was going to stop her from having this love child fathered by her thirteen-year-old one and only true love and lover.

Steve had also shared his suspiciousness about Mary Kay and Vili with some of his relatives but made them promise to keep the information to themselves. Most did. One didn't. On February 25, 1997, a cousin made two anonymous phone calls, one to Child Protective Services and the other to the Highline School District. Both took the report seriously.

The next day, Vili, now a seventh grader at Cascade Middle School, was pulled out of class and questioned by a detective. Vili was reluctant to reveal the nature of his relationship with Mary Kay but in the end told the detective that the relationship with his former teacher was sexual. Police then went to Shorewood Elementary School and arrested Mary Kay for statutory rape. Another Schmitz made headlines for a sexual scandal with a student.

Authorities conducted a thorough investigation fearing that Mary Kay may have victimized other students and her own children. While they found no evidence of additional sexual victimization, they found numerous children who were devastated by the news that their beloved teacher was a child molester.

To help understand why a dedicated teacher and mother of four children would risk everything by having sex with a grade school–age student, the court ordered a series of psychiatric examinations.

Given her history of impulsive sexual behavior as a teenager and her recent inappropriate sexual responses to a young boy, I expected the experts would find another secret in Mary Kay's life: childhood sexual abuse. And given her father's adoration of Mary Kay and his history of inappropriate sexual behavior, father-daughter incest shot to the top of my predictions. My predictions were wrong. Mary Kay repeatedly denied any form of childhood sexual trauma, although she admitted to a few episodes of sexual experimentation with an older brother.

A key finding that influenced the court's various decisions in this case was a clinical diagnosis of bipolar disorder. Experts thought Mary Kay had sex with a student because she had mood swings, but if she could be stabilized, her risk to reoffend would decrease significantly. A psychiatrist prescribed psychotherapy and a regimen of psychotropic medications known to help stabilize moods. Maybe the drugs would be the antidote to her problem.

In May 1997, out on bail and living alone, Mary Kay gave birth to her one and only true love's baby, a girl. In spite of the court's prohibition against contact with her teenage lover, Mary Kay allowed Vili to come into her home to see their child.

By July 1997 Mary Kay's lawyer negotiated a plea bargain that would avoid a lengthy prison sentence. All she had to do was plead guilty to child rape, take her prescribed psychotropic medications for six months, serve just three months in jail, then be released on probation and participate in a treatment program for sex offenders. It was a sweet deal most male sex offenders, bipolar or not, never see.

In August 1997 I watched as much of the televised court hearing as my busy schedule allowed. Anxious to hear what Mary Kay had to say to the judge about her bad behavior, I hoped to find clues, other than bipolar disorder, for her overwhelming attraction to Vili. I was disappointed when Mary Kay, well groomed but seemingly thin and frail, stood before the judge and sniffled only an admission that she had done "something that I had no right to do. Morally or legally," and a promise ". . . that it will never happen again." She finished with a flourish: "Please, please help me. Help us, help us all." Her admission was a start but left me unmoved. Her promise was hopeful. I agreed with her personal and universal plea for help. I remained skeptical that anyone in the courtroom truly understood why Mary Kay became a sex offender. After all, there was no abuse excuse to use. Instead, her attorneys had successfully linked the diagnosis of bipolar disorder to her crime.

The judge accepted the plea agreement but added two major conditions. Mary Kay must give up custody of her child to Vili's mother, and Mary Kay must never have any contact with Vili. After Mary Kay sniffled her agreement to both conditions, she was led away to begin serving the terms of her sentence.

For six months the public furor over Mary Kay's case seemed to settle down, except for a continuing debate about the soft sentencing and sexism. Then, in January 1998, Mary Kay was released from jail to begin her probation and again found herself in the spotlight. I was pulling for Mary Kay, but my gut told me she wasn't ready for release. Not yet. Barely a month went by before Seattle police found Mary Kay and Vili, now a high school freshman, together in a Volkswagen. So much for the antidote.

Back in court a few days later and charged with violating the no-contact conditions of her probation, Mary Kay stood before the judge and awaited her fate. The judge's eyes narrowed as she scolded Mary Kay for squandering a rare opportunity to get her life together, then she vacated the plea agreement and sentenced Mary Kay to six and a half years in prison, the maximum term for one count of child rape.

Had the judge known that the disheveled and confused Mary Kay standing before her was pregnant again, she could have sentenced her for an additional charge of child rape. But no one knew about the second love child until prison officials discovered Mary Kay's condition. No additional criminal charges were made, but another child, a daughter, was handed over to Vili's mother to raise.

Even in prison, Mary Kay maintained that Vili would be waiting for her and they would be together again. In 1999 prison officials intercepted love letters she had tried to send to Vili. For that violation she spent six months in solitary confinement. However, there were some bright spots for Mary Kay. A liberal mother-child visitation policy allowed not only Steve and their four children to visit, but it also allowed her and Vili's two children to visit.

While Mary Kay served her sentence and awaited her chance at parole in 2004, Vili grew up and defended his imprisoned lover. He claimed he was never a victim of his teacher and that he initiated the sexual contact. In February 1999 Vili told Oprah Winfrey that Mary Kay was "my world" and that he planned to marry her. At least that was his first story. He and his mother even coauthored a book, *Un Seul Crime, L'amour* (Only One Crime, Love), which was published in France only. Later, he and his mother sued the Highline School District and the Des Moines Police Department for failing to prevent the relationship between Vili and Mary Kay.

In civil court, Vili said that he was no longer in love with Mary

Kay and tried to make a case for being victimized and suffering emotional harm. The jury was not convinced and awarded no damages. I wondered what would happen if all the students Mary Kay befriended then betrayed sued for emotional damages.

On August 4, 2004, Mary Kay was released from prison on parole. She was required to register as a convicted sex offender in her county of residence and will have to do so for the rest of her life unless the order is lifted by the court. I was relieved to hear Mary Kay was also required by the court to undergo formal treatment as a sex offender, although I doubted that Mary Kay thought of herself as a sex offender.

The first step in a successful sex offender treatment program is admitting to the crime and accepting full responsibility. I was fairly certain that, in Mary Kay's eyes, she and Vili were lovers and soul mates, not victimizer and victim. She could only pay lip service to the first step, rendering the remaining steps virtually useless. She also had to retain the no-contact order with Vili, even though he was now an adult; the order referred to Vili's victim status, not his age. She is prohibited from teaching minors in the state of Washington and most likely in any other state where schools bother to do background checks. The world awaited the next chapter in the student-teacher saga.

The wait wasn't long. Vili quickly petitioned the court to lift the no-contact order and his request was granted. On October 11, 2004, I heard Mary Kay tell Larry King that she was engaged to marry Vili. She also said that she thought falling in love with a thirteen-year-old was not normal but her love for Vili had endured in spite of the age difference and her incarceration.

When Mary Kay also said that she had not realized that having sex with a minor was a felony, I wondered how this former teacher could be so uninformed about the laws associated with reporting suspected child sexual abuse and the possible criminal charges. Was love really that blind? Her attorney seemed to think so. He admitted that he saw something different in the relationship between Vili and Mary Kay, something not found in other cases of child sexual abuse. But he cautioned her client then that love was not a defense. On May 20, 2005, Vili and Mary Kay married at the Columbia Winery in a Seattle suburb. They tried to keep it mostly a blended family affair. Mary Kay's brother, Timmy, gave her away. The maid of honor was Mary Kay's teenage daughter, Mary Claire. The couple's two children, seven-year-old Alexis and eight-year-old Audrey, were the flower girls. Adding perspective to the spectacle, one of the bridesmaids was a woman Mary Kay met in prison. A horde of media surrounded the winery but only *Entertainment Tonight* had exclusive access to the ceremony. It was rumored *ET* had paid six figures for the right to interview Vili and Mary Kay and cover the wedding ceremony. Maybe love conquers all after all.

Maybe not. Mary Kay continues to describe her life with Vili in glowing terms and as not much different than other married couples with blended families and two children in the legal custody of another family member. But Vili may be showing some warning signs that all is not well in the marriage.

According to the *New York Daily News*, an officer in SeaTac, Washington, stopped a Cadillac for speeding on December 22, 2005. Vili was behind the wheel and appeared intoxicated. Another male was in the passenger seat. Vili was arrested for speeding and driving while intoxicated. The Cadillac was registered to Mary Kay. A jury convicted Vili of DUI in April 2006.

Vili also told *People Magazine* in 2006 that he sometimes thinks about how his life would have been had he not had sex with Mary Kay when he was thirteen. He also admitted to tension between him and Mary's children. It appears that the couple live on the money they received for the TV rights to their wedding, but Vili aspires to ply his creative talent in a tattoo studio.

On the seventy-fifth anniversary of the Lindbergh kidnapping, *Time* did a feature on the top twenty crimes of the twentieth century. "Mary Kay Letourneau's Forbidden Love, 1998" was included. With or without a bipolar diagnosis, Mary Kay's "crime of the century" certainly fits the teacher/lover category of female sexual offenders discussed in chapter 6.[4] But Mary Kay was not the last teacher to become a lover in the classroom.

Debra Beasley LaFave

The mother of a fourteen-year-old boy gets a phone call. The caller tells the mother that her son was seen spending a lot of time with a beautiful twenty-three-year-old middle school teacher, Mrs. LaFave. The boy's mother confronts the boy, who admits to a sexual relationship. She calls the police. With the boy's reluctant cooperation, investigators tape-record conversations between teacher and student.

As I listened to the tapes, it was difficult to tell that an adult female, let alone a teacher, was talking to the boy. The words and the quality of the voice were clearly that of a young adolescent girl. At one point in the conversation, the boy told the teacher she could come over to his house because his mother was out. They had this exchange.

LaFave: "Positive?"
Boy: "Yeah."
LaFave: "Promise?"
Boy: "Yes."
LaFave: "Pinky promise? Say pinky promise."
Boy: "Pinky promise."
LaFave: "All right."

When the unsuspecting teacher pulls up to the boy's house on July 21, 2004, she is surrounded by police. She is annoyed and doesn't understand why the police were involved. She said, "I was more thinking of it as being a young girl who just got caught with her boyfriend. And we shouldn't piss [off] our parents."

Debra Beasley LaFave was arrested and slapped with two separate sets of charges because the sexual activity occurred in two separate counties. After consulting with her attorney, John Fitzgibbons, Debra pleaded not guilty to four felony counts of lewd and lascivious battery and one count of lewd and lascivious exhibition. Each count carried a maximum fifteen-year prison term. Fitzgibbons made his defense strategy clear from the start: The twenty-three-year-old teacher was insane when she engaged in multiple sex acts with the fourteen-year-old student. After a hearing Fitzgibbons announced to the press that several mental health experts had examined his client since her arrest and their findings would explain what happened in this case. Without offering a diagnosis, Fitzgibbons said, "Debbie has some profound emotional issues that are not her fault." I wondered if this was the beginning of another abuse excuse defense.

Pushed by the boy's parents, prosecutors in both counties offered plea agreements stipulating that Debra must serve some prison time. Debra and her defense team rejected the offers, hoping to convince a jury of her emotional problems and avoid being sent to prison. When the boy's mother learned that Court TV planned to cover the first trial, she quickly moved to protect her son from having to testify on national television. At a hearing a psychologist testified that requiring the boy to testify with all the media coverage could be detrimental to the boy's emotional well-being. A new plea agreement stipulating no jail time was offered and accepted just before the first trial, in Hillsborough circuit court, was to begin.

On November 22, 2005, Debra was sentenced to three years of house arrest and seven years of probation, along with a number of other requirements such as registering as a sex offender, participating in sex offender treatment programs, wearing an electronic monitoring device, revocation of her teaching certificate, and prohibition against any contact with the victim.

On December 8, 2005, the judge in the second county refused to accept the new plea agreement. He announced that any deal letting Debra avoid prison time "shocked" his conscience, then he set a trial date for April 10, 2006. Caught between the boy's mother, who was trying to protect her son from national scrutiny, and a recalcitrant judge insisting on jail time, the prosecutor dropped all charges against Debra in Ocala County. No charges. No trial.

With no official opportunity for Debra to offer an explanation for her deviant behavior, she told the media that she wanted everyone to know her story so they could understand why she seduced one of her students. She went to the airwaves to tell her tale.

During an interview with Matt Lauer in 2006 on NBC's *Dateline*, Debra admitted that she was experiencing emotional problems and talked about her childhood and the trauma in her past. She discussed her rape at age thirteen by a boyfriend, which she believed set the stage for her twisted view of sex. She told Lauer: "I kind of developed this idea that it was my role. In order to make a man, guy, boy, happy—I had to do my part, which was pleasing him in that way."

I knew that her decision to never tell anyone about the rape prevented Debra the opportunity to learn that she, as a young girl, was developing a seriously dysfunctional attitude about interpersonal relationships and sexual behavior. And I was not surprised that by age fifteen she was drinking heavily and had attempted suicide, at least twice, once by slitting her wrists. At the time I wondered if she was a budding borderline personality disorder.

Inside, Debra appeared to be a smart but troubled young woman. Outside, she definitely was model material. But after a brief stint of posing for a car magazine, Debra got serious with her goal of becoming a teacher. In short order, Debra enrolled at the University of South Florida, majored in English, stopped drinking, and got into a stable relationship. Her grades were good and things were going well for Debra. Yet she was having bouts with mood swings. She saw a psychiatrist who told her she was depressed and prescribed Zoloft. At first the antidepressant worked, but later she said she experienced no improvement.

In April 2001, about a year before Debra was scheduled to graduate from college and some four years before she was arrested, her older sister, Angela Beasley, who was five months pregnant, was killed when a drunk army officer rammed a jeep into her car. At the officer's court martial, Debra testified that her sister's death left her depressed, angry, and unable to concentrate on anything except her sister's death. Debra's mother confirmed that Debra had been an emotional mess since Angela's death. Sometime after her arrest, Debra speculated that her sister might have been able to help her avoid her inappropriate responses to her student. In 2006, she told Lauer, ". . . she knew me well. And she always could tell if I was doing something that I shouldn't be doing."

In 2002 Debra graduated and took a job as an eighth grade reading teacher at a middle school in a Tampa suburb. By all accounts her first year as a teacher was successful. No one saw the trouble to come.

After her first year of teaching, Debra married Owen LaFave, the man she had been dating for about five years. He was smart, charming, romantic, and also model material. Debra had it all—a teaching career and a husband most women only dream about. Or so it seemed. Debra struggled with sexual problems in the marriage and, in spite of medication, serious bouts of depression and mood swings. Then she began to medicate herself with alcohol—lots of alcohol.

Starting her second year of teaching, Debra became an instant hit with students, even though she claimed she was "oblivious" to the impact she was having on the boy students. When Debra attended a football game in support of one of her friends, the coach, the young football players took notice. One fourteen-year-old in particular.

Since the student-athlete was not in her class, Debra paid little heed to the boy until she and her husband chaperoned a field trip to Sea World. Among the aquatic exhibits, she and the boy talked and got to know each other as more than just student and teacher.

But not much more. At about the same time, Debra's mood swings were becoming more intense. Although she didn't know it at the time, she was on the verge of a serious emotional meltdown.

Colleagues, family, and friends were astounded when Debra regressed from a professional and highly regarded twenty-three-year-old schoolteacher at the beginning of the school year to somebody who resembled one of her most difficult problem students. She seemed immature, listened to rap, smoked, and wore sexually provocative clothes. Debra was also spending a lot of time with a young student-athlete. Very soon she couldn't stop thinking about him.

Debra invited the boy into her classroom, they flirted, and she kissed him. A few days later, the boy returned but brought a friend with him. Debra claims the boy held her against a wall and exposed her breasts to his friend. She felt violated. The boy told investigators a different story. He reported that he asked Mrs. LaFave to flash him and his friend and she willingly raised her shirt, exposing her breasts to the teenagers.

Only Debra and the two teenaged boys know the true story, but everybody agrees that about a week later Debra had sex with the fourteen-year-old for the first time. By her own account, Debra drove to Ocala, about a hundred miles from Tampa, where the boy was staying with a cousin. She brought the two boys back to her apartment and ordered pizza and a pay-per-view movie. While the cousin watched the movie Debra led the boy to an upstairs bedroom and gave him oral sex.

Matt Lauer and I must have had the same thought. Why would a former rape victim initiate sex with somebody who had assaulted her a few days earlier? Debra told Lauer: "Well you gotta understand you've never been raped. You get caught up in a lot of emotions that are confusing and you don't understand. You don't understand why when somebody does something negative that you like it." Debra then went on to give a snippet of her emotionally absent father's negative parenting practices, which, she claimed, created an association of negative attention with love. She later said she was in the mode of wanting to please the boy, apparently a throwback to the impact of her rape as a teen. Debra must have needed a lot of negative attention and love because she continued to manufacture ways to have sex with the boy, like a teenager in love, until his mother found out and stepped in.

So there you have it. Without making excuses, Debra tells us she thinks she seduced a fourteen-year-old boy because her father was emotionally absent and she was a rape victim when she was thirteen. All this pushed her backward, from an adult teacher to a teenager in love. And had her sister been alive she may have detected the warning signs and put a stop to it before Debra went over the edge. But what about the medication and the mood swings?

Debra's attorney, John Fitzgibbons, hired three psychiatrists to evaluate Debra. Each arrived at the same conclusion. Debra was suffering from a serious mental illness: bipolar disorder. As we learned previously, when bipolar disorder is misdiagnosed as depression and treated with antidepressants, the bipolar symptoms, especially the manic episodes, can become more frequent and severe. And one of the symptoms of the manic phase can be impulsive behavior such as impulsive sexual behavior. It appeared that the defense had the support necessary to convince a jury that Debra was bipolar and had been misdiagnosed and treated for depression while her cases were settled without going to trial.

On November 24, 2006, Debra gave a statement to CNN's Nancy Grace about the media ignoring her bipolar diagnosis and challenged everybody "... to read a book or an article on bipolar illness." I was impressed. I contacted Debra's attorney and requested a series of interviews as an opportunity for Debra to tell her story, including her struggle with bipolar disorder, in this chapter. I thought her personal and candid account would help guide parents and professionals to a better understanding and prevention of teacher sexual misconduct.

Through her attorney, Debra declined. He added that he didn't anticipate his client would ever speak publicly about her case again. I understand and wish her well as she works on her recovery.

Debra and Mary Kay are only two, but they are arguably the most well-known female teacher sex offenders. Their cases are unusual because most cases of child sexual abuse do not involve a bipolar diagnosis, with or without a history of personal childhood trauma. I wondered how many more bipolar teachers were out there.

JENNIFER LYNN SANCHEZ

On December 22, 2005, Jennifer Lynn Sanchez, thirty-one, was arrested for having sex with a seventeen-year-old student at Buena Vista Continuation High School in Taft, California. In January 2006, Sanchez was formally charged with unlawful sexual intercourse, oral copulation, and sodomy. On June 30, 2006, the math teacher was sentenced to probation but no incarceration because of her history of mental problems. In exchange for pleading no contest to one misdemeanor count of unlawful sexual intercourse, all felony charges were dismissed. If she complied with the conditions set down by the court she would avoid a year in the county jail and have the opportunity to expunge her record of a sex charge.

Jennifer was not required to register as a sex offender but was ordered, as a condition of her probation, to receive psychiatric care, including appropriate medications. The diagnosis: bipolar disorder.

With bipolar defense becoming so popular with attorneys and mental health experts in cases of teachers sexually abusing students, perhaps Matthews and her colleagues should entertain adding a new category to their typology of female sexual offenders.[5] I think Bipolar-Teacher/Lover seems to have currency.

Other teachers abuse for a variety of reasons, and some seem familiar.

Sandra "Beth" Geisel

In June 2005, Christian Brothers Academy high school English teacher Sandra "Beth" Geisel was fired after she was caught having sex in a car with a teenage boy. Police subsequently charged her with raping a sixteen-year-old student, once in her home in a suburb of Albany, New York, and a second time in the press box on the CBA football field. She was also facing charges for a possible third sexual encounter with the boy. Mrs. Geisel was forty-two and a mother of four.

In a strange twist, Beth's attorney announced on August 5, 2005, that she was considering suing the sixteen-year-old because Beth was drunk when she had sex with him at her home and could neither have given her consent nor raped him. Too drunk to give her consent, so the boy is criminally responsible? How about the tryst in the field box? There's more.

According to affidavits filed by a couple of teenage boys, Mrs. Geisel gave "hand jobs" to a couple of boys in the back of a school bus, allowed her house to be used for a teenage party that included alcohol, and had sex separately with two boys after the party while her son was in the house. On another occasion she went to one boy's house and had sex with him and another boy who "took turns having vaginal sex with her." On another occasion Beth invited a boy to the press box at the school's football field, where she bent over a table and "had vaginal sex" while other students were listening nearby.

Apparently Beth and her attorney had second thoughts about the civil suit because they accepted a plea agreement requiring the former teacher to plead guilty to one count of rape in the third degree and one count of driving while intoxicated as a misdemeanor. According to the district attorney, a plea agreement was offered to protect the boy from "potentially hostile public questioning that is part of any trial," and the family was satisfied that "justice had been done."

Judge Stephen Herrick accepted Beth's acceptance of responsibility for her actions, then sentenced her to a mere six months in jail, which included time already served. Taking into account that Beth, by all accounts, was a good teacher before alcohol sent her into a spiral of sexual misconduct, he also ordered the former teacher to be placed in a residential treatment program for alcoholism. She would also need to serve ten years of supervised probation and register as a sex offender.

Judge Herrick told Beth, "You crossed the line from teacher to consort, and that's totally unacceptable." Then he stunned the courtroom: "The sixteen-year-old is a victim in the statutory sense only. He certainly was not victimized by you in any sense of the word." Apparently the good judge did not do his homework. Then he compounded his error: "You misunderstood attention as affection and failed to realize you were being manipulated and sexually abused, and you became a playmate." I recognized the "blame the victim" excuse. Gender bias in these cases is alive and well. I could not think of one case where a male teacher who molests a female student was called a victim. For very good reasons, the boy's parents were outraged.

MARGARET DE BARRAICUA

On a late Saturday afternoon in February 2005, Sacramento police approached a suspicious car parked behind an elementary school. When they looked inside the front seat they were surprised to find a thirty-year-old high school English teacher, Margaret De Barraicua, having sex with one of her students, a sixteen-year-old boy. Police were even more surprised when they looked in the rear of the car and were greeted by Margaret's two-year-old son strapped in a safety seat. Margaret was arrested and carted off to jail. The sixteen-year-old was questioned then turned over to his parents. The two-year-old was placed with his father, Margaret's husband.

The boy, a special education student at McClatchy High School, told police that having sex with his teacher was his idea and it happened only one other time. He said Mrs. De Barraicua never coerced him into having sex or threatened him to keep him quiet. On the other hand, Margaret told authorities she was in love with the boy and had an ongoing romantic relationship with him. She admitted to four separate sexual encounters, the first at her house in December, and the rest in her car. Margaret was charged with four felony counts of statutory rape.

It all began when Margaret was placed at McClatchy as an intern teacher by her program at California State University in Sacramento. Authorities reported that teacher interns are subjected to all the screening required of any teacher in a public school, including a criminal check and fingerprinting. The screening found nothing amiss in her background to suggest she would be a threat to children, and no complaints about her teaching surfaced.

At a preliminary hearing in July 2005, Margaret's attorney argued that his client was sorry and remorseful. He asked the judge to reduce the four felony charges to a single misdemeanor. The prosecutor stood firm and argued in favor of the four felonies because the young intern had violated her position of trust as a teacher by taking advantage of a vulnerable special education student, not once, but four times.

A legion of supporters, including college professors, teachers, friends, neighbors, and family members wrote letters to the judge describing Margaret as a loving mother, an excellent student, a devout Catholic, and a valuable member of the community. Her actions with the boy, most argued, were totally out of character.

A reverend who was a family friend even tried to deflect responsibility away from Margaret. He wrote that the boy should share some responsibility because he consented to the sexual encounters. I wondered if the reverend would have said the same thing had the student been a girl and the teacher a male. Some people who should know better still don't seem to understand the power differential between an adult in a position of authority and a child, regardless of the gender. And some still don't understand that children are *never* qualified to give consent to inappropriate sexual behavior.

In a strange twist, the prosecutor found unintentional support for his position in a letter written by Margaret's brother, a middle school teacher. Her brother told the judge that his sister sought his advice when she first started her intern position at McClatchy. Apparently some of her students were sexually inappropriate and he advised her to establish clear boundaries with any student who approached her sexually. In effect the prosecutor argued that De Barraicua ignored her brother's advice and knew what she was doing when she stepped across the line with her sixteen-year-old student. She should be held accountable for her actions, he argued.

Margaret's attorney never revealed any kind of a trial defense based upon childhood trauma or mental health issues; no abuse excuse, no Bipolar-Teacher/Lover excuse, no "the victim made me do it" excuse. Instead, he argued against requiring his client to register as a sex offender, which would prevent her from becoming a teacher again, because this was her first criminal arrest and she had no history of inappropriate sexual behavior with children. In the end, Margaret pleaded guilty to four felony counts of statutory rape as stipulated in a plea agreement offered by the prosecution but modified by the court.

On November 18, 2005, Margaret was sentenced to one year in the county jail, instead of prison, and five years formal probation. The judge did not require Margaret to register as a sex offender providing she abided by the conditions of her five-year probation.

Little was revealed in court documents about why Margaret had sex with one of her students, but her father, a retired Air Force medical technician who now works as a physician's assistant, tried to explain his daughter's inappropriate behavior to the judge. Without giving details, he wrote that his daughter was overwhelmed with a complex set of stressors and emotions.

Stress has been shown to be a contributing factor in a lot of child abuse cases, but is seldom, if ever, the core reason for the inappropriate behavior, especially the sexual abuse of a child. Also, teachers who don't seem especially stressed but are troubled in other ways find novel ways to seduce children.

PAMELA ROGERS TURNER

Go into any online chat room popular with teenagers and you will find lots of innocent comments from adolescents searching for friends. Many adolescents connect directly with others through cell phones and the Internet. Sometimes adults use the Internet to enter a child's world.

During a cyberspace chat, Pamela Turner told a thirteen-year-old boy that she thought he was cute. Soon, cyberspace gave way to sexual space and the twenty-eight-year-old teacher from Centertown Elementary School in McMinnville, Tennessee, initiated a sexual relationship with the boy, the son of a close friend. The sexual abuse went on for about three months before she was caught.

In February 2005 Pamela was charged with thirteen counts of statutory rape and fifteen counts of sexual battery. Initially, Pamela pled not guilty to all charges and a trial was set for November 2005. If convicted on all counts, she faced nearly a century in prison. When the boy's mother told prosecutors that she wanted to avoid putting her son and the family through the stress of a trial, a plea agreement was crafted, allowing Pamela to plead no contest to four charges of sexual battery by an authority figure.

At sentencing on August 12, 2005, a possible hundred years in a Tennessee prison dissolved into 270 days in the Warren County Jail. An eight-year sentence was suspended but she was ordered to serve seven years and three months on supervised probation, register as a sex offender, surrender her teaching certificate for life, and have no contact with the boy. The sentence also stipulated that she could not profit from the case in any way and barred her from granting interviews for eight years.

Pamela was a model prisoner and was released from jail after six months for good behavior. She apparently left her good behavior in jail because she soon began contacting the boy, a violation of her probation. She was arrested again on April 24, 2006, on charges that she had sent text messages, nude photos, and sex videos of herself to the boy using her father's cell phone, as well as contacting the boy through her Web site and blogs. Cybersex gone wild.

On July 14, 2006, an unsympathetic judge denied Pamela's impassioned plea for another chance to rehabilitate herself. He revoked her probation and ordered her to serve the remainder of the suspended seven-year prison sentence at the Tennessee State Prison for Women. But that didn't stop Pamela. In January 2007 she pled guilty to sending nude photos of herself to the boy and received two additional years in prison. Some of the pictures showing Pamela clad in underwear and dancing provocatively surfaced on the Internet.

So what went wrong with this young woman that led her to carry on a sexual relationship, openly and defiantly, with a young boy in spite of facing very serious prison time? A clinical psychologist hired by her family testified at the July sentencing that Turner suffered from a sexual addiction. She also said that Pamela experienced a great deal of trauma in her life and suffered from significant post-traumatic stress. Her final conclusion was that Pamela was extremely immature and vulnerable. The psychologist also argued against a prison sentence because Pamela might be vulnerable to same-sex advances if incarcerated.

Pamela's history offers few clues that would indicate trauma and a sexual addiction. She hails from a sports-oriented family. Her father had been the girls' basketball coach at Clarkrange High School for nearly thirty years, winning two state championships. Pamela played on one of the championship teams coached by her father. After high school Pamela remained interested in sports and coaching. She graduated from Tennessee Tech University with a degree in education and for about a year and a half she taught physical education in the Warren County school system in McMinnville. She was also a coach.

Pamela stayed close to the sports tradition when she married Christopher Turner on July 26, 2003. He was the head coach for the Warren County High School boys' varsity basketball team in McMinnville. But problems in the Turner marriage surfaced early and were ongoing for several months before she was arrested. He filed for divorce in January 2005.

Like most female teachers who cross sexual boundaries with their students, school officials initially saw Pamela as a good teacher and an excellent role model for students. She was beautiful. She was athletic. But she also liked showing off her body. In her past she was Ms. Monday Nitro of World Championship Wrestling at spring break festivities in 1997. Although many young women today enjoy flaunting their looks, in Pamela's case, her background may have been rife with symptoms of narcissism and compulsive sexual behavior no one bothered to explore.

KIMBERLY CORDREY-MCKINNEY

In October 2005 Maryland State Police and the Department of Social Services investigated a report that Kimberly Cordrey-McKinney, a thirty-year-old teacher, was having sex with a sixteen-year-old boy who was a student at the high school where she taught. The boy was not in any of her classes, but the two connected via steamy conversations and text messaging on the boy's cell phone. In November 2005 Kimberly was arrested and charged with several counts including sexual abuse of a minor, child abuse from a custodian, unnatural/perverted sexual practice, and second-degree assault. She entered an Alford plea, which means she didn't admit guilt but conceded the prosecution had enough evidence to convict her.

According to newspaper and television reports, Kimberly admitted she had a three-month sexual "affair" with a student. Or, as she explained, "I loved him the best way I knew how." I wondered what it was about teacher-student or adult-child love she didn't understand. And I wondered when sexual abuse of a child suddenly becomes an "affair." Sexual predators will love the new lexicon.

NOTES

1. Associated Press, "2,500 Educators Punished for Sex Abuse in Last 15 Years," *Arizona Daily Star*, October 21, 2007, p. A4.

2. For a review of prevalence rates and theoretical concepts presented in this chapter, see Robert J. Shoop, *Sexual Exploitation of Students: How to Spot It, and How to Stop It* (Thousand Oaks, CA: Corwin Press, 2003).

3. For a comprehensive examination of the Mary Kay Letourneau case, see Greg Olsen, *If Loving You Is Wrong* (New York: St. Martin's Press, 1999).

4. J. Matthews, R. Mathews, and K. Speltz, "Female Sexual Offenders: A Typology," in *Family Sexual Abuse*, ed. M. Q. Patton (Newbury Park, CA: Sage Publications, 1991), pp. 199–219.

5. Ibid.

8

THE OTHER SIDE
OF CLERGY ABUSE

BRIDES OF CHRIST
FALLEN FROM GRACE

O n June 13, 2002, the Catholic bishops of the United States met in Dallas to formulate a response to the burgeoning problem of child sexual abuse by priests. The president of the US Conference of Catholic Bishops (USCCB), Bishop Wilton Gregory, opened the conference with a moving call for forgiveness, an appeal to victims to report clergy sexual abuse, and a charge to all abusive priests to turn themselves in. His voice filled with passion as he attacked the failure of Church leaders to stand up and do what was right for the children. After hearing from Scott Appleby, a historian of Catholicism in the United States, and four victims of priest sexual abuse, the bishops gathered together to address the tragic issue.

After much debate and soul searching, the bishops overwhelmingly approved the Charter for the Protection of Children and Young People on June 14, 2002. The charter was divided into four sections. The first section called for parishes and dioceses to reach out and offer support to clergy sexual abuse victims. The second section called for all allegations of clergy sexual abuse to be reported to appropriate local civil authorities as well as be investigated by the diocese according to Canon Law. Section three was the establishment of a national Office for Youth and Child Protection at the USCCB and a national review board to monitor its work. The final section addressed prevention and called for the implementation of a number of preventive measures, including the removal of any abusive cleric from ministry.

The USCCB also commissioned a comprehensive study to survey the extent of sexual abuse by priests. All dioceses and religious orders of men in the United States were surveyed to determine the number of allegations and the number of priests and deacons accused of sexually abusing minors. Lingering voices of denial and minimization were muted when the John Jay College of Criminal Justice in New York released its findings. The results indicated that approximately 4 percent of all priests were credibly accused of sexually abusing children and youth during the years 1950 to 2002.[1]

While the actions by the USCCB were clearly a response to the growing problem of abusive priests, the policies, procedures, and programs contained in the charter seem to encompass any man or woman who sexually abuses a child within the household of the Church, but it was not binding on members of religious orders. The Catholic Church does not have jurisdiction over religious orders because members of religious orders report to leaders of their order who are accountable to Rome, not to diocesan bishops. Rome is the spiritual head but the bishops make the decisions. Most nuns belong to a religious order.

A female victim of sexual abuse by nuns and an activist for victims of clergy abuse offers this view: "Nuns can abuse children, teens, and vulnerable adult women in their care and NOT be held responsible for the healing of these victims and their equally devastated families, nor to provide restorative justice. Women religious are autonomous. Bishops have no real authority over nuns. Nuns are not included under the dictates of the Dallas Charter. They chose not to be. They answer only to the provincials of each

order and to Rome. Ah, Rome, Rome, the invisible, absentee land-
lord who can't be reached by injured tenants nor counted on to
respond honestly and justly when systems and people are broken.
NO ONE is approachable, reachable, or responsible to make the
improvements necessary for fullness of life." Her story of abuse by
nuns is presented at the end of this chapter.

So the charter does not apply to nuns. Does it really matter?
While I have had a number of patients who told me about verbal
threats of being banished to burn in hell and harsh punishment
with rulers and paddles by nuns in Catholic schools, reports of
nuns sexually abusing anybody were rare. In more than thirty
years of treating perpetrators of sexual offenses, including women,
not a single nun was referred for evaluation or treatment. Of
course I was aware of the practice of keeping the secret within the
Church and sending offending clerics to Church-sanctioned treatment facilities. Instead of referrals, I heard rumors. But I learned
that hundreds of victims of female clergy, as well as colleagues
who were better connected with the religious community than I,
knew the rumors were true.

In 1994 Paul Duckro, John Chibnall, and Ann Wolf of Jesuit-run
St. Louis University designed a survey specifically for Catholic sisters to assess the prevalence and impact of sexual abuse in childhood, sexual exploitation in professional relationships, and sexual
harassment in ministry. Several women religious congregations
nationally commissioned the study. After completing a pilot study
using three communities of sisters in the St. Louis area, Duckro
and his associates modified and expanded their project in preparation for launching the only national scientific survey of the
sexual victimization experiences of sisters ever conducted. The
results were disturbing.

The Leadership Conference of Women Religious (LCWR),
which was one of the major supporters of the study, expressed
concern that the results of the study might be taken out of context
and should be presented in a responsible manner. In response to

these concerns, Duckro and his associates agreed to prepare scholarly articles for publication in peer-reviewed professional journals, coordinate the timing and dissemination of the final report to "trustworthy" media people, and not do anything that would seek publicity or sensationalize the findings.

When the results of the study were published quietly in a respected religious research journal in 1998, the media hardly took notice.[2] Nearly five years later, Bill Smith, a reporter for the *St. Louis Post Dispatch*, published a story on the study, which was followed by subsequent reports about the study by religious and national media.[3] Soon, concerns within the Catholic religious community about a "cover-up of silence" and media distortions of the findings surfaced.

Other Catholics were compassionate and expressed more concern about the sexual abuse of women religious in their communities than a cover-up. As Precious Blood Sister Andree Fries, who was president of the LCWR when the study was conducted, told the *Catholic Telegraph*, "The results were not a big surprise. All of us had been dealing with the after-effects" of sexual abuse experienced by community members, especially those abused as children.[4] Like it or not the sexual abuse of and by nuns was under a microscope. What did the microscope reveal?

Nearly one in five nuns reported having been sexually abused as a child. This figure (about 19 percent) is a bit lower than the range of 30 to 40 percent of sexual abuse found in the female population of the United States. Like the general population of females, nuns reported that most abusers were male family members or friends. No real surprises there. That 6 percent were abused as a child by priests or other male religious was not too surprising either, now that more was known about the extent of clergy sexually abusing children. The real eye-opener was that a little more than 3 percent of the nuns surveyed identified their child sexual abuser as a nun or other female religious, about half the rate of priest abuse.

When asked about experiences of sisters' sexual exploitation during religious life (officially defined as sexually oriented behavior in the context of a professional relationship characterized by an inherent power differential such as teacher-student, counselor-client, doctor-patient, pastor-congregant, spiritual director-directee, or formation director-novice relationships), a little over 12 percent reported such abuse. Of these about half were exploited by a priest or other male religious figure and about 25 percent were sexually exploited by another sister. Nuns seem to be sexually abusing at a rate of about half that of priests.

Like the general population, children who have been sexually abused tend to be at a higher risk for future abuse and exploitation as an adult. Nuns who experienced childhood sexual abuse were at greater risk for sexual exploitation in religious life (about 30 percent exploited) than those not sexually abused as children (about 9 percent exploited). And only a little over 1 percent of the sisters who were exploited filed a formal complaint against their exploiter.

How about sexual harassment and the sanctity of the Church? Compared with national studies indicating that a majority of women experience some form of sexual harassment in the workplace, nuns seem safer from this unwanted intrusion in their ministry. Only about one sister in ten reported experiencing work sexual harassment. Not surprising, the largest categories of harassers were men (48 percent male lay, 39 percent male religious), but a little over 11 percent reported female harassers, including a female partner in ministry (about 3 percent).

Here's a particularly interesting finding: sexual harassment by a female religious or lay figure was more likely to involve genital sexual behavior than sexual harassment by a male religious or lay figure, with the female religious figure twice as likely to involve genital behavior than male religious figures, as well as male religious and lay figures combined.

Nuns who were sexually abused as children were also at

greater risk for sexual harassment during their religious life (about 15 percent harassed) than sisters who were not sexually abused as children (about 8 percent).

Overall, two sisters in five (about 40 percent) have been sexually victimized at some point in their lifetime, and close to 29 percent have been sexually victimized at some point during their religious life. Of the sisters who have been sexually victimized, 43 percent have experienced multiple (two or more) forms of sexual victimization. It seems that sisters are not strangers to these harmful behaviors.

The researchers pointed out that the results of the study more likely fall into the category of under-reporting than over-reporting. Disclosure of sexual abuse is difficult for most victims and can be especially troubling to many sisters who have never disclosed before or received any form of therapy to deal with the trauma. In support of the under-reporting hypothesis is the finding that only a few nuns (about 8 percent) filed a formal complaint against their harasser.

Clearly, the results of the Duckro study show nuns as victims of sexual victimization with long-term serious consequences common to most victims of sexual abuse: anger, shame, anxiety, confusion, and depression. And many victimized nuns were also having difficulty imagining God as Father and they experienced prayer difficulties as a result of the abuse.

As Sister Andree Fries pointed out, "We recognize that sexual abuse is a terrible violation of human dignity and a betrayal of trust, as well as a serious crime. Abuse has been perpetrated against the most vulnerable—children and women, as well as vulnerable men."[5] But what about nuns who sexually abuse?

In 2002, Donna Markham, the former director of Southdown Institute, a facility in Ontario, Canada, specializing in serving priests and religious men and women, presented findings from an ad hoc sample of women religious who were treated there.[6] With no distinction made between adult sexual encounters with peers and sexual exploitation of vulnerable adults, she found that about 9 percent of religious sisters admitted to sexual contact with other adults during religious life. She also found that less than 1 percent of religious sisters admitted to sexual contact with minors.

Since we know from other research that only about a third of all suspected sex offenders confess to their crimes when evaluated, Markham's results may be an underestimate of the problem.[7] On the other hand, her sample was drawn from a clinical population, sisters in treatment, so the prevalence rate may be lower in the general population of religious sisters.

Nobody has any idea of the actual number of nuns who sexually abuse children or adults, but the Duckro and Markham studies shine more light into the dark corner of the Church, thought to be occupied only by renegade priests.

In August 2006 an echo of the cascade of successful civil law suits in cases of predator priests rumbled across the Louisville, Kentucky, landscape. This time, an order of nuns, the Sisters of Charity of Nazareth, agreed to settle lawsuits by forty-five plaintiffs who alleged that they were sexually abused at orphanages and schools supervised by nuns between 1930 and 1970. While most of the plaintiffs reported abuse by a longtime orphanage chaplain, Reverend Herman Lammers, this was no simple case of another clergy member sexually abusing vulnerable children. No, this time several nuns and a couple of laymen were also indicated. One plaintiff reported abuse by the reverend and by a nun.

William McMurray, the plaintiff's attorney, told Peter Smith of the *Courier-Journal*, "This marks the first time in United States history any victims of a Catholic orphanage have recovered (a payment due to) childhood sexual abuse. The settlement restores dignity to folks that have deserved it for so many decades."[8]

Attorneys who have litigated cases of clerical sexual abuse over the past decade or so report significantly fewer cases, but there are a growing number of victims suing nuns. The reasons sexual abuse by nuns has been slow to surface are many. At the top of the list are our cultural biases about gender roles, victims, and victimizers. Our society fully expects that men will be victimizers and females will be victims, especially in sex crimes. Few people expect women to rape, pillage, and plunder. Another major reason rests in the main cultural belief that clergy, any clergy, adhere closely to God's commandments and would not sexually abuse children or sexually exploit others. This is especially true for priests and nuns, who pledge sexual abstinence.

As people were not ready to hear about priests as predators just a few years ago, they certainly are not yet ready to hear about nuns as sexual offenders. Thus, victims of sexual abuse by sisters face a double whammy. Their sexual abuser broke not one but two taboos: Females do not sexually abuse, and nuns certainly do not sexually abuse. Even as our culture fights its way through the two broken taboos, victims of sexual abuse by sisters are faced with the daunting task of assigning responsibility for the abuse within a complex labyrinth of more than 450 women's religious orders that often have used similar defensive strategies demonstrated by the Catholic Church earlier on in the sexual abuse by clergy scandal.

Often the victim's pain and suffering created by sexual abuse by clergy is compounded when religious organizations responsible for the abuse take such a defensive posture. Some litigation has dragged on for years, an eternity for victims who hunger for recognition, redemption, and healing. But other victims hope to see their perpetrators in another kind of court.

Although hundreds of nuns have been accused of sexual abuse, only a few are accused formally in civil court, and fewer still in criminal court. But some nuns have been arrested and faced criminal charges. According to the *New York Times*, a seventy-nine-year-old Roman Catholic nun, Norma Giannini, pleaded no contest on November 12, 2007, to two counts of indecent behavior with a child in connection with accusations from two men, now in their fifties.[9] The men accused Giannini of sexual assaults, including intercourse that occurred in numerous locations such as a convent and a classroom in the 1960s, when she was a principal and teacher at St. Patrick's Congregation grade school in Milwaukee. One victim reported he was also sexually abused by Giannini in his home. Sister Giannini, a member of the Sisters of Mercy, is one of the first nuns to face criminal charges for sexual misconduct.

On February 1, 2008, Milwaukee County Circuit Judge M. Joseph Donald first sentenced Sister Giannini to five years in prison on each of two felony charges, stayed the sentences, then sentenced her to a year in the house of correction and ten years probation.[10] She faced up to twenty years in prison. The two victims had given impassioned pleas for prison time for their abuser. One said, "Please don't give her a pass . . . she belongs in prison." Pointing to the devastating long-term effects of the sexual abuse on the two victims, prosecutor Paul Tiffin had argued for at least eight years of prison time, essentially a life sentence for the seventy-nine-year-old Giannini. Reading from a prepared statement, Sister Giannini asked for forgiveness ". . . for all those I've injured." If forgiveness doesn't come she could also be prosecuted for sexually abusing four other boys in the 1960s and 1970s, including one in Chicago.

It took more than forty years to get Sister Giannini in criminal court to face her victims and admit her crimes. Other victims wait but keep their stories out there, hoping somebody will listen and act.

Leading the charge is Ashley Hill, the founder of the first national effort addressing the issue of sexual abuse by women religious. In *Habits of Sin*, the first book to help victims of sexual misconduct by the "Brides of Christ," Hill told her own story of child sexual abuse by a nun and provided a forum for others abused by women religious. The book, published in 1995, remains a "must read" for anyone caught in the quagmire of religious deceit and denial.[11]

In July 2004 the Survivors Network of those Abused by Priests (SNAP) asked the LCWR to allow victims to tell their stories of sexual abuse by nuns at the conference's annual meeting. In conjunction with its request, SNAP held a news conference where several victims of sexual abuse by nuns spoke out for the first time. One victim, Patricia Cahill, described the seduction by a nun when she was fifteen. "She took me under her wing and then into her bed. I didn't know sex between women was an option; she taught me." The nun's sexual control over Patricia continued until she was in her mid-twenties. When Church officials stepped in they followed the tried-and-true method of shuffling offending clerics around various parishes and positions. The nun was removed from her job as principal of an elementary school in New Jersey but continued working at a nursing home where girls serve as volunteers.

Over the years, two members of SNAP and survivors of sexual abuse by Roman Catholic nuns have compiled a list and descriptions of abuses of male and female children, teens, vulnerable adults, and other nuns by members of up to forty different orders of female religious. Approximately 650 cases are documented, including chilling stories of rape, brutality, sexual abuse, and murder. The list gets longer. Over the past year or so an estimated four to five hundred male and female victims of sexual abuse by nuns have come forward to tell their stories. Here are a couple.

ANDREW RICHARDS*

In chapter 6 of this book, Andrew discussed sexual abuse by his mother, other relatives, and being pimped by his father into a child sexual abuse ring in a rural community near his home. And now the rest of Andrew's story.

Near that rural community there was a large Catholic institution that included a seminary and a large convent. Eventually I was passed from the sex abuse ring into the convent. When my relatives dropped me off at the convent, the nuns removed my clothing, bathed me, gave me a laxative and an enema, all to prepare me to enter in a more "pure state." From then on I was only dressed as a female. They disciplined me harshly and I was made to be inordinately submissive and obedient. Many times I was restrained and molested sexually for hours. I was told I was in the company with Jesus as a suffering lamb of God. I felt holy.

After some period of "formation" I was delivered over to another very large Catholic convent (a motherhouse) in a large city. While being transported by the nuns in what was then called a panel truck, I was restrained and mildly sedated.

At the motherhouse, which had an associated asylum for mental patients, I was submitted to a process that seemed designed to erase my sense of self and eliminate any volition to act on my own. At various times I was deprived of food, light, sense of time, restrained, caged, mildly drugged, and electrically over-stimulated. At times I was strung up with my arms above my head and whipped with the kind of whip that stings but does not leave permanent marks.

The associated asylum had cages from the 1800s that mental patients were confined in. At times I was kept in such a cage. I was also electrically tortured with a device that in the past was called a uterine exciter (formerly an electrical device inserted into the uterus to cure women of their "mental problems"). I was also restrained in wet-packs; that involved total wrapping of the body in a rubber sheet surrounded by regular wet sheets (which shrunk as they dried). There were times when I was restrained in bed for days and molested incessantly. The treatment thoroughly "tamed" me and I became supremely compliant.

There were other little boys who went through this process, too, because the nuns took in groups of boys and girls during the summer. Boys had our male clothes taken away. From then on we were dressed as females, either in the novice's habit or other varieties of female clothing including the bride's dresses worn by nuns when they took their vows. A foundation garment used to feminize us boys typically involved wearing a rectal dilator and suppressing the genitalia by a tight girdle.

The whole process seemed aimed at erasing and humiliating my male gender. The nuns continuously promoted the belief in us that we were privileged to have an opportunity to atone for the sins of others by suf-

fering with Christ. So, submission, discomfort, and overstimulation were to be accepted willingly, supposedly engendering a form of ecstasy.

The boys and girls who were taken into the convent were formally referred to as "aspirants," just as young prospective nuns are often similarly labeled. Informally, we were called "the servants of the sisters."

The culmination of my stay in the convent was to take part in a pageant. A main theme of the pageant was to have boys perform as girls, dressed in elaborate female attire. The goal of the contest was to determine which of the boys could act the most submissive in a stylized feminine way; the better contestants received lavish praise. Of course the feminine foundation garment described earlier had to be worn. After the pageant I was returned home, and my parents seemed to feel privileged that their son was chosen to spend time with the nuns. Many years later I met a former nun at a survivors' symposium who had lived in that motherhouse. She said she had heard about the pageants.

More than fifty years later, my wife and I went back to the grounds of that convent for me to seek more closure. A very elderly nun came out of the main entrance and greeted us. I told her that I had been an "aspirant" there in the 1930s–1940s. It didn't phase her that I was a male who said that. She only asked if I had become a priest.

At nine years of age I came under control of the nuns at my Catholic grade school. They, no doubt, knew of my prior experience. The nun who taught my class was the primary conduit into the convent in which the grade school teachers resided. My classroom nun was moved along with me to teach each next grade that I was promoted to, thus there would be no loss of continuity.

I was kept after school several days a week to be the object of sex abuse by the nuns. The abuse had an aura of caring, kindness, and love even if discomfort was involved. Again, any discomfort was valued as helping Jesus atone for the sins of others. My classroom nun would say that she gave up a family to serve God and he rewarded her by sending me to her. My classroom teacher and the nun who was the principal, along with selected other nuns, took part in the abuse activities. I was quite a gift to them because I was trained to be so compliant.

The after-school sessions often started with milk and cookies slightly laced with a sedative. On various occasions I would be stripped and bathed, and/or given an enema, or dressed as a girl to do some chore, or restrained and molested. Soft protective cloth around my extremities prevented the restraints from leaving marks.

I recall that upon being returned to my home, my mother would notice some things were different, like my hair being wet; but she did not ask and I did not tell what happened because I thought she would be jealous of other lovers.

During the summer months I would be smuggled into the grade school convent for most of the day or overnight. My classroom nun would meet me in the church basement. She would take me to a storage room, remove my clothes, and dress me in a nun's habit. I would then wait at the top of the stairway leading to the convent while she took another route to unlock the door from the inside. I recall being anxious that the janitor would see me.

On some occasions the nuns would have me provide sexual "service" for the parish priests. I recall being dressed as a nun, and with a nun on each side of me, I was escorted across the sacristy from the nun's side to the priest's side. As we crossed the sacristy we had to genuflect in front of the alter, and I speculated about shocking those who were praying in the church proper by turning around and saying, "I'm a boy!" In later years my wife was amazed that I knew in detail how a nun puts on the wimple and various parts of her habit.

This went on for several years during which time all tuition was waived for me at school. As time went on I wanted it to stop, and I wanted to spend some time playing with other children. As I grew a little resistive, threats were made by the nuns that they would publicly say that I had been extremely inappropriate and that I would be expelled from school. Since I couldn't count on my parents protecting me, I unrealistically prayed that one of my classmate's fathers would be told of my being abused and intercede on my behalf.

The abuse at school ended abruptly one day when I was twelve. As usual the nun asked me to stay after school, and as usual my classmates taunted me about being a teacher's pet. In an attempt to show them that I was not, I stuck my tongue out at the nun behind her back. She caught me, she slapped me, and my silent anger showed. The abuse stopped immediately and she was transferred out of state in the middle of the school year.

I eventually learned to cope in life by watching how other children behaved, having no valid reference myself. I felt like my true identity was with the abusers dressed as a girl. "Normal" behavior seemed unreal to me, but I managed to serve in the military, earn a college degree, and have a family in which the children were not abused.

All of the abuse I underwent was framed in the context of "love." Love of God and love of me. I was never blamed or shamed, and I always felt safe with the abusers. And above all, they said God approved of these special relationships and sacrifices. I never felt responsible for what I later realized was inappropriate behavior. I have never experienced shame or guilt about what happened.

PRISCILLA CLARK[*]

Here is another personal story of sexual abuse by clergy, this time from the perspective of a female victim.

I was raised by my divorced mother in my grandmother's home. My father was adulterous and absolutely not present at anytime in my life. My mom had to work every day and most weekends. Because my freshman year was a failure scholastically at a day school run by the Sisters of Charity, I was sent to a Catholic boarding school for the next three years of high school. I managed to get through my sophomore year relatively unscathed but at the beginning of my junior year, Mother Mary, who had recently returned from a year in Rome, entered my life.

Mother Mary was floor monitor and "mother" to the twenty-seven girls in my class. She lived on the same floor as we did and was assigned the responsibility for our well-being and for our academic and spiritual formation. Mother Mary "groomed" me for a time then began her nightly visits. Each evening when the girls had settled down in their rooms, and lights were out, she quietly left her private room at the end of the hall and came into my room to spend the next one to three hours with me.

I was from a broken home. My mother worked. My father, who had remarried, never came to see me or take me anyplace. My grandmother cared for me but she was elderly. And the parish school nuns treated me differently than they did children who had intact "proper" families. I was a child very much in need of attention and nurturing. Over time Mother Mary made me feel special, listened to, important. She told me she loved me and that I was intelligent and talented. Gradually she began abusing me sexually.

After lights out Mother Mary would enter my room and close the door. She removed her clothing from her waist up including her veil and headpiece. She kissed me at length on my mouth. Then she would pull my head down to her naked breasts and urged me to kiss and suck her nipples. There were constant assurances of how much she loved me yet she degraded my mother and my boyfriend. She also shared confidences about the nuns with whom she lived and girls whom she taught and oversaw.

It didn't matter that I had a roommate whose bed was less than four feet from mine. My roommate also suffered abuse when she had to pretend to sleep each night through my junior year as Mother Mary decimated my body, soul, mind, and future.

During my senior year Mother Mary arranged for me to have a single room though we could not afford one. She also moved herself down to my floor and took on oversight of the seniors. This afforded her easier, safe access to me. Mother Mary also managed to separate me from my best friend by forbidding anyone in the senior class to speak to her.

I never told anyone about what happened to me because I thought I had had an affair with a nun even though I had no sexual attraction for women. Not until 1990 when information about priests who abused children broke in the media, did I begin to figure out that I had been abused sexually, emotionally, spiritually, and physically.

As with so many other victims of sexual abuse, I have had many effects from the abuse: difficulty forming and maintaining healthy relationships, alcohol/chemical abuse, food addiction, chronic depression, thoughts of suicide, self-destructive behaviors, serious and chronic health problems, and a huge burden of shame and self-hatred. The toll this abuse has exacted in my life and the lives of my loved ones is many faceted and ongoing. Mother Mary stole my innocence, enthusiasm, awe, trust, and soul.

I liken sexual abuse by clergy to abortion, the most hated of all sins in the minds of Catholic authority figures. The fledging life of the abuse victim is ripped out and the "fetus" discarded in a trashcan. The Catholic Church fights to protect the lives of the unborn, and rightly so. I agree that all human life is precious from conception to death, yet in its support and cover-up of predatory nuns and priests who have sexually abused children and vulnerable adults, the Catholic Church commits the very sin it abhors. The Catholic Church as a whole, in its deceit and delay when these crimes are exposed, abort their victims. But aren't abuse victims as important as fetuses? Don't we deserve the protection, support, and healing of the Catholic Church so we can live too? Don't throw away the bodies, souls, and lives of your aborted sexual abuse victims. Help us to live.

My hope is that any women or men who were abused by nuns realize that there is help in talking about the abuse and sharing their stories with their churches, their families, their friends, a good therapist. Abuse by priests is out in the open now. Abuse by nuns needs to be dealt with by the Catholic Church, honestly, justly, prayerfully. There is no peace for any of us unless there is justice for each of us. Victims should be the main consideration.

Without question, most people who are drawn to a religious life do so for pure and spiritual reasons. They adhere to whatever vows their respective religion requires with little or no hesitation. They are the selfless, tireless workers of their faith. Yet, like most other professions, some individuals are attracted to religious life in the unrealistic hope of finding a safe haven for their serious emotional problems. They often become disillusioned and even more dysfunctional. Others purposely select a path within a religious community because it provides them with a perfect venue for their perversions: a protective community, lots of prey, and God's wrath. The Holy Trinity of sexual abuse.

Little is known about the sexual abuse by women religious and less is known about why they do it. But psychotherapist Myra Hidalgo, using a systems approach, thinks she is on to something.[12] First, she carves up the Catholic Church into systems, each an interactive and contributing factor in the perpetration of sexual abuse. Then she proposes "a new twist on an old idea," the Cycle of Sexual Trauma. From her analysis of the Catholic Church through this lens, Hidalgo concludes that the Catholic Church is an incestuous family system with ". . . oppressive sexual beliefs; rigid, idealized gender roles; and a shaming, patriarchal leadership style [which] fosters optimal conditions for sexual abuse to emerge and thrive among the Church's most devout followers."[13] So how does sexual shame and sexual trauma foster sexual abuse?

Hidalgo points out that we have known for a long time that many perpetrators of sexual abuse have been victims of childhood sexual trauma, the so-called cycle of abuse, but she expands the net of trauma to capture multiple sources of childhood sexual experiences beyond the traditional concept of direct sexual abuse. Examples are sexual humiliation, gender-based degradation, sexual neglect or gross misinformation, homophobia, stigmatization due to teenage pregnancy or sexually transmitted disease, and any form of sexual disempowerment. She believes that a cycle of sexual trauma, fed by systemic sexual shame, particularly related to homophobia, operates as the root cause of the sexual abuse crisis in the Catholic Church. And the source, according to Hidalgo, can be traced back to the perpetual sexual shame and dysfunction of Catholic leaders since the time of the Church's formation.

Based upon her Cycle of Sexual Trauma model, Hidalgo proposes that priests and nuns are more likely to have been traumatized as youth by sexually shameful beliefs, especially regarding both female sexual expression and homosexuality, than the general population. She argues that this sexual trauma was more likely to have been severe and most likely not to have been resolved before entering the seminary or convent, where there is exposure to more of the same dogma. Taken together the mix feeds the Cycle of Sexual Trauma and places priests and nuns at a higher risk for sexually offending. Hidalgo presents a compelling analysis but additional scrutiny and research is necessary in order to fully support her thesis. For example, one could argue that such a powerful systemic dysfunctional approach to sexuality would produce even greater numbers of abuse by clergy than currently documented. Even so, her Cycle of Sexual Trauma appears worthy of consideration.

Two colleagues and I proposed a concept similar to Hidalgo's Cycle of Sexual Trauma for the general population in 1989. We called it the Abuse of Sexuality, and a later version the Socioculture Abuse of Sexuality. I will discuss our concept in the final chapter of this book with an eye toward prevention.

But, first, a look at girls behaving badly.

Notes

1. John Jay College of Criminal Justice, *The Nature and Scope of the Problem of Sexual Abuse of Minors by Catholic Priests and Deacons in the United States*, Washington, DC: US Conference of Catholic Bishops.

2. John Chibnall, Ann Wolf, and Paul Duckro, "A National Survey of the Sexual Trauma Experiences of Catholic Nuns," *Review of Religious Research* 40 (December 1998): 142–67.

3. Bill Smith, "Nuns as Sexual Victims Get Little Notice," *St. Louis Post Dispatch*, January 4, 2003.

4. Staff report, "Local Congregations Respond to Abuse Report," *Catholic Telegraph*, January 17, 2003, p. 1.

5. Ibid.

6. Donna Markham, "Some Facts about Women Religious and Child Abuse," *Covenant*, September 3, 2002.

7. Gene Abel and N. Harlow, *The Stop Child Molestation Book* (Philadelphia: Xlibris Corporation, 2001).

8. Peter Smith, "Order of Nuns Agrees to Pay $1.5 Million in Abuse Suit," *(Kentucky) Courier-Journal*, August 25, 2006.

9. Catrin Einhorn, "Nun Pleads No Contest in Sex Abuse," *New York Times*, November 13, 2007.

10. Georgia Pabst, "Catholic Nun Sentenced in Abuse of Boy 40 Years Ago," *Milwaukee Journal Sentinel*, February 1, 2008.

11. Ashley Hill, *Habits of Sin* (Philadelphia: Xlibris Corporation, 1995).

12. Myra L. Hidalgo, *Sexual Abuse and the Culture of Catholicism: How Priests and Nuns Become Perpetrators* (New York: Haworth Maltreatment and Trauma Press, 2007).

13. Ibid., p. 68.

9

BAD SEEDS
GIRLS WHO MOLEST AND MURDER

Karen waited until her parents left for work then crept into her brother's room. She looked at her younger brother, Karl, who was awake but having difficulty getting out of bed. He suffered from a mild form of cerebral palsy, and today he just couldn't get his limbs coordinated. Karen went to Karl and offered to help. When Karl reached for his sister's hand, she pushed him down, pulled a rope from her pocket, and quickly tied him spread eagle to the head and foot posts. As Karl struggled with his restraints and screamed for his parents, Karen forcefully masturbated her brother until he ejaculated. She laughed at him when he came and when he threatened to tell their parents later. Karen told Karl their parents would never believe the story, and he would get into a lot of trouble for coming all over himself and the bed.

Most members of our society want to believe that young girls don't commit sexual crimes. They do. But the incidence of girls who sexually abuse remains elusive because recognition and reporting are inhibited by our society's reluctance to accept the notion that females, especially young girls, are capable of such dastardly deeds. They are.

In 1991 the FBI reported that the arrest rate for sexual offenses committed by adolescent girls rose nearly 32 percent between 1980 and 1990.[1] While some studies suggest that about 10 percent of juvenile sexual offenders are girls, most researchers and clinicians believe this figure is lower than the actual rate due to the under-reporting of female sexual abuse in general. Another glimpse of girls behaving badly comes from studies suggesting that anywhere from 2 to 74 percent of childhood sexual abuse victims were abused by a female, often an adolescent girl.[2]

When we examine studies of girls who sexually abuse, we find that the majority of sexual offenses committed by girls under the age of eleven years and an even larger majority by girls ages eleven to seventeen involved hands-on behavior ranging from child molestation to rape. The term "hands-on" means nonconsensual behavior such as sexual kissing, simulated intercourse, breast fondling or sucking, genital fondling, digital or object penetration of the vagina or anus, cunnilingus, fellatio, and intercourse; and many are committing so-called "hands-off" sexual offenses such as making obscene phone calls, voyeurism, exhibitionism, and fetishism. Some girls even get involved in bestiality, prostitution, and pornography.

While most girls sexually offend against family members or someone they know, many abuse strangers, and a majority select either male or female victims, usually twelve years old or younger. How young are our daughters and sisters when they commit their first sexual offense? Very young. The median age seems to be at about nine years, with some as young as five.[3] Perhaps the seeds of sexual misconduct are planted early.

SUSAN DEWEY*

While I waited for Susan Dewey to arrive for her appointment, I studied her school records again. Although she had earned "good" grades from kindergarten through sixth grade, she had been enrolled in mostly special education classes. Periodic evaluations by school psychologists noted that Susan's potential was "below average with significant weakness in auditory/vocal abilities." I knew from my work with dyslexic kids a number of years ago that Susan's school achievement and test scores showed the typical pattern of a learning disabled child. Susan's mother had requested records for the seventh grade through high school but I did not receive them in time for the evaluation. Since I had no idea about how well she did in these grades, I decided to informally assess Susan's reading and comprehension levels before I administered any assessment instruments that required Susan to read, comprehend the material, and respond.

I also knew that I would have to structure the evaluation to accommodate Susan's documented overall low-average intellectual functioning. I was particularly concerned that she would have difficulty understanding the complexities of the warning of confidentiality I had to discuss with her before I could even start the evaluation. In a lot of ways the warning is close to Miranda rights read to suspects who are being arrested. In this case it meant that anything Susan told me, including an admission that she molested two young children, would be used as part of my consultation to her attorney and could show up in a report if her attorney asked me to write one as well as be used as part of my testimony in court. While the warning or so-called full disclosure was required of all forensic psychologists to present prior to proceeding with the evaluation, it was always a difficult way to establish trust and rapport, even in the best of circumstances.

When Susan came into my office she smiled broadly, introduced herself with a clear and confident voice, then offered her hand. I thought her actions were a bit formal for a girl who was barely eighteen, but often learning disabled kids learn to overcompensate to hide their deficiencies. After we exchanged greetings she took her seat and maintained eye contact as I explained the purpose and procedures of a forensic evaluation. I was careful to explain that I was going to be asking her questions about the charges against her and her statements to me would not be confidential. I also told her that her attorney, Craig Summers, and the court had questions about her risk for recidivism and the need for therapeutic intervention. Her face flushed when I told her the court said it wouldn't do to have her continue molesting three- and four-year-old children. Her attorney and the court wanted to know how much of a risk to other children she was and if she was a good candidate for therapy.

When Susan launched into a full-blown angry denial of the charges, I knew my fears about the warning were real. Susan wasn't ready to face the charges, let alone have me discuss her admission with anyone, even though I knew her attorney told her to be truthful with me. I listened until Susan was finished building a protective wall of denial and rationalizations, then told her we would get back to the allegations later but first I had to have her permission to continue with the evaluation. I added that if she gave me permission to evaluate her I would start with the easy stuff first: her background information.

It was my experience that discussing the charges too early in an interview was usually much less productive than waiting until later, after the person has become used to sharing intimate information. An early confrontation about the charges, as required by the warning, often results in a strong defensive posture and an entrenchment of denial followed by a lower level of cooperation with the evaluation overall.

I told her I understood her position and that I didn't want her to admit to anything that was not true. I again asked for permission. When she started to squirm in her chair and looked at the door, I thought I had lost her. I was wrong. She slowly shifted her eyes from the door to me and said, "My lawyer told me I needed this evaluation. I guess I better do it."

Susan settled down when I asked her about her childhood. She seemed to enjoy talking about her family experiences even though they were hardly typical. She told me her parents were never married and that they only lived together off and on over a two-year period when Susan was a baby.

Although her mother was absent a lot because she had to work three jobs in order to support herself, Susan, and two younger boys, Susan denied any form of neglect or abuse by her mother. Susan described her as a loving and caring mother who interacted with her children in nurturing ways whenever she could. However, Susan also said, "I knew I had to hurry up and grow up to help my mother with my brothers and the house."

She also said that a total of three or four men had lived with her mother, each for about a year, until her mother terminated each relationship. When I asked Susan how she was treated by these men, I expected to hear stories of abuse and neglect so common to families with a stream of live-in boyfriends. I was surprised when Susan said, "They treated us okay, like they were our own father." I was relieved to learn that her mother's boyfriends did not abuse Susan, but my relief was short lived.

Susan's cheerful demeanor changed when she told me that she had been molested when she was about five or six years old. She said, "My brother's friend's father did multiple sex acts on me when I was over at his house once." Susan expressed the fear that many children have after they have been sexually abused: she was afraid that her mother would become angry with her so she never told her. Susan eventually told a friend who may have told Susan's mother, but if Susan's mother knew she never discussed it with Susan. After the abuse, Susan avoided the abuser by "not going over there anymore or having someone else go with me."

It is true that many sexually abused kids, especially those with learning disabilities, have problems with protecting their boundaries and end up being abused again. It was true with Susan. At fifteen Susan met three men, all between the ages of twenty and forty, through a female friend. She said she had no romantic interest in these older men and considered them "friends of my friend."

On one occasion Susan went to the apartment of one of these men for an egg. The man invited Susan inside then overpowered and raped her. Afraid, she did report the rape. Seemingly, Susan didn't learn from her experience with the first man, and went to the apartment of another of these men to use the telephone about a month later. She said, "It happened again but it wasn't so violent. But he threatened to kill me if I told anyone. I didn't." I waited for the story about the third man. Susan went on, "He made advances and I told him I wasn't interested. He insisted and wouldn't let me go and had sex with me against my will."

Susan eventually told some people at the apartment complex where the men lived and someone told Susan's mom. As a result of the report Susan was referred to a sexual abuse counseling program at a local community mental health facility. No charges were ever filed against the men. I hoped the counseling program worked and Susan learned how to make better decisions about relationships and protecting herself. My hopes were dashed.

At seventeen, Susan started dating a nineteen-year-old man. After dating for a few months she had her first consensual intercourse. She said, "It just happened at his house one day. I liked it." When Susan turned eighteen the couple became engaged and told their families about their plans to marry.

She reported that, until a few weeks before the evaluation, she was living with her fiancé and a mutual friend in an apartment. She and her fiancé had been having sex for several months. One night Susan was not feeling well and went to bed. She awoke to find her fiancé on top of her trying to have intercourse. She resisted and told him that she was sick and didn't want to have sex. Susan said, "He wouldn't stop then something happened and he became crazy or something." Susan later threw him out of the house and stopped seeing him. But he wouldn't take no for an answer and he started to harass and stalk her. This time she reported him to the police.

Susan told me she was curious about sex as a child but she did not play sexual games with other children. She explained, "Mother told me it was wrong to touch someone or let someone touch. I wouldn't do something that was wrong." Susan also received information about sexual matters from her mother and sex education classes in school. Her mother told her that sex should be reserved for the person you loved and planned to marry. "Mother also told me about the monthly and where babies come from." Susan's mother, a sex abuse victim herself, was overprotective of Susan and did not let her date until she was about sixteen. Even then, Susan had few dates.

At eighteen, Susan secured employment as a phone solicitor for a local charity. She was fired after about six months because she was unable to solicit the required number of donations. She was determined to be self-sufficient and got a job as a cook at a local fast-food restaurant a couple of weeks later. Susan beamed when she told me she had recently been promoted to cashier and she was sure more promotions were soon to follow.

After I collected all the information I thought I needed about Susan's background, I asked her if she was ready to talk about the allegations. Susan started to fidget again but said she was ready. I encouraged her to begin by telling me what happened. She said immediately that the allegations were untrue. She stared at me right in the eyes, and said, "It's wrong, totally wrong."

I gave her ample time to explain why the allegations were wrong but she couldn't explain why children who were known to be truthful would accuse her of molestation. She then confronted me with pointing out that the four-year-old had actually told the physician who examined the children that "Sandy," not Susan, had molested her. Susan was correct. I countered by asking Susan why she eventually told the police that she did, indeed, engage in inappropriate sexual behavior with these children, if she didn't do it.

Susan looked at the floor. "Before I went into the interview with the investigators from CPS and the police, my case worker told me to admit to it and I wouldn't have to go to jail. I would just get treatment. I wasn't going to do that but I got nervous in the interview. I started to have flashbacks of my own molestation. I got real confused and I admitted to it in order to stop the interview." Susan looked up and added, "It was also getting late and I had to get to work."

I realized that Susan had just told me that she confessed to molesting children in order to get to work on time. This time she refused to confess to anything. Maybe she wasn't working today, I thought.

A few days after I evaluated Susan, Craig Summers called for the results. He was anxious to cut a deal with the prosecutor. I told him that my evaluation confirmed Susan's history of borderline intellectual functioning and learning disabilities. I pointed out that Susan had managed to complete the requirement for a high school diploma, secure gainful employment, and was a resourceful young lady in spite of her deficits.

I also told him that I worried about how her history of multiple personal sexual victimization experiences, including sexual molestation as a young child and four rapes as a teenager, impacted her responses to the two alleged young victims in this case. We discussed the statistics: while only about a third of abused children grow up to become abusers themselves, a large majority of perpetrators of sexual abuse have an abuse history similar to Susan's.

"How about the confession?" Summers asked.

I explained that Susan attempts to present herself as functioning at a level higher than her cognitive abilities allow, but her educational history suggested that she may not clearly understand important details in a complex situation and could be easily confused while under pressure. Responses in such a situation may appear to be adaptive but instead are often based upon anxiety, confusion, and poor analytical abilities. If Susan was not the perpetrator in this case, her confession in a pressured situation could reflect her low ability to adequately assess the complexity of her situation and the serious ramifications of confessing to a crime she did not commit.

I told Summers I was surprised by her comment that one of the reasons she finally admitted to the allegations was to terminate the interview so she could go to work. While her work ethic is commendable, this comment reflects a very poor understanding of the investigative process and her ability to adequately assess and select potentially less harmful alternatives to resolve the situation. Regardless, it is foolish for someone to confess to a crime he or she did not commit in order to get to work on time.

I then told Summers what he already knew: no psychological evaluation can accurately assess a person's guilt or innocence regarding the commission of sexual offenses. Since Susan denied she molested the two girls, the major step toward rehabilitation—accepting responsibility for her acts—was absent. Therapy begins at that threshold and I could not provide an accurate assessment of her amenability for treatment in the event she was the perpetrator.

I did point out that if she were to accept responsibility for her actions, her overall history would suggest a lack of compulsive sexual attraction to or behavior with young children as seen with so-called pedophilic offenders. In fact, pedophilia is rarely found in females, but research with female sexual offenders suggests several typologies,[4] one of which could match Susan: The adolescent female sexual offender who engages in inappropriate sexual behavior with young children as a form of sexual curiosity and experimentation. These girls usually negotiate the experimentation phase of sexual development successfully and seldom go on to perpetrate sexual crimes as an adult. Therapeutic intervention with this type of female sexual offender is typically very effective and reduces the potential for recidivism even further.

I then assumed, for the sake of argument, that Susan was the perpetrator and, if she accepted responsibility for her acts, it was my opinion that probation with mandated appropriate sex offender treatment as well as treatment for her own sexual victimization issues would be a reasonable alternative to incarceration. I also stressed that Susan not be allowed unsupervised contact with young children until her therapist recommended otherwise.

A couple of months after I discussed my report with Summers, he requested a second evaluation of Susan. When I interviewed Susan a second time she was more forthcoming about inappropriate activities with the two alleged victims. She hung her head down and admitted that she had touched the kids "on their private parts" but didn't do anything else. When I asked her to explain her inappropriate behavior, she said she couldn't explain it because she didn't understand why she touched the kids the way she did. She added, "It just happened."

I remembered from the first interview with Susan that she had used the same phrase when she told me about her first consensual sexual intercourse. Susan seemed embarrassed when I asked if she became sexually excited while touching the kids, then she replied with a simple, "No, they're just young kids."

Since Susan had a history of admitting, albeit under duress, to molesting the children then denying it, I asked her why she was now admitting again. She told me that her attorney had gotten upset with her because she had not been truthful to me and her denial was going to land her in jail for a long time. "He said I had a chance at probation if I admitted and got into therapy." I was concerned that Susan's present admission was also a product of duress, so I told her that I wanted to be sure she was telling the truth this time rather than admitting to something she didn't do because she was afraid of going to jail. She looked at me through teary eyes and said, "I know I sometimes don't understand things very well, but I'm telling the truth this time. I touched those kids and I shouldn't have done it and I don't know why I did it."

I called Summers and told him about Susan's admission of guilt. I also told him that I was not totally comfortable with Susan's confession because I felt she was experiencing fairly significant stress associated with the possibility of being sent away for quite some time. Summers agreed that the stress was real because he was convinced a jury would believe at least one of the kids and find Susan guilty of at least two sex crimes, which would require several years of incarceration under Arizona's mandatory sentencing statutes for sexual offenses against children. "I don't want to go to trial and I'm working with the prosecutor on a plea agreement with probation available. But, as you know, Susan must come clean about what she did with these kids before the prosecutor will offer the agreement." He then tried to reassure me that Susan's admission was truthful and not just a ploy to avoid prison time.

This was not the first time I had heard this story. Since the mandatory sentencing went into effect, a lot of defense attorneys were advising people accused of sexual crimes to avoid trials and try to cop a plea with lesser time in prison or probation. In some cases I knew the accused was innocent but had confessed anyway in order to avoid the risk of being found guilty by a jury and spending the rest of a life time in jail. In Susan's case I decided to give her and her attorney the benefit of the doubt.

I wrote a follow-up report to Summers stating that Susan's admission was an important step toward rehabilitation and the reduction of risk factors associated with recidivism. I added that since Susan had assumed responsibility for her inappropriate sexual behavior with both young children, she would be eligible to participate in a treatment program with a focus on female sexual perpetration. I also recommended that the treatment program address Susan's personal sexual abuse trauma and her borderline intellectual functioning.

But the seeds of childhood misdirection often bear an even more bitter fruit.

Melinda Loveless, Laurie Tackett, Hope Rippey, and Toni Lawrence

Fifteen years ago in my home state of Indiana, fifteen-year-old Melinda Loveless and three other teenagers lured, attacked, tortured, and brutally murdered twelve-year-old Shanda Sharer.[5] Each was convicted and sentenced to prison for their parts in the crime that shocked the residents of Madison, a small town along the Ohio River. At an age when most girls in small towns in Indiana were concerned with friendships, school sports, clothes, and boys, many asked what drove these four teenage girls to murder a twelve-year-old girl.

According to most accounts, Loveless and fourteen-year-old Amanda Heavrin were best friends and lovers. Heavrin was also seeing a lot of Shanda Sharer. Loveless didn't like Sharer and was very possessive of Heavrin. Loveless had warned both of them repeatedly and in no uncertain terms to stop seeing each other. They refused.

To make her point, Loveless dreamed up a plan to scare Sharer into compliance and Heavrin back into her arms. But she needed help and a car. She called another friend, seventeen-year-old Laurie Tackett, and asked her to come over to her house. When she showed up, Tackett had a couple of fifteen-year-old friends, Hope Rippey and Toni Lawrence, in tow. Rippey didn't know Loveless. Lawrence had met her maybe once or twice before. These young girls didn't know it at the time, but they were in the wrong place at the wrong time.

As the girls chatted about nothing in particular, Loveless suddenly pulled a large kitchen knife from her purse. She told the other three girls that she was upset about the relationship between Sharer and Heavrin and she wanted to scare Sharer so badly that she would stay away from Heavrin forever. Loveless was a strong young woman with a long knife. She convinced the girls to help and they all piled into Tackett's car and headed for Sharer's house.

When the four teenagers pulled up at Sharer's house, Loveless sent Rippey and Lawrence to the front door to lure Sharer out. Loveless and Tackett waited in the car.

When Sharer opened the door, Rippey and Lawrence spun a compelling tale concocted by Loveless. They posed as friends of Heavrin and told her that Heavrin was waiting for her at a popular deserted place known as the Witches Castle. All Sharer had to do was get in the car and off they would go. But Sharer couldn't leave the house just then. After all she was only twelve years old and her father was home. She knew he wouldn't give her permission to go out into the night without a good reason. She would have to wait until her father was asleep, then she could sneak out without anyone knowing. She told the girls to come back around midnight.

After midnight the four girls returned to Sharer's house. Even though Sharer seemed hesitant to leave, Rippey and Lawrence eventually convinced her to go. They went to Tackett's car. Sharer climbed into the middle of the front seat and Rippey took shotgun. Loveless was hiding in the backseat under a blanket.

As the car approached the Witches Castle, Loveless sprang from her hiding place, yanked Sharer's head back by the hair, and pressed the business end of the knife against her throat. If Loveless just wanted to scare Sharer, she succeeded. Sharer broke into deep sobs and begged for her life. But Loveless wasn't satisfied, not just yet. She and Tackett dragged her out of the car and into the castle. Loveless handed the knife to Rippey so she could tie Sharer's hands. Rippey got into the spirit of the moment and used the knife to taunt the hapless young girl.

While Loveless was taking some of Sharer's jewelry and sharing the spoils with Rippey and Lawrence, several cars drove by. The girls became concerned about unexpected visitors, so they dragged Sharer back into the car. Tackett suggested they go to a secluded area near her home, but first she needed to stop for gas.

At a gas station, the girls jammed the terrified Sharer behind a seat and covered her with a blanket. To make sure Sharer didn't escape or cry for help, Loveless watched her prey carefully. Tackett and Rippey took care of the gas. Lawrence made a phone call to a friend without revealing that the foursome was having great fun terrorizing a twelve-year-old girl. The fun was just beginning.

When the girls got to Madison they pulled by Tackett's house on the way to a more secluded area a few miles down the road. There, Tackett promised, was an old logging road. A perfect place to attend to the problem of Sharer without interruption. When Tackett stopped the car, Rippey and Lawrence got out. Loveless and Tackett grabbed Sharer and forced her outside on one of the coldest nights of the season. Sharer stood waiting for whatever was going to happen next.

As Loveless untied Sharer, Rippey and Lawrence fled to the warmth of the car. They watched as Loveless threatened Sharer with the knife and ordered her to take off all of her clothes. Sharer protested and pleaded but did what Loveless commanded. When Sharer was down to her panties, Loveless grabbed the clothes and tossed them into the car. Rippey mockingly put on Sharer's polka-dot bikini bra and Lawrence flipped on the radio.

Tackett grabbed Sharer and held her hands behind her back. When Loveless approached, Sharer repeatedly pleaded for her life and promised to never see Heavrin again. Loveless was not moved and screamed back at Sharer to "shut the fuck up." Then Loveless shifted from trying to scare to trying to hurt.

A sickening thud shot through the frigid air as Loveless plowed her fist into Sharer's bare stomach. Sharer went down. But not for long. Loveless pulled her up by the hair then repeatedly smacked Sharer's face into her knee until the battered young girl's braces ripped through her lips. Loveless tossed her aside like a rag doll then grabbed the knife. She yanked Sharer's head back and tried to cut her throat. But no matter how hard Loveless sawed, the dull knife would not do its job.

Rippey jumped out of the car to help. She held Sharer down as Loveless switched to stabbing Sharer in the chest. Stabbing caused some damage but not enough to kill. Even Tackett took a few turns before running to the car for some rope. If the knife wouldn't work, a rope might. Tackett wrapped the rope around Sharer's neck and pulled it tight until she felt Sharer's bloodied body go limp. The girls threw Sharer's body in the trunk and drove back to Tackett's house.

The four girls went upstairs to Tackett's bedroom, where they tried to predict their future with mystic stones. When I think of a bunch of teenage girls in a bedroom together, I normally think about a slumber party with pranks and pizza, not four girls trying to divine their future while a battered, nearly nude, young girl lay in the trunk of a car.

The fortune-telling was suddenly interrupted when Tackett's dog began barking at the car. Sharer was alive. Tackett took charge. She ran to the kitchen, grabbed a sharp knife, and headed for the car. She opened the trunk and stabbed Sharer several times. When Sharer was quiet, a bloodied Tackett closed the trunk and went back to the girls in her room. She announced that they all needed to go for another ride. Apparently Rippey and Lawrence had had enough and refused to go. Loveless and Tackett left them behind and headed back to the car.

Tackett and Loveless didn't have a plan so they drove around trying to figure out what they should do. To make sure Sharer was dead, they stopped. When they opened the trunk, they were surprised when a bloodied and battered Sharer sat up and tried to speak. Tackett grabbed a tire iron and smashed it on Sharer's head. When Sharer fell back, Tackett closed the trunk.

Tackett and Loveless still couldn't decide what to do but stopped again when they heard strange sounds coming from the trunk. Tackett stopped the car and again went to trunk. Loveless stayed in the car. When Tackett opened the trunk she found Sharer gasping for air and in the throes of what seemed to be the final death rattle. Tackett grabbed the tire iron again and repeatedly beat Sharer.

This time certain that Sharer would not move or make a sound again, Tackett closed the trunk. She took the tire iron and got back in the car with Loveless. Loveless watched as Tackett placed the tire iron under her nose and smelled it. She seemed almost giddy as she told Loveless about bashing Sharer.

Thinking Sharer must be dead by now, Tackett and Loveless finally conceived a plan to dispose of her body. They decided to return to Tackett's house where they could burn the body on a trash pile. But Sharer was not dead, so they had to stop a number of times and use the tire iron on the young girl.

When they finally got to Tackett's house, Rippey and Lawrence were asleep. Tackett woke them up and told them about Sharer and the plan to burn her on the trash pile. They soon realized that the plan was no good because the ground was covered with frost and they didn't have anything to start the fire. The foursome were sitting around trying to concoct a new plan when Tackett suggested they take another look at Sharer. They went to the car.

Lawrence didn't want to look so she got into the car and started the engine. She kept it at a high rev to drown out any sounds Sharer might make once the trunk was opened. After all, Sharer was the little girl who would just not die. Tackett opened the trunk. Rippey looked at Sharer's mangled body and decided to get in a few licks of her own. She picked up a bottle of Windex lying in the trunk next to Sharer and sprayed her. Sharer sat up.

Tackett started to talk to Sharer but was interrupted by the sound of her mother's voice calling her from the house. Sharer suffered more when Tackett quickly slammed the trunk closed on her head and ran to the house. It would not do for her mother to discover what her daughter had been up to all night.

When Tackett returned to the car, the girls piled in and drove off to dispose of Sharer. They decided burning the body was still a good idea and Rippey knew a perfect place, another old logging road. The girls stopped at a gas station, topped off the tank, filled a two-liter soft drink bottle with gasoline, and then headed for

Sharer's proposed final resting spot. Once there, Lawrence stayed in the car as the other three went to the trunk to gather Sharer. They used the blanket to carry Sharer a few feet away from the car then dumped her on the ground. Rippey poured gasoline on Sharer until she was satisfied the body would burn. Tackett struck a match and tossed the tiny flame at the young girl who had endured the longest and most terrifying night of her young life. Sharer's body ignited in a flash.

The girls watched for a moment then got back into the car and drove off. Suddenly Loveless ordered Tackett to turn around and go back to the fire. Apparently she wanted to make sure Sharer would not survive this final insult. Back at the burning body, Loveless seemed transfixed as she watched excited flames lick at Sharer. Loveless then poured the remainder of the gasoline onto Sharer and headed back to the car.

On the way from the gruesome scene, a remorseless Loveless told the other girls how funny Sharer looked as she twisted into a final fetal position and her tongue shot in and out of her mouth. No respect for the living. Or the dying.

Sharer's charred corpse lay there a few hours out in the field where her tormentors left her until a couple of hunters on a quest for quail discovered the body and called authorities. The authorities were also notified when, that same day, Lawrence and Rippey told their parents some of the saga of poor Sharer.

The residents who lived in and around Madison along the Ohio River were increasingly horrified as they learned more about the gruesome details of the torture and murder of Sharer. The county prosecutor initially charged all four girls with murder, arson, battery with a deadly weapon, aggravated battery, criminal confinement, and intimidation. Loveless and Tackett were also charged with seven additional crimes, including child molesting and criminal deviant conduct. Later, the prosecutor decided to add felony murder to the long list of charges against Loveless and Tackett.

Lawrence and her attorney were the first to work out a plea agreement. In exchange for her testimony, all charges except for a guilty plea to criminal confinement and intimidation were dropped. About four months later Lawrence took an overdose of antidepressant medication prescribed by jail medical staff. After she recovered in an intensive care unit, Lawrence was transferred to a secure mental health facility where she was evaluated and treated for a couple of months then returned to jail.

Faced with Lawrence's impending testimony, a long list of felony charges, and the prosecutor's decision to seek the death penalty, Loveless and Tackett finally accepted a plea bargain about eight months after the torture and murder of Sharer. When they both agreed to plead guilty to murder, torture, arson, and criminal confinement, the prosecutor agreed to drop the remainder of the charges and withdraw from seeking the death penalty. The agreement also required that both cooperate with the state. Loveless and Tackett each testified to their part of the crime. Both were sentenced to sixty years in prison, a lifetime for teenagers.

When fifteen-year-old Lawrence stood before a judge, she faced six to twenty years in prison. She hoped for something in the lower range but got the maximum. She was disappointed in the judge's decision but got to work on her rehabilitation in prison. She quickly earned her GED then completed the requirements for an associate's degree in about four years. Her hard work paid off. Twenty-four-year-old Lawrence was released from prison on parole in 2000 after serving nine years of her twenty-year sentence.

Rippey decided to take her chances at trial. It was a bad decision. She was found guilty on enough charges to land her in prison for sixty years, minus ten for mitigating circumstances such as a troubled family background and mental health issues. But she, like Lawrence, set out on a course of rehabilitation. In prison, Rippey earned a bachelor's degree in the Ball State University's college program for inmates. She also became a spokesperson against teen violence and helped train dogs for the visually handicapped. In

2004 Judge Jenny Manier was impressed with Rippey's efforts and expression of remorse. She reduced Rippey's sentence from fifty to thirty-five years. Still a lot of time, but Rippey walked out of prison in 2006 after serving thirteen years.

Probably buoyed by the success of Lawrence and Rippey to be released early, Loveless pursued an early-release scheme of her own. Her attorney, Mark Small, filed a postconviction relief petition alleging she was provided ineffective counsel following the murder of Sharer. Among other things, Small argued that Loveless accepted the plea agreement because she was psychologically impaired and her attorneys and the prosecutor "exaggerated" the death penalty to her. I wondered how a death penalty could be exaggerated. A hearing was scheduled for October 2007 to debate Loveless's release from her sixty-year prison sentence or have a new trial. When Small claimed that he was denied access to his client prior to the hearing, it was rescheduled for December 2007.

Tackett, now thirty-two years old, is the only one of the four girls who has not made a serious effort to be released from prison early. According to some media reports, Tackett attempted suicide while in prison in 2004, found God, and spends most of her time studying the scriptures and trying to forgive herself for what she did to young Shanda Sharer.

It doesn't take a mental health expert to understand how these four girls brutally murdered one of their own. In many ways Sharer's murder was the culmination of a perfect storm of four tragic lives folded into one.

By all accounts, Melinda Loveless, the third of three girls born to Marjorie and Larry Loveless, was raised in a swirl of alcohol, infidelity, domestic violence, and sexual abuse. Her father, a Vietnam veteran, worked sporadically and poorly at a variety of occupations and used most of his earnings to satisfy his need for personal pleasure. At times the family lived fairly well, but most of the time finances were tight.

According to Marjorie, Larry liked to cross-dress using

makeup and his wife's and his daughters' underwear. Sometimes he would smell his daughters' underwear in front of other family members. He had sex with countless other women and pressured his wife into participating in sexual activities with others, including orgies and gangbangs. He was also an emotionally unstable and violent man who beat his wife so viciously that she had to be hospitalized after she refused to let him bring home two women he had met in a bar.

There were reports that when Larry was a probationary officer with the New Albany Police Department, he and his partner beat a black man Larry thought had had sex with his wife. He also shot at his daughter, Melisa, when she was seven years old. It is unclear if Larry molested children, but court records contain reports that Larry may have fondled one of his infant daughters and molested Marjorie's thirteen-year-old sister, a family cousin, as well as his two older daughters. And then there were the rapes.

After being denied sex for a long period of time, Larry allegedly raped Marjorie while his three daughters watched. A cousin, Teddy, testified that Larry tied them up and raped each one in succession. The girls refused to corroborate Teddy's rape story. Melinda also denied that she was sexually molested by her father, but she did confirm she had slept in the same bed with her father until she was fourteen years old.

Melinda's mother provided little stability for her three daughters. She had a history of alcohol abuse and suicide attempts. And she often participated in her husband's open-marriage lifestyle. She once attacked her husband with a knife when she found him spying on Melinda and a friend. Shortly after this episode and another suicide attempt, Larry moved out and the couple divorced.

When Melinda's father moved to Florida and remarried, she became even more emotionally troubled. She got into fights at school and disobeyed her mother. Melinda went into therapy. In 1990 she started dating Amanda Heavrin. In 1991 she told her mom she was gay. Her mother was not amused but may have learned to accept her daughter's sexual preference.

Laurie Tackett's background was different but no less traumatic. Her mother was a fundamentalist Pentecostal Christian who demanded strict compliance with her faith-based beliefs. Breaking the rules could bring harsh punishment, including an attempted strangulation by her mother over a dress code violation. Child Protective Services stepped in and initiated unannounced visits to protect Tackett.

On another occasion, Tackett's mother was so outraged when she learned that Rippey's father allowed Tackett and Rippey to play with a Ouija board she went to the home and demanded that the Ouija board be destroyed and the house exorcised. Her father, a felon who served time in prison in the 1960s, worked in a local factory. Tackett also claimed that she was molested at age five and again at twelve.

Tackett was often at odds with her parents, especially her mother. By the time she was fifteen she found a religion of her own: the occult. She was also beginning to show the signs of emotional instability. Her mother discovered signs of self-mutilation in 1991 and moved quickly to have Tackett hospitalized, where she was prescribed an antidepressant and released.

I wondered why hospital personnel did not pick up the very obvious signs of something more troubling than a temporary bout with depression. Teenagers who self-mutilate need to be evaluated and treated carefully. An in-and-out approach usually leads to serious problems down the road. And sure enough, in two days, Tackett was at it again. This time the wounds on her wrists were so serious she required emergency treatment and confinement to the hospital's psychiatric ward. About three weeks later Tackett was discharged.

I expected the borderline personality disorder diagnosis and Tackett's admission to having hallucinations since childhood. One of the hallmarks of a borderline personality disorder is self-mutilation, especially cutting. Some borderlines I have known reported that seeing the blood somehow makes them feel real; others refer to a compulsion to hurt themselves. Abused children raised by seriously dysfunctional parents often struggle with a multitude of emotional problems. As mentioned earlier, borderline personality disorder is a common outcome of abuse.

Tackett dropped out of school in September 1991 and headed to Louisville in October to be with friends. Tackett's emotional turmoil was a strong indicator of the terror to come. Then she met Melinda Loveless.

Background information about Hope Rippey and Toni Lawrence is not as detailed as with the other two girls, but there were some hints of trouble. Hope was born in Madison, Indiana, in June 1976. Her parents divorced when she was seven years old, a vulnerable developmental age for most children. Hope's mother moved to Michigan with the kids for about three years then reunited with Hope's father back in Madison.

Hope, now about ten years old, resumed her previous childhood friendships with Tackett and Lawrence. Even though Hope's parents were concerned that Tackett was a troubled young girl and a bad influence on their daughter, they allowed the relationship to continue. Then a real clue to serious emotional problems emerged: at about age fifteen, Hope began to self-mutilate. More fuel for the blaze to come.

Toni Lawrence was born in Madison just a few months before Hope. She and Hope formed a close childhood relationship before Hope moved to Michigan. Reports indicate that Lawrence was molested by a relative at age nine and raped by a boy at age fourteen. Skilled counseling usually helps children with sexual abuse and rape trauma, but it often requires a long-term commitment by both therapist and victim. Unfortunately, Lawrence stopped going to therapy before her trauma could be adequately repaired, and serious signs of trouble came to the surface. She became promiscuous, began to self-mutilate, and made at least one suicide attempt.

So we have three young girls scattered along the Ohio River, each with an emotional storm brewing deep inside, waiting for the right climate to thunder. And along comes a supercell of anger — Melinda Loveless.

It is possible but very doubtful that any of the four girls could have committed such a horrific crime alone. It took the fusing of their collective emotional anger and outrage to capture a young girl and torture her for nearly ten hours before setting her on fire while she was still alive. Not one of the girls acted to stop the events.

Group rape and murder is not a new phenomenon, and the need to kill resides in all of us as a primitive urge. Fortunately the urge to kill is kept in check by civilized social environments, but dysfunctional social environments can stimulate homicide. While this concept applies to all the social environments created by our ancestors over the sordid history of mankind, the concept also applies to smaller clusters of social environments such as a group of dysfunctional girls. It works like this: within the group the prevailing attitude can act as a restraining force against homicide or it can stimulate the urge until a homicide occurs.

Stimulated by Loveless, the gang of four formed a society of sick individuals who administered their own brand of justice on another individual who threatened one of their members. Loveless was certain that Shanda Sharer was taking her teenage lover, Amanda Heavrin, away from her and she must be stopped. She needed a little help from her friends.

Sigmund Freud took this concept a few steps further.[6] He theorized that a group is more than a collection of individuals gathered together with similar ideas and motivations. A group takes on its own identity and becomes a dynamic entity. For example, individuals in a group often shed their own individual identity and self-control in favor of unconscious urges and the demands of the group mentality. When this happens, individuals become more suggestible and can get caught up in a collective feeling of power. Within this group arrangement, individual responsibility is dissolved. Within a subgroup of individuals with personal psychopathology, for example, individual responsibility, self-monitoring, and restraint are insidiously muffled by the strength and security of the group, which allows horrific behavior to come forward with permission and without sanctions.

As noted forensic psychologist Louis Schlesinger points out in his book *Sexual Murder*, ". . . ordinary people can easily be made to engage in all sorts of potentially aggressive behavior if the context or environment condones it."[7]

NOTES

1. Federal Bureau of Investigation, *Uniform Crime Reports for the United States, 1990* (Washington, DC: Government Printing Office, 1991).

2. For reviews of prevalence rates summarized in this chapter, see Kurt Bumby and Nancy Halstenson Bumby, "Adolescent Female Sexual Offenders," in *The Sex Offender: New Insights, Treatment Innovations and Legal Developments*, ed. Barbara K. Schwartz and Henry R. Cellini (Kingston, NJ: Civic Research Institute, 1997), p. 10-2-10-16; Barbara K. Schwartz and Henry R. Cellini, *The Sex Offender: Corrections, Treatment and Legal Practice* (Kingston, NJ: Civic Research Institute, 1995), p. 5-1-5-22; Gail Ryan and Sandy Lane, eds., *Juvenile Sexual Offending: Causes, Consequences, and Correction* (San Francisco: Jossey-Bass, 1997).

3. Ibid.

4. J. Matthews, R. Mathews, and K. Speltz, "Female Sexual Offenders: A Typology," in *Family Sexual Abuse*, ed. M. Q. Patton (Newbury Park, CA: Sage Publications, 1991), pp. 199–219.

5. For a comprehensive account of the Shanda Sharer case, see Aphrodite Jones, *Cruel Sacrifice* (New York: Pinnacle Books, 1994).

6. Sigmund Freud, "Group Psychology and Analysis of the Ego," in *The Standard Edition of the Complete Psychological Works of Sigmund Freud*, ed. and trans. J. Strachey (London: Hogarth Press, 1921), vol. 18, pp. 67–143.

7. Louis B. Schlesinger, *Sexual Murder: Catathymic and Compulsive Homicides* (Boca Raton, FL: CRC Press, 2004).

10

THE PATH TO PREVENTION

WHY DO GIRLS AND WOMEN BECOME DANGEROUS AND WHAT DO WE DO ABOUT IT?

When I first discussed writing a book on dangerous women with a group of colleagues, the majority response went something like this: "Do we really need another book on female sexual abuse victims?" I thought they didn't quite hear my proposal correctly, so I became clearer about my intentions to write about female perpetrators of dangerous acts, not female sexual abuse victims. Or, in the language of the criminal justice system, "perps not vics."

This time their response was "But haven't you found in your forensic and clinical work that most girls and women who engage in aberrant acts are childhood abuse victims?" While the answer to their question is that a history of child abuse is certainly present in many dangerous girls and women, the answer is way too simplistic to account for the growing number of cases of girls and women behaving badly. Other factors are also at work. Understanding those factors is the first line of prevention.

WHY DO GIRLS AND WOMEN BECOME DANGEROUS?

Research and clinical literature has uncovered a number of factors generally thought to propel girls and women into killing their children, partners, or others, as well as sexually abusing children and adults. Here's a "sperm to worm" look.

GENES

A child is born with a unique blend of all the genetic material from her parents and generations before—ancestral memories that make us what we are. Genomics, the study of genes, has shown that many individuals have a genetic makeup, including but not limited to certain mutated genes, that may carry a higher risk for health problems like cancer or psychological problems like depression, for example. Alcohol and drug abuse problems are thought to have a genetic base as well. While no one has identified a gene or a cluster of genes clearly associated with dangerousness so far, a person's overall temperament and personality character traits seem prewired to a certain extent. Some women are born to be nice. Some women are born to be not so nice. But genetic factors alone do not produce dangerous people.

PRIMITIVE PARENTING

About three decades ago a social worker ushered me into a room at the rear of a youth center in one of many impoverished areas in New York City. Betty, a fourteen-year-old girl, stood and shot me a big grin when I entered the room. The social worker introduced us. I smiled back as Betty and I sat opposite each other in surprisingly new lounge chairs. The old busted bean bags were history. My back silently thanked whoever was responsible.

Betty had sparkling green eyes, a pleasant face with smooth

blemish-free skin, and a bubbling personality. Except for the tell-tale signs of the second trimester of pregnancy, Betty could have been just about anybody's dream daughter.

During the 1960s and 1970s, child development specialists worried that many parents, especially young parents and potential young parents, lacked the information and skills necessary to raise their kids to be intellectually sound and psychologically healthy. They believed young people who knew more about parenting would make better decisions about sex and pregnancy, as well as increase their chances of become more informed and skilled parents once they had children. Research showed very clearly that informed and skilled parents were at much less risk to neglect and abuse their children.

Funded by several federal grants, a program called Education for Parenthood was launched to test this bold idea. Behavior Associates, a group of research, developmental, educational, and clinical psychologists, of which I was a member, was chosen to design and implement a comprehensive evaluation of this nationwide program. I was selected to direct the evaluation project. As part of my duties, I traveled across the country and to Puerto Rico interviewing preteens and adolescents about sexuality, pregnancy, and parenthood.

Betty was one of about a dozen pregnant teens I interviewed that day. When I asked Betty to tell me about her plans for her baby, she threw out a smile that could have melted any heart. She said, "Why, I'm just going to love it to death."

I worked hard to suppress the images in my head of mothers I had evaluated over the years who had done just that. I fought these images off with a private review of the research that showed love mattered and was essential to brain development in the early years of life, especially social and emotional development. I reassured Betty that love was one of the most important things a parent could give to a child, then I asked her what else she planned for the child.

Betty's smile faded and her sparkling green eyes slowly went blank.

About five years later our evaluation data found that the majority of adolescents who participated in a variety of Education for Parenthood programs could answer the question of plans for parenthood and many others about the subject without going blank. We found statistically significant positive changes in the parenting knowledge, attitudes, and self-reported behavioral skills of the teenage participants. For example, when asked what makes a good parent, teenagers like Betty said:

> *Understanding the child. The child is a person with certain ways of doing things. It is wrong to raise a child to be just like yourself.*
> *Having a good education so you will be aware of things. If you don't know anything, you can't help your child learn and know things.*
> *Love.*

Those who were connected with the project were excited that we had data to support the notion that education for parenthood could be a viable approach to reducing pregnancy by teens and the number of abandoned, neglected, and abused children by less-informed and less-skilled parents. But the idea of teaching potential parents, such as preteens and adolescents, about healthy sexuality and how to be a parent met with political, religious, and societal resistance. After visiting a program site in the middle of the Bible Belt, I received hate mail warning that I, and others like me, would be punished by God for meddling in the purview of parents.

Never mind that our data also showed the majority of teenage participants had received little to no information about sexuality and parenting from their parents or anybody else, for that matter. Their information came mostly from peers and the media. Like many proven beneficial programs that counter mainstream thinking, a national initiative to move forward with Education for Parenthood never took root.

Now, more than thirty-five years later, I am encouraged to hear that child development specialists and mental health professionals are revisiting the idea. But I can't help but wonder where our society would be today if we had followed the directions of the data discovered so long ago. As one teenager told us: "Too many kids who become parents don't know what they're doing, and that's why there are so many messed-up kids."

From the cases in this book we have learned that primitive parenting practices are alive and well. Many of the women who became dangerous were children who were neglected, abused, or abandoned when they were young by parents and other family members. A child not wanted, not nurtured. A child wanted, not nurtured. Dangerous.

SOCIOCULTURAL MESSAGES

On an early morning in late August or early September, I forget which, I was rushing around the house trying to leave for an important meeting. In the background I heard the sound of a vaguely familiar female voice on television. It was Laura Ingraham, the former white-collar criminal defense attorney who now hosts her own conservative radio talk show. She is a best-selling author and a political and cultural commentator often on television and other radio shows.

She was hawking her latest book, *Power to the People*, and an interviewer set her off with a controversial question about something she wrote. I was late for my meeting and paid little mind as she answered by railing against all things liberal, Marxist, and scientific, as she is wont to do. But I tuned in when I heard her send out a call to all parents to fight back against the sex-saturated antifamily messages pushed by nearly all forms of media.

On the way back from my meeting, I stopped at my favorite bookstore for a look at *Power to the People*. Some chapters interested me enough to pay the discounted price for a first-run hardcover.[1]

Even though Ingraham states that she does not take the position that large families are better than small families, her rhetoric testifies otherwise. She readily embraces and espouses the biblical command for married couples to go forth and multiply. She takes to task just about anybody who accepts the notion of being fruitful and multiplying but is moderate about how fruitful and how much multiplying.

Ingraham argues that large families are worth the numerous sacrifices endured by parents and children but doesn't present a credible argument for her position. She either does not understand or completely ignores the psychological stress and financial factors inherent in the mandate that poor families produce more children than they can handle.

Perhaps she hasn't seen the pain and suffering of countless disadvantaged and poor families barely eking out a survival after following the "go forth and multiply" command and quickly producing more children than they can feed. Contrary to Ingraham's position that parents who reduce the number of children do so to have money for selfish and frivolous things, many parents simply do not have the resources for either selfish means or for their children.

Ingraham further supports her position with an argument that people who multiply greatly and pass their values on to their children are more likely to see their values survive and have a stronger impact on the future. Her logic is impeccable. This is called the intergenerational transmission of values. Most functional parents pass on functional values but many dysfunctional parents pass on dysfunctional values. The bottom line is, who is at the most risk for the intergenerational transmission of child abuse? Families with lots of kids and few resources.

This cultural message of producing lots of children is steeped in strong religious dogma and plants the seeds of child abuse and neglect. In fact, it is my opinion that those who champion the notion that parents should produce more children than they can nurture are perpetrating preconception child abuse. Who suffers? The parents, the children, and society.

As I considered the strong religious underpinnings of Ingraham's charge to reluctant and "selfish" parents, I was reminded of Warren Jeffs, the prophet of the fundamental sect of the Latter-day Saints. Jeffs stood trial in Utah in September 2007 for being an accomplice to the rape of a fourteen-year-old girl by coercing her to marry her nineteen-year-old cousin and "go forth and multiply."

Within this religious sect, men are allowed to have more than one wife. Young girls are often forced into marriages with older men and expected to produce as many children as possible, as soon as possible. Young boys of the sect are often run off with little or no resources. No one knows for sure, but reliable reports suggest Jeffs has about seventy wives, including some of his deceased father's younger widows, and hundreds of children.

The children are taught by the tenets of the religion to have no intimate contact with the opposite sex until the prophet arranges and performs a marriage ceremony. The arrangement and the ceremony occur often within days of each other. At the core of this sect's values is the truth of Ingraham's argument that "the more children you have . . ."

The victim in this case told the court that she protested against the marriage but finally had to give in to the pressure from all her family members and, of course, Jeffs. She had no resources to escape to safety and felt betrayed by her family, which was operating on the words of the Bible interpreted by the prophet.

The defense in the case claimed that no force was used. I think they forgot about religious and cultural intimidation. The defense also claimed the young girl "sugared up" to her husband on occasion. I guess nobody understood how victims learn and use techniques to survive an abusive situation. Fortunately, she escaped the marriage and the sect before she was transformed into a dangerous woman. The prophet was convicted and still faces similar charges in Arizona.

Women don't have to listen to a member of a religious sect to receive harmful cultural messages. Research studies in the psychology of women are generally consistent in their findings that American society differentially values gender and promotes specific gender roles. This process can be seen in lower pay for women for the same job responsibilities, differential expectations of assertive behavior, and the sexual objectification of females, to mention only a few examples.

Although the sexual objectification of females has long been part of our cultural messages about women, over the past decade or so the messages about female sexuality have changed significantly. Messages glorifying promiscuity and bad girl behavior have intensified and now permeate mainstream media. Ingraham calls it our "Pornified Culture," and Ariel Levy, author of *Female Chauvinist Pigs*, is a little kinder when she calls it "Raunch Culture."[2]

Whatever we call it, the girls are wild about it and our society can't seem to get enough of the girls gone wild. If young girls will show it, people will buy it. And young girls, especially drunk young girls trying to out-party their narcissistic celebrity idols, are more than willing to seek fame and perhaps fortune by showing their stuff and sticking their tongues down each other's throats. After all, one good photo or good French kiss may land a movie contract. And later you can show the tapes to your kids and grandkids at family gatherings.

Sexualization of girls can be found everywhere, even with toys. While the number one best-selling doll, Barbie, has always come under criticism for her bust size and other subtle sexualized features, she pales in comparison to Bratz, the number two best-selling doll line in the country. Bratz dolls, which are rapidly gaining in popularity over Barbie, boldly portray the "sexpot" look of heavily made-up faces and sexually provocative clothes. But there's more. With accessories, a young girl can create her own prostitute! Just what every four- to eight-year-old girl needs to help her become, as one mother put it, a prosti-tot.

But the barrage of sexual messages targeting preteens has been shown to have a negative impact on nearly all aspects of a girl's healthy development, and psychological wounds become a fertile breeding ground for the growth of dangerous women. Or at least women who look dangerous.

I was at a writers' conference a few months ago attending a workshop on screenplays. I got there early and sat down near the front of the room. A pretty, late-twenty-something woman came over and offered me a handout. I looked beyond the handout and saw a naked, tightly sculpted midriff adorned with a petite, sapphire-encrusted navel ring. As I reached for the handout, she bent low and explained something about one of the sheets. Her crop top fell open with ease, revealing supple young breasts with firm pink nipples. I was relieved to see no nipple rings, but I had no idea what she said about the handout. I was praying as hard as I could that my inner adolescent would not come out.

I believe this lovely young woman, who was the speaker's assistant, was not purposely trying to be sexually provocative. At least not to me. She gave each person in the room the same view when she bent over to explain the handout. I believe that she, like so many other young girls and women, embraced the prosti-tot look early on and now was so desensitized to it that she wasn't aware that her attire was inappropriate for the setting.

Ariel Levy tells us raunch knows no boundaries. Even girls who are hopelessly overweight try to compete by baring more flesh and tattoos than anybody should. From the anorexic to the supersized, young girls are baring it all. For what? According to Levy, the raunch is for show, to be hot, but not to ask for sex. Girls feel they must be hot and slutty to attract and compete for boys, but the girls' show is not meant to ask boys for sex, just attention. I understand. The young assistant was just wearing her "normal" slut uniform. And it worked. I and just about everybody else in the room took notice, but I didn't see her give any other messages about sexual behavior. At least not to me.

Some sexualized cultural messages about girls and women are even more sinister. Earlier this year I was filled with anguish when I learned that the number one downloaded song in America was Akon's "I Wanna F— You" from his rap album *Konvicted*. As a psychologist who has spent a lot of time evaluating convicts in prison, I still have difficulty understanding how we allow our youth to get hooked on all things representing the worst of our culture. It is a mystery to me why girls and women still tolerate and support misogynistic gangbangers who demean women and advocate violence against them and just about everybody else. What is it about criminals and gang culture that we forgot to tell our children? I also wondered how the cultural message about interpersonal relationships turned so mean and vicious.

The rappers and the gang-wannabes with their "in your f—k-ing face" clothes, music, messages, and violence have a strong hold on many of our country's children who will grow up, if they don't murder each other, and have children of their own. What kind of lullabies will those parents sing to their children? And what will they tell them about sex?

THE SOCIOCULTURAL ABUSE OF SEXUALITY

In 1989 a couple of my colleagues and I became increasingly concerned that children were being sexually abused in ways beyond the traditional definition of direct sexual abuse. As a response, we introduced a concept, Abuse of Sexuality, in *Males at Risk*, one of the first books written about males sexually abused as children.[3] Later, I revised the concept and presented it as the Sociocultural Abuse of Sexuality in *The Male Heterosexual*.[4]

The Abuse of Sexuality model rests on the solid foundation of developmental psychology, the study of how humans develop, from conception to death, or, as a director of one of the Education for Parenthood programs quipped a number of years ago, "from sperm to worm." Developmental psychology tells us that most humans pass through numerous developmental stages on the way to adulthood and beyond. During each stage we are faced with challenges such as learning how to walk, talk, read, and where to deposit urine and feces. In most cases people in our learning environment help us face those challenges successfully and usually without a lot of fuss. When they don't help out the challenge becomes more difficult and sometimes these skills are never properly developed.

We proposed a bold idea: Sexuality is just like any other developmental task. It is a constant developmental process from infancy on that may be either nurtured or hindered in multiple ways along the way, and hindrances to normal sexual development may reach abusive proportions at any time. As such, the Abuse of Sexuality model describes a continuum of eight somewhat overlapping developmental environments that range from the promotion of healthy sexual development in boys and girls to approaches that are overtly abusive and significantly reduce the probability of normal sexual development regardless of gender.

The Ideal Environment. If one accepts our bold idea that sexuality is nothing more than just another developmental task, then it should be relatively easy to design a social environment to foster, rather than hinder, the development of healthy sexual attitudes and behavior. Accurate sexual information appropriate to the child's level of curiosity and understanding would be presented within a supportive, understanding, and nurturing family setting. Individuals who play significant roles in a child's life would consistently model appropriate expressions of sexuality and feelings. Aggressive and other forms of exploitative sexual expressions would be absent.

Because the ideal environment provides a positive approach to the development of sexuality, such as used in the development of other human activities like speech, walking upright, and eating with utensils, the results could be very positive.

The Predominantly Nurturing Environment. Even though ideals of any kind are seldom actualized, realistic striving for something better usually produces something better. If a child is provided with accurate information about sexuality in a *mostly* supportive, understanding, and nurturing setting, the probability of developing positive sexual attitudes and healthy expressions of sexuality would seem enhanced. But most people in Western society do not accept the notion that sexuality is just another developmental task. Developmental tasks are okay for walking and talking but not for sex.

Over the centuries, sex has been glorified and vilified, sometimes at the same time. Philosophers, romantics, scientists, religious zealots, and commercial enterprises have all staked their claims. Misinformation and myths about sex, rather than accurate information about the development of sexuality, provide the foundation for attitudes toward sexuality in Western society.

Suppose we had the same attitude about using our legs. We might still be crawling around on the ground. And how about our hands? Not too long ago children who were naturally left-handed were thought to be possessed by evil spirits and were punished for using the hand they were wired to favor. Our attitude about sexual behavior is not too far removed.

The Environmental Vacuum. Bombarded with all sorts of misinformation and religious proscriptions against most sexual activities, it is not surprising that many families feel compelled to protect their children from exposure to any type of information about sexuality. Ignorance is bliss, goes the logic. But remember physics tells us that the universe abhors vacuums and will fill a vacuum as quickly as possible with whatever is available. If parents don't do the job, somebody else will, and it might not be good for the child.

The Evasive Environment. Some families may be willing to provide information about sexual matters, but the information is typically meager and inaccurate, barely filling the vacuum. Thus the child's natural expressions of curiosity about sexuality are met with little information or vague responses based on myths and misinformation. Children reared in these settings are left to their own immature thoughts and interpretations of sexuality.

These children, and the children from the environmental vacuum, are also especially vulnerable to extrafamilial sources of information about sexuality, such as uninformed peers, media-controlled and commercially driven messages about sexual behavior and gender roles, and sexual materials designed to fill the informational void through titillation and exploitation. Think media and other predators.

The Negative Environment. Although some families try to avoid dealing with a child's natural curiosity about sex by providing no information or evasive misinformation, others actively promulgate religiously driven ideas that most sexual behavior is evil, harmful, and a sign of moral weakness.

Negative attitudes about sex and fear tactics predominate this environment. Attempts by children to explore their sexuality through normal experimentation often result in assorted types of punishment. The all-too-familiar consequence of this aversive approach to sexuality is a pervasive sexual angst consisting of confusion, guilt, ambivalence, and shame, hardly a formula for the development of a positive self-image or healthy adult sexual relationships.

The Permissive Environment. Some individuals renounce sexual repression and adopt, instead, a nonrestrictive and nonpunitive approach to teaching children about sexual matters. This "let it all hang out" philosophy appears well meaning and useful on the surface, but it often lacks proper pacing and timing considerations dictated by the child's developmental level. That is, sexual information and experiences are provided at such a level and frequency that they exceed the child's capacity to process and understand them.

A young child can easily become overwhelmed with too much information, even accurate information, and may become confused and frustrated. Some children also become overstimulated with sexual information and experiences beyond their developmental level. Precocious ideas about personal sexuality and sexual experimentation may follow. Think raunch culture.

The Seductive Environment. Within some families, a drama of "innocent" seduction occurs. Children are faced with messages about their sexual desirability and a possible sexual interest in the child by an adult family member, usually a parent. Although overt sexual contact usually does not occur, the child may be exposed to "accidental" partial or full nudity, seductive posing or gestures, and teasing with an underlying sexual motive. Even accurate information about sexual matters is presented in a way to titillate rather than satisfy the child's sexual curiosity. This highly charged environment often confuses the child about sexual feelings, sexual behavior, and appropriate partners. Sometimes, seduction goes too far.

The Overtly Sexual Environment. Transcending Abuse of Sexuality settings is the overtly sexual environment. Included here are adult-child sexual activities commonly referred to in the criminal justice system as child sexual abuse. Examples are intercourse, cunnilingus, analingus, fellatio, genital fondling, digital penetration, simulated intercourse, sexualized kissing or touching, intentional genital exposure, and directed exposure to adult sexual behavior. Exposing a child to educational or pornographic materials for the purpose of sexual titillation and exploitation, as well as encouraging developmentally inappropriate sexual contact between children under the guise of normal sexual experimentation, are also considered overt sexual responses. The negative consequences of this type of abuse of sexuality are well documented in the cases presented in this book.

A LIFESPAN OF VIOLENCE

Tragically, violence is a far too frequent visitor in the lives of girls and women. We know that about one out of two women have experienced some form of physical, sexual, or psychological abuse in a lifetime. From an early age girls are warned about stranger danger, but only a small percentage of assaults are committed by a stranger. Most females are physically or sexually assaulted by someone they trust, such as a parent, date, acquaintance, boyfriend, or husband. Nearly a third of women in this country have been physically battered by their partners.[5] Sometimes both sex and violence are combined.

In the United States, about one wife in ten is forced against her will to have sex by her husband. While these acts are clearly rape, laws in more than half of the states give husbands immunity from prosecution for the crime of rape because the woman he forced to have sex is his wife. The marital rape exemption essentially converts the marriage license into what researchers David Finkelhor and Kersti Yllo call a "license to rape."[6] Many husbands often use their license. About half of women reporting marital rape also reported that they had been raped by their husbands more than twenty times.

Like most rape victims, sexually abused wives report feelings of betrayal, anger, humiliation, and guilt. On a long-term basis most marital rape victims develop an aversion to intimacy and sex, problems with trusting men, and a persistent fear of another sexual assault. Many marital rape victims describe feelings of hate and thoughts of murder, and some, like other battered wives, turn thoughts into action.

Beginning in the 1970s, feminists spurred the public to address issues surrounding violence against women. By 1990 a number of national policy reports had identified violence against women as a serious economic, criminal justice, and public health issue, but the health community was one of the last to act and its response lagged behind. To help the health community catch up, the American Psychological Association's (APA) Committee on Women in Psychology formed and directed a task force to review current psychological research on the prevalence, causes, and effects of different forms of violence against women and to describe existing and recommended interventions, legal changes, and policy initiatives to address the problem. This was the "What do we know and what do we do about it?" approach to violence against women.

When APA published the task force's report in the book *No Safe Haven* in 1994,[7] it was hailed as one of the most comprehensive reports on the issue of violence against women, with one caveat. The report addressed only male violence against women. In all fairness, the APA task force was not alone in its myopic view of violence against women. The issue of female violence against women was almost completely ignored or denied by just about every researcher or policymaker for years.[8]

When I was doing research for my book *The Male Heterosexual*, I found that reliable studies of gay and lesbian domestic violence were virtually absent from the interpersonal violence research literature prior to 1984. At the time, lesbian relationships were presumed to be free from the practice of patriarchy, which, according to many feminists, was largely responsible for intimate violence against women by heterosexual men. But the new findings regarding studies of interpersonal dynamics in same-sex relationships were beginning to challenge the feminist domestic violence theory, which was based upon power dynamics, sexism, gender oppression, and misogyny.

In 1986 P. A. Brand and A. H. Kidd created quite a stir when they found that 25 percent of lesbians and 27 percent of heterosexual women reported physical abuse in committed relationships, and 7 percent of lesbians and 9 percent of heterosexual women reported rape in dating relationships.[9] It was surprising that partner violence rates for lesbians and heterosexual women were virtually the same.

Although disagreement still exists among researchers about the number of lesbians who are battered each year, most reliable research since Brand and Kidd has consistently found that lesbian, gay, and bisexual male domestic violence equals or surpasses heterosexual wife abuse.[10] As Ellyn Kaschak points out in her groundbreaking book *Intimate Betrayal: Domestic Violence in Lesbian Rela-*

tionships: "It has been difficult for many members of the lesbian community and feminists, whether lesbian or not, to accept that there are among us women who batter and abuse other women. Yet, unfortunately, they exist in large enough numbers to require the systematic attention of researchers and therapists alike."[11]

MENTAL DISORDERS

In 1952 the American Psychiatric Association published the first edition of the *Diagnostic and Statistical Manual of Mental Disorders* (*DSM-I*), commonly known as the "gray bible" for its color and psychiatric importance. As a clinical psychology graduate student enrolled in a neuropsychiatric seminar in the mid-1960s, I was required to memorize and regurgitate on demand the *DSM-I's* diagnostic nomenclature and definitions from the manual's 125 pages. In 1968 the American Psychiatric Association published the *DSM-II*, a modest revision of the first edition but still within the range of memorization and regurgitation. Since then the *DSM* has grown through four revised editions from a tidy list of mental disorders into the *DSM-IV-TR*, a memory-busting compendium of more than 300 mental disorders crammed in about 950 pages.[12]

While the majority of the mental disorders listed and described in the various *DSMs* are mostly gender blind, some disorders seem to afflict men and women in different ways and at different rates. Some are particularly related to girls and women becoming dangerous.

Narcissistic Personality Disorder. Let's start with a trend in our society to manufacture and worship narcissists, or what I like to call *cultural celebrophilia*. While most dangerous women like the "XXXs of Evil" would not necessarily qualify for an official diagnosis of a narcissistic personality disorder, many seem close. The key characteristics of a narcissist are: a grandiose sense of self-importance, a belief that one is superior and should be recognized as such, a need for excessive admiration, a sense of entitlement, a lack of empathy for others, envy of others and a belief that others are envious of them, and snobbish, disdainful, or patronizing attitudes.[13] Recognize anybody?

Many of these characteristics may help some individuals to become celebrities, but these can also quickly become serious handicaps when trying to cope with the rigors of normal life—maintaining relationships, parenting children, and staying out of jail. We should not forget the secondary impact on young children who crave to be worshiped like their badly behaving narcissistic idols.

Mood and Anxiety Disorders. Arguably the most insidious and potentially the most harmful mental disorders for girls and women are mood and anxiety disorders. The *DSM-IV-TR* describes thirteen subcategories of anxiety disorders.[14] Especially relevant is post-traumatic stress disorder (PTSD).

PTSD, or many features of PTSD, are often found in female victims of childhood or adulthood trauma who commit crimes. Some examples are persistently re-experiencing a traumatic event through intrusive images, dreams, or feelings; efforts to avoid thoughts, activities, places, or people that trigger recollections of a traumatic event; feelings of detachment and a restricted range of feelings; a sense of bad things to come; sleep disturbances; difficulty concentrating; hypervigalence; and anger management problems.[15]

Mood disorders capture the complex array of depressive disorders, including bipolar, commonly known as manic depression, and postpartum features.[16] The research on women's mental health issues is clear: women are much more likely to suffer from more forms of anxiety and depression disorders than men. Major reasons for the increased risk range are thought to be genetics, physiology, and gender role orientation. Girls and women who struggle with anxiety and depression are thought to be at higher risk for suicide, matricide, and other antisocial behavior, the trifecta of lethality.

Anxiety and mood disorders are often difficult to diagnose accurately due to the similarity of symptoms among the various disorders. Girls and women who are misdiagnosed often receive improper treatment, which increases the risk of exacerbating the disorder and potentially dangerous behavior.

Borderline Personality Disorder. Another predominately female mental disorder is borderline personality disorder (BPD). The essential features of BPD are a pervasive pattern of instability in interpersonal relationships, self-image, and affects, and marked impulsivity that begins by early adulthood and is present in a variety of contexts.[17] BPD is found frequently in girls and women who commit impulsive criminal acts and is often associated with a history of childhood neglect and sexual abuse.

Dependent Personality Disorder. The essential feature of a dependent personality disorder is a pervasive and excessive need to be taken care of that leads to submissive and clinging behavior and fears of separation.[18] Individuals suffering from a dependent personality disorder need a steady stream of reassurance from others and often go to excessive lengths to obtain nurturance from others, even to the point of engaging in unwanted and sometimes criminal behavior. They also have exaggerated fears of being unable to care for themselves and urgently seek another relationship as a source of care as soon as an intimate relationship ends.

Antisocial Personality Disorder. Often associated with dangerous and violent behavior, individuals with this disorder exhibit a pervasive pattern of disregarding and violating the rights of others that begins in childhood or early adolescence and continues into adulthood. These individuals are often deceitful, impulsive, aggressive, reckless, irresponsible, and show a lack of remorse for their inappropriate behavior.[19] As one might expect, individuals with antisocial personality disorder often show up in substance abuse treatment, prison, and forensic settings. While this disorder is more often associated with males, females are far from immune.

In 2002 Terrie Moffitt, Avshalom Caspi, Michael Rutter, and Phil Silva won the American Psychological Association's Maccoby Book Award for their groundbreaking research on gender and antisocial behavior.[20] They concluded there were two forms of antisocial behavior, which turned out to be good and bad news for women. The good news: one form appeared to be a low-prevalence, early-childhood onset neurodevelopmental disorder afflicting only males. The bad news: the second form was more common and appeared to be related to social relationships, but it afflicted both males and females.

They also found that males have a higher rate of exposure to the most important risk factors for developing antisocial behavior, exhibit more physical aggression and violence, and develop a more persistent life-course pattern of antisocial behavior than females. But for girls, depression is a frequent companion to conduct problems, and the depression becomes more severe as antisocial girls enter womanhood.

Substance-Related Disorders. The all-too-frequent accomplice to most any criminal behavior or abusive family situation is the use and misuse of drugs. Substances range from our country's drug of choice, alcohol, and various popular illicit drugs such as methamphetamine and cocaine, to prescribed and over-the-counter medication. The use or abuse of substances can induce mental problems or exacerbate symptoms of a mental disorder.[21] It is no secret that drug-related crimes, including domestic abuse, have increased over the past several years. Add to this the list of girls and women acting out or putting themselves or others at risk while intoxicated.

WHAT DO WE DO ABOUT IT?

Many researchers complain that the more notorious cases, such as those of Andrea Yates, Aileen Wuornos, or Mary Kay Letourneau, are atypical and offer a slanted view of dangerous women. Even so, I believe we can use these cases as a platform to educate the public on the risk factors common to the majority of so-called "ordinary" cases that seldom get media attention. For example, Andrea Yates suffered from a serious emotional disorder exacerbated by poor healthcare management and religious dogma. Aileen Wuornos was a throwaway child who learned fragile and risky survival skills and grew up fueled by anger and substance abuse. Mary Kay Letourneau was born into a family with two faces and may be the first example of using bipolar disorder to explain compulsive and dangerous sexual behavior with a student.

A history of primitive parenting practices, childhood trauma, religious dogma, mental disorders, and/or substance abuse are at the root of many "ordinary" cases presented in this book. So what do we do to help prevent girls and women from becoming a danger to themselves or others?

PUBLIC EDUCATION PROGRAMS

Over the past several years we have learned a lot about dangerous women, and the research base is expanding. But most of the information stays buried deep in the brains of professionals working in the area rather than distributed to the general public. Most of what the public knows about dangerous women comes from media accounts of cases that have the highest probability of increasing readership or viewership, not to educate the public. While this is a start, the reporting is often fraught with errors and sensationalism. Even if the accounts are accurate and less sensational, the public is usually spared an in-depth analysis of the problem.

For instance, to help the public understand and prevent maternal filicide, forensic psychologist Geoffrey McKee suggests using a variety of venues to tell the stories of ordinary women who have resolved their childcare crises by killing their children.[22] He recommends a proliferation of made-for-television movies or documentaries, cable interviews, and series in girls' and women's magazines. This approach could be adapted very easily to include stories of other "ordinary" women, such as presented in this book.

Although the public has been saturated with high-profile cases of some dangerous women, the overall educational value of those presentations is questionable. I believe the personal stories of dangerous girls and women, augmented by a focus on the underlying causes of their tragic solutions to life, are essential. But the stories must include a broader look at how gender role socialization and our society's dangerous dance with sex and violence plays into undermining the healthy psychological development of girls and women. An increase in studied but public-friendly accounts could reach at-risk girls and women and their families before tragedy strikes.

PARENTHOOD EDUCATION PROGRAMS

Several years ago I presented a major address at the International Childbirth Association about the Education for Parenthood project. During the question-and-answer part of the talk, someone asked something like this: "Given the problems many parents seem to have in raising functional children, would you agree that it makes sense to require a minimum amount of information and skill before producing children?" When I agreed, she went on, "Maybe it makes sense, then, for states to mandate passing an examination before allowing people to have children — sort of like requiring a test to secure a driver's license." Before I could answer, her comments set off a heated debate among the participants, who were very divided in their opinions. Privately I thought it was a good idea but offered that it would never see the light of day because it was too controversial.

Later, at another conference, I threw the parent license idea out for discussion and received the same kind of controversy with an added twist: Someone recommended we also ask potential parents to pay a damage deposit before having children. If their children do no damage to our society by the age of eighteen years, the money, plus interest, is returned. I thought that it was a brilliant idea but another one that would never see the light of day.

Imagine my surprise when I learned recently that conservative talk show host and writer Laura Ingraham seemed to support a similar notion of pairing education and licensing. After attacking the "no-fault" divorce laws as responsible for the high divorce rate in this country, she offered this: ". . . many scholars and family rights activists are encouraging states to mandate classes preparing couples for marriage before granting their licenses. Seems sensible . . ."[23] I was disappointed she didn't address the damage deposit idea.

Ingraham also got it right when she championed the cause for biological parents to parent their children, especially from birth through about age six years. As support she summarized studies showing nonparental childcare from birth to kindergarten was linked to an increase in children's assertive, noncompliant, and aggressive behaviors through the sixth grade.[24] A lot of these kids were girls.

The results suggest that children need a competent parent to not just love them but to also take care of them and teach them the skills they will need when they leave the family and enter society, a process that begins in earnest at about age five or six. But most parents and potential parents need the information and skills necessary to provide children with the best opportunity to develop a healthy self-esteem and the skills necessary to negotiate an increasingly difficult world.

Many well-adjusted families do a good job of parenting and pass good parenting practices on to their children. But many children are born into families who are without resources and employ primitive parenting practices that are also passed on to the children. The best way to stop the intergenerational transmission of poor parenting is to intervene and help. One of the best ways of preventing a breeding ground for dangerous girls and women is to intervene and help.

I propose a government-supported national Education for Parenthood program designed by successful parents and the best and brightest working in the fields associated with fostering the psychological health of children. I also propose a two-tier system with each tier designed to meet the educational needs of the participants. The first is for individuals who already have children. The second is for potential parents such as tweens and adolescents. States considering the successful completion of parenting classes as a requirement for a marriage license can use the national Education for Parenthood program as a model.

Then there is the hot issue about who should provide information about sex to children. My position has always been to encourage and help parents provide appropriate information about sexuality to their own children. But parents need to be well informed about sexual matters as well as the most effective ways to present information to children according to the child's developmental level.

Studies show that most children do not receive adequate information about sex from their parents. Instead they receive it from sources that do not always have the child's best interest in mind and/or peers who may be even less informed than the child. Some schools offer sex education classes or sex education topics in health classes, and some faith-based organizations offer "abstinence" classes. I do not support providing information about sexuality to children without parental permission.

Parenting is one of the most difficult challenges anyone can accept. A well-designed Education for Parenthood program could empower parents to foster psychologically healthy behavior in their children and take on the merchants of misinformation who are competing for our children's money, minds, and souls.

PREEMPTIVE THERAPEUTIC INTERVENTION

Preemptive therapeutic intervention begins with a firm understanding of girls and women and why some of them kill their children, murder their partners or others, molest children, or kill themselves. While the research base on girls and women who behave badly or commit crimes is increasing, more directed research is needed to assist clinicians in assessing risk factors and treating the problems. Any therapist who works with girls and women must remain current with emerging research, be expert in women's health and cultural issues, and gain the necessary training to assess risk factors and provide appropriate intervention strategies in a timely fashion.

Also crucial to a successful preemptive therapeutic approach is an increase in the availability of community resources for information, support, treatment, and protection related to women's issues. Charitable and governmental agencies can supplement the therapy provided by private agencies or therapists, but many at-risk women and girls may have to rely solely on community resources such as shelters, hotlines, women's centers, and self-help groups.

As a nice bonus, research will also improve forensic assessments of dangerous women, which will assist the courts in making effective decisions about the cases and protection of the public. Some legal researchers propose a form of therapeutic jurisprudence, an interdisciplinary approach that pulls the law and the social sciences together to assess the psychological and physical impact of legal rules and practice on those to whom the law applies.[25] For example, recognizing how a murderous mother with a serious postpartum mental disorder differs from a thug on the street who kills for profit. Or a battered spouse who kills after being abused may be acting in self-defense even though she was not being attacked at the moment she killed her partner. In this way issues of child and spousal protection and perpetration prosecution may be addressed in a more informative and less adversarial manner and eventually assist in reducing the frequency of dangerous acts by women.

PERSONAL SAFETY

In Gavin de Becker's provocative book *The Gift of Fear*, he describes survival signals that protect us from violence. De Becker, a leading expert on predicting violence, argues that our prewired powers of intuition are the best protection we have from dangerous predators.[26] At the risk of oversimplifying a complex concept, de Becker's position is that we predict and make decisions about the behavior of other human beings based upon an innate ability to read certain signals and an unconscious response to the meaning of the signals. As partial support for his position, de Becker offers Desmond Morris's finding that at least sixty-six signals are universal to all human beings on the planet.[27] One example is stroking the chin. It means "I am thinking" in every culture.

The essence of de Becker's position can be adapted to protecting yourself and your loved ones from dangerous girls and women. The strategy uses your answers to three questions: "What do you see?" "What do you feel?" "What do you do?"

What Do You See? Most girls and women are not dangerous and the ones who are may not look much different from the ones who are not. But there are signs that suggest there may be trouble ahead. Here are a few risk factors "seen" by professionals in the field. You can develop your own list based upon your experiences with dangerous girls or women.

- Provocative or other socially inappropriate clothing
- Using or abusing alcohol or other drugs
- Physically or verbally aggressive behavior
- Sexually provocative behavior or promiscuity
- Lying and other deceptive behaviors
- Demanding and selfish
- Unrealistic expectations of self or others
- Shows little or no remorse for bad acts or empathy for others

- Signs of a mental disorder (anxiety, depression, mood swings, psychosis)

What Do You Feel? For each risk factor you experience, you should have an emotional response. You know, the nagging feeling that you should take your toys and go home? Now! In other words, trust your instincts. Don't second-guess yourself. The first-gut response to these signals is usually the right one. Here are some common emotional responses to warning signs:

- Feel uncomfortable
- Feel manipulated
- Feel exploited
- Feel abused
- Feel afraid

What Do You Do? If what you see makes you feel uneasy in any way, make a decision right away to protect yourself or others you believe may be at risk. Depending upon the level of risk and the situation, many options may be available. Your instinct may help guide you to the most effective solution. If the level of risk is high, immediate action may be needed, such as avoiding contact with the dangerous person and preventing contact with children or other family members. In some cases the risks can be lowered by guiding the dangerous individual to competent mental healthcare. Do not be afraid to contact the proper authorities for intervention if you think you or your loved ones are in danger.

Notes

1. Laura Ingraham, *Power to the People* (Washington, DC: Regnery Publishing, 2007).

2. Ariel Levy, *Female Chauvinist Pigs: Women and the Rise of Raunch Culture* (New York: Free Press, 2005).

3. Frank G. Bolton, Larry A. Morris, and Ann E. MacEachron, *Males at Risk: The Other Side of Child Sexual Abuse* (Newbury Park, CA: Sage Publications, 1989).

4. Larry A. Morris, *The Male Heterosexual: Lust in His Loins, Sin in His Soul?* (Thousand Oaks, CA: Sage Publications, 1997).

5. For a review, see Lenore Walker, *Abused Women and Survivor Therapy* (Washington, DC: American Psychological Association, 1997).

6. David Finkelhor and Kersti Yllo, *License to Rape: Sexual Abuse of Wives* (New York: Free Press, 1985).

7. Mary P. Koss, Lisa A. Goodman, and Angela Browne, *No Safe Haven: Male Violence against Women at Home, at Work, and in the Community* (Washington, DC: American Psychological Association, 1994).

8. J. L. Ristock, "The Cultural Politics of Abuse in Lesbian Relationships: Challenges for Community Action" in *Subtle Sexism: Current Practices and Prospects for Change*, ed. V. Benokraitis (Thousand Oaks, CA: Sage Publications), pp. 279–96.

9. P. A. Brand and A. H. Kidd, "Frequency of Physical Aggression in Heterosexual and Female Homosexual Dyads," *Psychological Reports* 59 (1) (1986): 1307–13.

10. For reviews of prevalence rates and issues associated with lesbian domestic violence, see Ellyn Kaschak, ed., *Intimate Betrayal: Domestic Violence in Lesbian Relationships* (New York: Haworth Press, 2001).

11. Ibid., p. 2.

12. American Psychiatric Association, *Diagnostic and Statistical Manual of Mental Disorders: DSM-IV-TR* (Washington, DC: American Psychiatric Association, 2000).

13. Ibid., pp. 714–17.

14. Ibid., pp. 429–84.

15. Ibid., pp. 463–68.

16. Ibid., pp. 345–428.

17. Ibid., pp. 706–10.

18. Ibid., pp. 721–25.

19. Ibid., pp. 701–706.

20. Terrie Moffitt, Avshalom Caspi, Michael Rutter, and Phil Silva, *Sex Differences in Antisocial Behavior* (Cambridge: Cambridge University Press, 2001).

21. American Psychiatric Association, *DSM-IV-TR*, pp. 191–295.

22. Geoffrey R. McKee, *Why Mothers Kill: A Forensic Psychologist's Casebook* (New York: Oxford University Press, 2006).

23. Ingraham, *Power to the People*, p. 37.

24. Ibid., p. 23.

25. D. B. Wexler, "Therapeutic Jurisprudence and the Criminal Courts," *William and Mary Law Review* 35: 279–99; D. B. Wexler, "Therapeutic Jurisprudence in a Comparative Law Context," *Behavioral Sciences and the Law* 15: 233–46; B. J. Winick, "The Jurisprudence of Therapeutic Jurisprudence," *Psychology, Public Policy, and the Law* 3: 184–206.

26. Gavin de Becker, *The Gift of Fear: Survival Signals That Protect Us from Violence* (Boston: Little, Brown, 1997).

27. Desmond Morris, *Body Talk: The Meaning of Human Gestures* (New York: Crown, 1995).

ACKNOWLEDGMENTS

F irst and foremost, I would like to express my gratitude to my clinical patients and forensic clients over the past thirty years who had the courage to share their tragic and compelling personal stories about growing up dangerous in America. I am also most grateful to two survivors of sexual abuse by nuns who stepped forward with their stories and gave me permission to use their names even though I chose to keep them anonymous. I owe a huge debt of gratitude to my agent, Claire Gerus, whose vision of this book stimulated the project, for her excellent guidance and unbounded encouragement over the past two years. Special thanks to Robin Sax Katzenstein for her review of the manuscript and taking time from her demanding criminal justice schedule to write the foreword. I would also like to thank esteemed colleagues Donald Dutton, Richard Gartner, Mic Hunter, David Lisak, and acclaimed author Diane Fanning for their incisive reviews and comments. I am especially grateful to Paul Duckro, who answered my clarion call for information about nuns who sexually abuse by providing access to his research and wonderful counsel about the issue. And to Lenore Walker, the intrepid pioneer who forever changed how we must address interpersonal violence in women's lives, heartfelt thanks for your support and comments during the beginning stages of this book. To Joe Gramlich, an exceptional copyeditor at Prometheus Books: thank you for making this a better book. Special love and thanks to my wife, Patty, who stood by for months waiting patiently for her turn while I and my computer danced with one dangerous woman after another.

INDEX